- MEDITATION -
LIBERATION OR ATTACHMENT?
Exploring the Two Facets of Meditation

BHIKKHU NYĀNADASSANA
(IOANNIS TSELIOS)

Publications

"THE FOUR NOBLE TRUTHS"
THERAVADA CENTER FOR STUDY AND PRACTICE

2024

Non-profit Organisation

Apostolou Pavlou 5
Agia Paraskevi 153 42
Athens

https://www.theravada.gr

info@theravada.gr

ISBN 978-618-86185-3-4

Printed at:

AFI ILIOPOULI & P. RHODOPOULOS LTD.
Orpheus 200 (5 Agapis Street)
122 41 Egaleo - Athens

Contents

PART II — INSIGHT MEDITATION

PART III — NIBBĀNA OR NIRVĀNA

PART IV — QUESTIONS AND ANSWERS ON MEDITATION

PART V — THE GREAT DISCOURSE ON THE ESTABLISHMENT OF MINDFULNESS *MAHĀ SATIPAṬṬHĀNA SUTTA*

Abbreviations

All references to abbreviations refer to editions of the *Pali Text Society*, London, in Latin script. Pāli, a common language (lingua franca) in ancient India, part of the middle Indo-Aryan language group, Prakrit, was used by the historical Buddha Gotama.

A: *Aṅguttara-nikāya*
D: *Dīgha-nikāya*
DA: *Dīgha-nikāyatthakathā*, Commentary on *Dīgha-nikāya*
Dhp: *Dhammapada*
DhpA: *Dhammapadatthakathā*, Commentary on *Dhammapada*
Dhs: *Dhammasaṅganī*
DhsA: *Dhammasaṅganī-aṭṭhakathā,* Commentary on *Dhammasaṅganī*
It: *Itivuttaka*
KhpA: *Khuddakapāthatthakathā,* Commentary on *Khuddakapātha*
M: *Majjhima-nikāya*
MA: *Majjhima-nikāyatthakathā*, Commentary on *Majjhima-nikāya*
Nd1: *Mahāniddesa*
Nd2: *Cullaniddesa*
Ps: *Paṭisambhidāmagga*
PsA: *Paṭisambhidāmaggatthakathā*, Commentary on *Paṭisambhidāmagga*
PED: *Pāli-English Dictionary*, T. W. Rhys Davids and W. Stede, Pāḷi Text Society (PTS), London
S: *Saŋyutta-nikāya*
SA: *Saŋyutta-nikāyatthakathā,* Commentary on *Saŋyutta-nikāya*
Sṭ: *Saŋyutta-nikāya-ṭīkā,* Subcommentary on *Saŋyutta-nikāya*
Sn: *Suttanipāta*
SnA: *Suttanipātatthakathā,* Commentary on *Suttanipāta*
Ud: *Udāna*
Vibh: *Vibhaṅga*
Vin: *Vinaya-piṭaka*
Vism: *Visuddhimagga*

Publisher's Note

The current publication stands out as a notable highlight in the extensive literature on meditation. While thousands of books have been published describing various meditation methods, few delve into the subject of meditation and attachment. This book aims for a deep understanding of the mechanisms of attachment and liberation, additionally examining how one can overcome the deception of attachment by realizing the impermanent nature of even the most sublime feelings of well-being and bliss that arise from meditation. It is an outstanding manual that is much more than a simple introduction to meditation. It is the result of years of study, practice and teaching by the author Ioannis Tselios (Venerable Nyānadassana), a Buddhist monk of Greek origin, who has devoted over forty years of his life to understanding and practicing meditation.

This remarkable work is addressed not only to those who are familiar with the practice of meditation, but also to beginners. Its writing is clear and easily understood, making it a comprehensive guide for readers regardless of prior knowledge or background. It can help us discover the true nature of the material and mental phenomena that govern our world. This understanding is the beginning of the complete liberation of our minds from the existential suffering inherent in all beings. We invite you to read, study, and apply the knowledge found in this insightful handbook. The path to self-knowledge and inner peace is before you.

In conclusion, I wish to express my deepest gratitude to the author for his dedication and the wisdom he has shared since his arrival in Greece in 2019, serving as a beacon of knowledge and spiritual guidance for us, the Greek community.

Michael Xynos
President of Athens Theravada Centre
Honorary Consul of Sri Lanka in Greece

Athens, January 2025

*Observing the nature of rise and fall
in the material body, in feelings, in thoughts, in mind
and mind-objects,
abide independent, not clinging to anything in the world.*[1]

- THE BUDDHA -

[1] D II, *Mahāsatipaṭṭhāna-sutta.*

GENERAL INTRODUCTION

Meditation is a word that encompasses many meanings and practices. When related to the spiritual life, however, it usually refers to mental exercise in which the practitioner uses the techniques of concentration and awareness to achieve inner harmony and peace. It also brings about deep relaxation, mental calm, and clarity, enhances emotional well-being and happiness, and increases attention, intelligence, and self-awareness, as well as self-fulfilment, self-confidence, self-esteem, and creativity. Furthermore, meditation helps to overcome anxiety, stress, depression, and other negative emotions.

When applied correctly, the concentration of the mind, the most fundamental principle of meditation, collects the usually scattered and fragmented stream of mental states, thereby inducing mental unification. The two main characteristics of such a concentrated and unified mind are unbroken attention to an object and the consequent calming of mental functions, qualities that distinguish it from the non-concentrated mind.

A mind untrained in concentration moves in a manner that the Buddha likens to the quivering of a fish pulled out of the water and thrown onto land.[1] It cannot remain still but jumps from idea to idea, thought to thought, and emotion to emotion without internal control. This fragmented mind is also filled with illusion and delusion. Overwhelmed by anxieties, it perceives things in a distorted manner due to the fluctuations of random thoughts. Therefore, the Buddha advises:

> This fickle, unsteady mind, difficult to guard,
> difficult to control, the wise person straightens it,
> as a fletcher straightens an arrow.

---

[1] Dhp, 34.

> Wonderful, indeed, is the taming of the unruly, swift, and wilful mind. A tamed mind brings happiness.[2]

A mind that has been trained and tamed with concentration can remain focused on its object without distraction. By focusing the mind on a chosen object, the practitioner can eliminate mental distractions. The mind then achieves stillness, becoming fully absorbed in its object. This freedom from distraction brings further peace, joy, happiness, and bliss. However, it can also lead to intense attachment to mental phenomena, especially the aforementioned emotions of well-being and bliss. This occurs because the meditator does not understand that these achievements are also impermanent and transient, have their own limitations, and do not lead to liberation from existential suffering within the continuous cycle of birth and death.

Therefore, in addition to the practice of meditation, this book will also address the issue of attachment and liberation, especially when analysing insight meditation (*vipassanā*), on pages 30, 41 and in Part II. Before that, however, we will examine the general history and evolution of meditation.

History and evolution of meditation

Meditation traces its roots back to India. The first evidence of meditation appeared in the Vedas, which are sacred texts of Hinduism, around 1500 BC.[3] Stone seals found in the Indus valley, which date back to 2500 BC, depict a human figure seated cross-legged in a posture widely considered to be 'yogic' or 'meditative'. Many researchers disagree, however, on the interpretation of this pose. One reason is that the cross-legged posture is a common habit in Indian culture. Many merchants, salesmen,

---

[2] Dhp, 33, 35.

[3] Antonio de Nicholas (2003), *Meditations Through the Rig Veda: Four-Dimensional Man*, pp. 273–274.

tailors, speakers, musicians, and others adopt the pose in everyday life, sitting in front of their shops and homes, or in public spaces, during routine tasks or conversations. This specific figure also has a bovine face, is ithyphallic, bears the horns of a bull or buffalo, and is flanked by various combinations of tigers, cattle, rhinoceroses, elephants, fish, snakes, and other creatures. Therefore, according to many scholars, there is no straightforward evidence that it depicts a meditator or yogi.[4]

Nevertheless, it is a fact that the various concepts of meditation and its practice most likely originated from ascetics in ancient India. The historical Buddha Gotama, the greatest meditator the world has known, whose profound influence and teachings spread beyond the Indian subcontinent to many countries in the ancient and modern world, mentioned that the first inclination towards meditation manifested when great corruption appeared in Indian society. Those who felt revulsion towards the evil (*pāpa*) deeds they witnessed, such as theft, slander, lying, murder, punishment, and exile, decided to retreat to forests (*arañña*) where they built huts. In these quiet places they began to meditate (*jhāyanti*, Sansk. *dhyāyanti*) and lead an ascetic life. They were called 'Brahmins' (*brāhmaṇā*) because they discarded evil (*pāpa*), meaning they were the pure ones. They were also called 'meditators' (*jhāyakā,* Sansk. *dhyāyaka*) because of their devotion to the practice of meditation.

Later, however, those who could not live in huts and meditate settled around villages and towns, composing hymns for gods and deities, thus creating the three Vedas.[5] Since they did not meditate, people called them 'non-meditators' (*ajjhāyakā*). Thus, the Brahmins were divided into two groups, the meditators and the non-meditators, with the latter succumbing to

---

[4] Doris Srinivasan (1975), *The So-Called Proto-Śiva Seal from Mohenjo-Daro: An Iconological Assessment*, George Mason University, pp. 47 et seq.

[5] D III.93, *Aggañña-sutta: ganthe karontā*; Sn 32, vs. 304-8, *Brāhmaṇadhammika-sutta: mante ganthetvā*; DA III. 870: *tayo vede abhisaṅkharontā.*

sensual pleasures and composing hymns for this purpose.[6] Among other things, they used psalms, ritual verses, prayers, songs, chants, mantras, magical phrases, incantations, rituals, and sacrifices to seek favours from gods and deities, as is common in many other religions. They became the well-known Brahmin priests of the Vedic religion, characterized predominantly by its worldly nature.

As time passed, people from other social groups, such as the nobility, merchants, and artisans, as well as some Brahmin priests, were critical of their own social status because it could not bring about moral and spiritual purity. They therefore decided to give up on family life and practice asceticism, believing that ascetic practice could lead to purification (*suddhi*). This is how the ascetic order emerged in India, whose members were called *samaṇā* (Sansk. *śramaṇa*),[7] meaning those who have calmed or subdued the evil within themselves (*samitattā pāpānaṃ*)[8] or, at least, were attempting to subdue it. However, it is important not to confuse the ascetic *samaṇas* with the animistic magician-healer shamans (*šamán*) of Siberia and other regions, who draw their power by identifying with animal-spirit guardians.

Although the ascetic *samaṇa* order comprised many social groups, contemporary scholars generally agree that most *samaṇas* came from the Brahmin social class.[9] Some *samaṇas* cultivated meditation as a means of purification, while others resorted to extreme practices, such as self-mortification, in order to achieve the same goal. Some meditators succeeded, through deep concentration, to attain the meditative absorptions (*jhāna,* Sanskrit *dhyāna*) which allow the practitioner to transcend the

---

[6] Sn 32, vs. 304-8, *Brāhmaṇadhammika-sutta.*
[7] D III.95, *Aggañña-sutta.*
[8] Dhp, 265.
[9] Patrick Olivelle (2011), *Ascetics and Brahmins: Studies in Ideologies and Institutions*, Anthem, pp. 60.

consciousness of the sensual sphere of existence. In doing so, they gain an immaculate purity of mind that brings about deep peace, rapture, happiness, and bliss. Contemporary scholars acknowledge that the diverse concepts of *dhyāna* and its practice originated from the ancient Indian movement of *samaṇa*,[10] which predates the 6th century BC (pre-Buddha, pre-Mahavira)[11] and influenced various Hindu traditions.[12] Many meditators of that era associated their experiences with theistic, metaphysical, mystical, and occult beliefs, while others aligned with atheistic, non-theistic, or materialistic views. In general, as in the Vedas or other religions, there was no uniformity in practice or interpretation within the *samaṇa* movement, leading to the creation of new beliefs, philosophies, and theories. Nevertheless, the practice of meditation, especially the attainment of the meditative absorptions (*dhyāna*), was the blossom of this movement. Through these, many meditators managed to acquire supernatural powers, recall past lives, and be reborn in blissful realms.[13]

Before his enlightenment, the Buddha practiced many of the techniques of the *samaṇa* movement. Indeed, after persistent meditation, he attained, under the guidance of two teachers, eight meditative absorptions. The culmination of these was the eighth absorption, where the pure mind reaches the immaterial 'base of neither perception nor non-perception' (*neva-saññā-nāsaññ'āyatana*).[14] However, he realized that even these had limitations and did not lead to non-attachment, dispassion (*vi-*

---

[10] Bronkhorst, Johannes (1993), *The Two Traditions Of Meditation In Ancient India*, Motilal Banarsidass Publ.

[11] Andrew J. Nicholson (2013), *Unifying Hinduism: Philosophy and Identity in Indian Intellectual History*, Chapter 9, Columbia University Press.

[12] William Mahony (1997), *The Artful Universe: An Introduction to the Vedic Religious Imagination*, State University of New York Press, pp. 171-177, 222.

[13] D I.77, *Sāmaññaphala-sutta;* A II.126, *Paṭhama-nānākaraṇa-sutta.*

[14] Please see p. 28 below.

rāga), enlightenment (*sambodha*), or Nibbāna (Sansk. Nirvāna).[15]

The Buddha began his own investigation into what was 'wholesome' (*kusala*) through systematic and methodical observation of mind and matter. Through this, he discovered the unstable and impermanent nature of all mental and material phenomena of every form of existence—human, non-human, and divine—even of the most exalted and transcendental absorptions. These absorptions are incapable of providing absolute satisfaction, and although they lead to rebirth in blissful realms, these realms are not permanent.

His deep observation (*anupassana*) enabled the Buddha to see the rise (*samudaya*) and fall (*atthaṅgama/vaya*) of the five aggregates of existence—material body, feelings, perceptions, mental formations, and consciousness. Through this knowledge, he eliminated the mental corruptions (*āsava*) that create attachment to these aggregates and bring about suffering in our unstable and fragile world.

Liberated from all mental corruptions and attachments, the Buddha attained Nibbāna—the perfect state of equilibrium that transcends the painful cycle of rebirth,[16] marking the redemptive liberation from *saṃsāra* (continuous wandering in the cycle of birth and death).[17] The systematic method of observation and analysis that the Buddha applied, which enabled him to see the rise (*samudaya*) and fall (*vaya*) of all mental and material phe-

---

[15] M I.166, *Ariyapariyesana-sutta* or *Pāsarāsi-sutta*. For the term **Nibbāna**, please see the elaborate explanation in Part III of the book, on p. 193.

[16] Rebirth or reincarnation is a topic that has intrigued many scientists in our era, and there is much compelling scientific evidence for it. See the article *Reincarnation or Rebirth — Scientific Research and Evidence*, www. theravada.gr/en/library, Various Topics.

[17] M II.93, *Bodhirājakumāra-sutta*. Cf. D II.35, *Mahāpadāna-sutta,* where the observation of rise (*samudaya*) and fall (*vaya / atthaṅgama*) of the five aggregates of clinging (*pañca upādāna khandha*) is clearly mentioned as the method of liberating the mind from all mental corruptions (*āsava*) and attaining enlightenment.

nomena in every form of existence, is called 'insight meditation' (*vipassanā*), a term he first used himself. It is this meditation, which enables one to remain independent and detached by not clinging to anything in the world, that we will discuss in Part II of the book.

The spread of meditation

Although meditation first appeared in India, over time it spread to neighbouring Asian countries. By the 19th century, Asian meditation techniques even permeated Western cultures, where they have been adopted into both spiritual and non-spiritual settings, like business, education, and health.[18]

In the West, the Parliament of the World's Religions, convened in Chicago in 1893, was a landmark event that heightened interest in meditation. It marked the first time that Western audiences on American soil received Asian spiritual teachings from Asians themselves. Following this, the Hindu Swami Vivekananda established several Vedanta *ashrams* (spiritual centres). In 1904, the Sri Lankan Buddhist Anagārika Dharmapāla lectured on Theravāda Buddhist meditation at Harvard University, and Soyen Shaku toured in 1907 teaching Zen meditation.[19] Both Vivekananda and Dharmapāla had also delivered formal speeches at the Parliament of the World's Religions.[20]

The 1960s then saw a renewed surge of interest in meditative practices among Western audiences, prompted by Asian spiritual teachers travelling to Western countries. Besides spiritual

---

[18] *The Benefits Of Meditation In Business*, https://shorturl.at/tKTWX.
[19] Eugene Taylor (1999), Michael Murphy; Steven Donovan; Eugene Taylor (eds.). "*Introduction", The Physical and Psychological Effects of Meditation*: A Review of Contemporary Research with a Comprehensive Bibliography 1931-1996: 1–32.
[20] *Parliament of the World's Religions*, https://shorturl.at/aciz4.

forms of meditation, secular meditation also developed, focusing on stress reduction, relaxation, and self-improvement.[21]

TYPES OF MEDITATION

After millennia of development and dissemination across many geographical regions, meditation today presents a vast diversity with hundreds of variations and types, each with different advantages and disadvantages, incorporating practices from different traditions, cultures, spiritual disciplines, and religions.

Nonetheless, all types of meditation can be classified into two broad categories: serenity meditation and insight meditation.

Serenity meditation

The most common and dominant type of meditation is serenity meditation, which has two main characteristics:

- Concentration: This involves focusing or unifying the mind on a single object or concept/idea for an extended period through undivided attention, excluding other objects.
- Resulting calmness: This state brings about tranquillity, serenity, and peace of mind, which create pleasant feelings of well-being, joy, rapture, elation, bliss, and euphoria.

Nevertheless, there is wide variation even among forms of serenity meditations, with each one differing from the others in terms of the object and focus of concentration. The most common include the concentration of the mind on a specific object or concept, such as:

- **Breath**: focusing on the breath.

[21] George S. Everly, Jeffrey M. Lating (2002), *A Clinical Guide to the Treatment of Human Stress Response,* eds. 200.

- **Mantra**: repeating one or more syllables, words, phrases, or verses, which may or may not have meaning. For example, transcendental meditation uses mantras, similar to other religious practices that use phrases for repetition. They function as self-suggestion, where an individual submits certain ideas to themselves.
- **Koan**: repeating a riddle, puzzle, paradox, or a short saying or story commonly used in Chan (Zen) meditation.
- **Chakras**: focusing on energy centres in the human body.
- **Kundalini**: concentrating on the 'dormant' sexual energy at the base of the spine, which rises (in the meditator's imagination) through the energy centres. Often used with *kriyas* (set of exercises), *pranayama* (breath control), *mantras*, *mudras* (symbolic hand and finger positions and movements), and *bandhas* (locks).
- **Visualisation**: using words and images (sceneries, people, deities, etc.), by exercising the imagination.

The meditator returns to this object, concept, or image whenever his attention is diverted or his mind wanders.

Moreover, since Buddhism is deeply concerned with human psychology, it teaches suitable meditations according to the temperament or character of each individual. These meditations act as antidotes to certain negative tendencies in humans. For example:

- For the deluded or speculative temperament: mindfulness of breathing (*ānapāna-sati*) is practised to abandon distracted thoughts.
- For the hating temperament: meditation on friendliness (*mettā*) is practised to counteract ill-will, anger, hate, jealousy, fear, sorrow, stress, and depression.
- For the lustful temperament: meditation on the foulness (*paṭikkūla*) of the body is practised to combat lust.
- For the intelligent temperament: meditation on the four

primary material elements (*dhātu*) of the body is practiced to overcome conceit, vanity, and narcissism by countering the innate tendency to identify with the body, which is achieved by exposing the body's essentially impersonal nature.

These meditations, among others, were taught by the historical Buddha Gotama himself and can suppress mental hindrances such as sensual desire, anger, sloth and torpor, restlessness and remorse, and doubt, facilitating the purification of the mind and the fruitful pursuit of wisdom. They can also lead to the attainment of meditative absorptions (*jhāna*).

The aforementioned meditations vary in terms of the degree of concentration achieved through them. Some, when practised diligently, can lead to exalted degrees of concentration, even to the level of meditative absorptions (*jhāna*), creating blissful feelings of well-being, rapture, elation, bliss, and euphoria. Others, however, can lead to only a lower degree of concentration, with milder feelings of relaxation, tranquillity, peace, clarity, sobriety, well-being, and happiness. Contemporary techniques, in which meditation is performed simply as a form of relaxation in which the practitioner visualizes pleasant scenes such as idyllic landscapes while listening to calming music, offer a comparatively brief moment of respite. They cannot lead to an elevated degree of concentration or to meditative absorptions that provide long-term bliss.

The meditative absorptions

Meditative absorptions are states of deep inner unification of the mind characterized by its complete absorption and immersion in the object of its attention. These states arise from highly increased and profound concentration on a specific object to such a degree of attention that, for the most part, discursive thought is suspended. However, feelings of rapture, bliss, and equanimity are greatly enhanced to the point of culmination. Therefore, although the meditator may occasionally experience some degree of rapture and bliss before attaining an absorption, these feelings of euphoria don't reach their highest point until the attainment of the full absorption.

The mind, experiencing these meditative absorptions, withdraws more deeply internally, transcending the sensual sphere (*kāmāvacara*) of consciousness and moving away from the sensory objects and stimuli that impinge on the senses from the external world. The mind therefore achieves a level of heightened self-awareness, tranquillity, calmness, and purity that far surpasses discursive or wandering thought.

Meditative absorption is, generally speaking, a mental state that transcends the five sensory functions and can typically be attained through seclusion and in silence, with unremitting persistence in the practice of concentration. During attainment, all activity of the five senses is suspended, and external visual, auditory or bodily impressions are not perceived. Despite the lack of external sensation, the mind remains active, fully alert, awake, and lucid, with full awareness of the object of concentration and the blissful experience that arises from it.

In the *Yoga Sūtra*, a seminal text by the Hindu author Patañjali, which many scholars consider to have been influenced by Buddhism in many aspects,[22] there is a mention of *dhāraṇā* (focusing). It is defined as *deśa-bandhaś cittasya dhāraṇā*, which means: focusing is the binding or fixing of the mind in one place or object (*deśa*). In the same text, *dhyāna* is defined as *tatra pratyayaikatānatā dhyānam,* meaning that *dhyāna* is the continuous flow of the mind towards that same object. However, this

[22] Karel Werner (1994), *The Yogi and the Mystic*. Routledge, pp. 26. White, David Gordon (2014), *The Yoga Sutra of Patanjali*: *A Biography*, Princeton University Press.

definition corresponds more closely to the conventional concept of concentration (*samādhi*).

In Buddhism, commentators derive the word *jhāna* from the root *jhe*, meaning 'to meditate upon, reflect on', or from the root *jhā*, meaning 'to burn'. Thus, *jhāna* means: a) 'meditation on an object' (*āramman'ūpanijjhāna*) or b) 'burning of adverse states' (*paccanīka-jhāpana*). Adverse states are those that oppose concentration. These are the five mental hindrances (*nīvaraṇa*), namely: 1) sensual desire, 2) ill-will or anger, 3) sloth and torpor, 4) restlessness and remorse, and 5) doubt.

Meditations that require the presence of sensual desire and passion in one's consciousness, such as tantric practices, therefore completely preclude the attainment of meditative absorption (*jhāna*).[23]

Commentators also use the word *appanā* for *jhāna,* which means 'unifying or fixing the mind on an object' (*ekaggaṃ cittaṃ ārammaṇe appeti*).[24] In English, *appanā* is also translated as 'ecstasy',[25] referring to meditative ecstasy.

The eight kinds of meditative absorption

There are eight types of meditative absorption, which differ mainly in the degree of intensity of concentration and the resulting feelings of well-being, bliss, and equanimity. These absorptions are divided into two categories: absorptions of the fine-material sphere and absorptions of the immaterial sphere.

---

[23] B. Alan Wallace (1998), *The Bridge of Quiescence: Experiencing Tibetan Buddhist Meditation*, Carus Publishing Company, pp. 215–216.

[24] DhsA.142.

[25] PED: *appanā* - ecstasy.

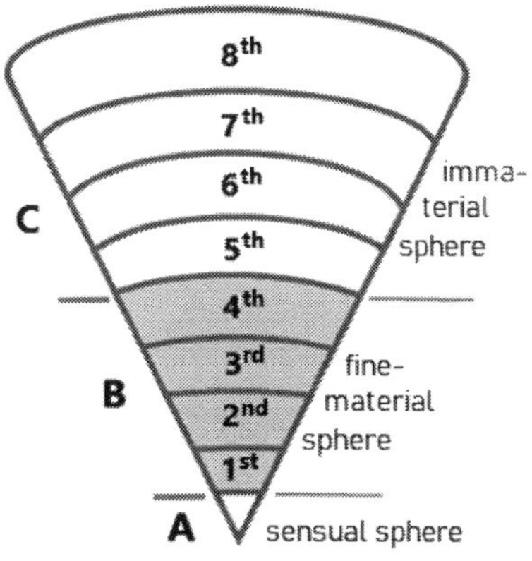

In this diagram, the point marked as '**A**' indicates the initial stage of concentration, during which the meditator may occasionally experience some degree of rapture and bliss, but his consciousness is still at the level of the sensual sphere.

'**B**' indicates the level of the fine-material sphere and the first four absorptions that the meditator's consciousness can experience.

The **1st** meditative absorption has five significant mental factors, known as 'the five factors of meditative absorption' (*jhānaṅga*), which are as follows:

1. applied thought (*vitakka*), which directs the associated mental factors towards the object of concentration,
2. sustained thought (*vicāra*), which maintains them there,
3. rapture (*pīti*), which brings about pleasure towards the object,
4. bliss (*sukha*), which is the feeling of experiencing elated happiness within the absorption, and
5. unification or one-pointedness of the mind (*ekaggatā*), which has the ability to unite the mental factors on the object of concentration.

When the meditator continues to attain the **1st** meditative absorption and repeatedly enters into it, then applied thought (*vitakka*) and sustained thought (*vicāra*) begin to appear gross to them, and their mind inclines more towards rapture and bliss, which appear more refined and pleasant.

Over time, the meditator's mind detaches from applied and sustained thought, resulting in the attainment of the **2nd** meditative absorption, which has as its factors only rapture (*pīti*), bliss (*sukha*), and unification of the mind.

When the meditator continues to attain the **2nd** meditative absorption and repeatedly enters into it, rapture (*pīti*) also begins to appear gross to them, and their mind inclines even further towards bliss (*sukha*), which appears more refined and pleasant. Gradually, their mind detaches from rapture, leading to the attainment of the **3rd** meditative absorption, which has only bliss (*sukha*) and unification of the mind as its factors.

Continuing to attain the **3rd** meditative absorption and entering it repeatedly, even bliss (*sukha*) begins to appear gross to them, and they incline more towards the unification of the mind, which appears yet more refined and pleasant. Eventually, their mind detaches from bliss, resulting in the attainment of the **4th** meditative absorption, which has only the unification of the mind and equanimity (*upekkhā*) as its factors.

The difference among rapture, bliss and equanimity can be understood with the following example. If someone, thirsty and exhausted in a desert, saw a lake at the edge of an oasis, they would feel rapture or joy (*pīti*). However, if they went to the lake, drank the cool water, and enjoyed it, they would feel bliss or happiness (*sukha*). Once they had quenched their thirst and sat under the shade of the oasis trees to rest, they would feel equanimity (*upekkhā*).

In this way, we are able to conceive of rapture as the pleasure one feels at the prospect of obtaining a desired object, and bliss as the actual experience of pleasure when obtaining it. Where there is rapture, there can also be bliss. Where there is bliss, however, there is not necessarily rapture, as in the case of the 3rd meditative absorption.

‘**C**’ indicates the level of the immaterial sphere and the four other meditative absorptions that the meditator’s consciousness can experience. The mental factors are the same as in the **4th** absorption, namely unification of the mind and equanimity. But the object of concentration is different for each of these, as is the degree of concentration and equanimity, which becomes progressively higher.

The **5th** meditative absorption refers to the consciousness based on infinite space (*akāsānañc'āyatana*). To attain this absorption, the meditator must first have mastered the 4th absorption of the fine-material sphere, which is based on an object like a coloured disc (*kasiṇa*), etc. They must then expand the mental image of the disc until it becomes infinite in extent. Next, by mentally removing the disc, they pay attention only to the space it once occupied, considering it 'infinite space'. With repeated attention in this manner, a consciousness emerges within the absorption, having the concept of infinite space (*ākāsapaññatti*) as its object.

The **6th** meditative absorption refers to the consciousness based on infinite consciousness (*viññāṇañc'āyatana*). The consciousness denoted here as infinite is that of the 5th meditative absorption. Since this meditative absorption takes the concept of infinite space as its object, it means that the corresponding consciousness, which pervades or apprehends this space and perceives it as its object, also partakes in its infinity. Therefore, to attain the 6th meditative absorption, the meditator takes as object the consciousness based on infinite space and considers it 'infinite consciousness' until the absorption based on infinite consciousness emerges as a concept.

The **7th** meditative absorption refers to the consciousness based on nothingness (*akiñcaññāyatana*). This absorption takes the emptiness (*suññatā*) of consciousness as its object, which is related to the concept of infinite space, perceived as vast and empty (*suñña*). Given that the 5th absorption takes as its object the concept of infinite, boundless and empty space, this means that the corresponding consciousness, which pervades or apprehends this space and perceives it as its object, also partakes in its emptiness or nothingness. Thus, the meditator takes as object the consciousness based on empty space and considers it as 'empty or nothing' until the absorption based on the consciousness of nothingness emerges as a concept.

It should also be understood that during this absorption, the activity of the mind is reduced, achieving such a high degree of tranquillity and equanimity that it gives rise to the perception that there is *nothing* (*na kiñci* or *ākiññcañña*). Nevertheless, there still exists the perception (*sañña*) of the state of 'nothingness'. This perception is weakened in the next meditative attainment, called the 'base of neither-perception-nor-non-perception'. This can be considered a *grey zone*, where the meditator cannot determine with certainty the existence or non-existence of perception, because a much higher degree of tranquillity and equanimity has been achieved.

The **8th** meditative absorption refers to the consciousness based on neither-perception-nor-non-perception (*nevasaññānāsaññāyatana*). This fourth and final immaterial absorption is so named because it cannot be said to either include or exclude perception. In this state of consciousness, the mental factor of perception (*saññā*) has become so subtle that it can no longer perform its decisive functions. Hence, it cannot be said that perception exists in this state. And yet, since perception is not completely absent but remains in a latent form, it would be equally inaccurate to say that the 8th meditative absorption does not contain perception.

Although only perception is mentioned here, all the other mental factors in this consciousness also exist in a state of such extreme subtlety that they cannot be characterized as either existent or non-existent. This immaterial absorption has as its object the consciousness based on 'nothingness', namely the 7th absorption.

The Bliss of Meditative Absorptions

During a meditative absorption, the meditator can remain motionless for hours, sometimes even days. They become deeply immersed in it, fully enjoying the bliss or equanimity without feeling the need to move due to discomfort. These absorptions bring a bliss that cannot be experienced in everyday life.

The Buddha refers to the absorptions of the fine-material sphere as 'pleasant abidings here and now' (*diṭṭhadhamma-phāsuvihārā*),[26] due to the blissful feelings they generate, and the absorptions of the immaterial sphere as 'peaceful abidings' (*santā vihārā*),[27] due to the deep tranquillity and equanimity they create. Meditators who have attained them often consider all other earthly and worldly pleasures insignificant in comparison. The bliss of the absorptions is their sustenance, allowing them to sit and enjoy it. This can become a form of attachment, however. Later, when discussing insight meditation, we will see how one can overcome this attachment through understanding the impermanent and transient nature of even sublime feelings of bliss and equanimity.

The nature of meditative absorptions

Although the meditative absorptions are blissful and delightful experiences, it should be noted that they lack the wisdom of insight and are thus insufficient for attaining ultimate liberation and enlightenment.[28] They are impermanent and temporary achievements. Moreover, the intense pleasurable feelings and emotions generated both before and after the absorption have sometimes been misinterpreted and mystically experienced by

---

[26] M I.40, *Sallekha-sutta.*

[27] Ibid.

[28] **Enlightenment** (*Bodhi*) is the moment when the Four Noble Truths (*ariya-sacca*) are understood. Please see p. 286.

meditators. These experiences are often personified as 'the union of man with the divine', 'the union of the human soul with the divine soul', 'the experience of the living God', 'the infinite self', 'the cosmic/universal soul, consciousness or energy', 'the immortal, indestructible, pure, and infinite soul or consciousness', 'the primordial powers', and 'the Absolute'. Many other meditation practices have also been experienced religiously and erroneously ascribed religious sentiments.

Similar misinterpretations existed even in the time of the Buddha. However, having experienced these absorptions himself, he explained the fallacy of such feelings and emotions, namely how 'feelings condition craving; craving conditions attachment; attachment conditions becoming; becoming conditions birth; birth conditions ageing and death, sorrow, lamentation, pain, suffering and distress.'[29]

He also explained that he had fully understood the actual occurrence of the arising (*samudaya*) and passing away (*atthaṅgama*) of feelings, their enjoyment and danger and the deliverance from them, and how he had liberated himself through non-attachment (*anupādā-vimutto*).[30]

Despite the fact that the absorptions are impermanent attainments, the Buddha included them in his teachings, discarding mystical and other similar interpretations, and retaining their essence, which is the high degree of concentration they produce. This concentration calms the five mental hindrances (*nīvaraṇa*) on one hand, while, on the other, creates deep serenity and equanimity, which can be utilized for insight meditation (*vipassanā*).

Insight Meditation

Insight meditation is unique among meditation practices and was first taught by the historical Buddha Gotama more than

[29] D I.45, *Brahmajāla-sutta.*
[30] Ibid. I.39.

2,500 years ago. In fact, it was through insight meditation that he attained enlightenment and became a Buddha. He conceived the truths he discovered through deep insight meditation, namely the analytical and systematic observation of mind and matter—particularly the mind, with all its illusions and the suffering it creates—and their transcendence through non-attachment, non-identification, and liberation, something no one had dared to do before.

Insight meditation exists today in its original form in Theravāda Buddhism, which has preserved the authentic Teachings of the Buddha and is considered to be early Buddhism. The term the Buddha used for this meditation is *vipassanā*, which means 'special (*vi-*) seeing (*-passana*)'. In a sense, it refers to the ability to be aware of things that are not perceived in the usual ways.

Insight meditation, which is independent of religious or cultural contexts, does not use conventional meditation methods. Instead, it employs systematic and methodical observation of material and mental phenomena in order to penetrate their true nature. It involves the practice of mindfulness[31] and awareness, which are used to observe and understand the unstable, transient, and impermanent nature of all mental and material phenomena, and to overcome the attachment to them that leads to existential suffering.

In insight meditation, observation with mindfulness and awareness extends to four areas: a) the body, b) feelings, c) thoughts, and d) mind-objects. This consists of two parts:

1) Knowledge of the object of observation, such as the body, feelings, thoughts, and mind-objects.
2) Insight into the nature of their rise (*samudaya*) and fall (*vaya*).

---

[31] *Mindfulness meditation*, as a separate practice that is popular today, is a derivative of insight meditation, though it is simplified or, in some cases, distorted and altered. See Ron Purser, David Loy (2013), *Beyond McMindfulness*, https://shorturl.at /cHNR3.

Essentially, the fundamental principle of insight meditation is the observation of the rise and fall—a characteristic of phenomena that are transient, temporary, fleeting, impermanent, unstable, and not lasting. Through insight meditation, it can be confirmed and verified that this characteristic prevails and is omnipresent in all phenomena of mind and matter. This knowledge leads to the insight of the three universal characteristics of our existence:

- impermanence (*anicca*),
- existential suffering (*dukkha*) caused by our attachment to impermanent phenomena, and
- non-self (*anattā*) within the impermanence of phenomena.

The three universal characteristics of existence

1. *Impermanence (anicca)*

Impermanence signifies the fundamental reality that nothing in the world is stable, permanent, unchanging, fixed, static, unalterable, enduring, or eternal. Change prevails in all activities and energies, as well as in all mental and material phenomena, all of which have the nature of rising and falling.

Although the phenomena surrounding us give the impression of being permanent and unchanging, they are in reality fleeting processes that are in constant flux. We are not the same people, physically, emotionally, or spiritually, as we were ten years ago or even ten minutes ago. Living as we do like moving beings in quicksand, it is therefore not possible to achieve lasting security and happiness. Every individual is essentially subject to constant change, as their bodies, feelings, perceptions, thoughts, and so on, change from moment to moment. Thus, change and impermanence are closely intertwined and interrelated with existential suffering, unhappiness, and pain.

2. *Existential suffering (dukkha)*

Dukkha refers to physical and psychological suffering experienced because of attachment to impermanent and unstable things, such as material and mental phenomena, and generally the unsatisfactory and imperfect nature of life itself.

Suffering arises due to the unstable nature of all material and mental phenomena which are constantly subjected to the rise and fall, and thus become the basis for distress, anguish, suffering and pain within the unstable world. It is not the instability in itself that causes our suffering, though. What makes us suffer is our desire for things to be stable and permanent, when in reality, they are not. So, we experience anxiety, stress, disappointment, and frustration in our attempts to maintain balance, permanence, and security amidst the flow, impermanence, and instability of life.

That is not to say, however, that life is only pain and suffering. There are moments of happiness in life, but they do not last, because they are subject to the law of change and impermanence. This causes fear of change, which is experienced as insecurity. In this way, suffering (*dukkha*) is closely linked with impermanence (*anicca*).

3. *Non-self, non-soul (anattā)*

The concept of non-self indicates that ultimately nothing eternal or immutable exists either in- or outside human nature that can be identified as 'self', 'soul', 'permanent entity', 'permanent personality' or 'ego'. The whole concept of 'self' or 'I' is, in reality, an idea, a mental construct trying to establish itself in an unstable and temporary aggregate of material and mental elements. It is the basis for all wrong views and the continuous suffering in *saṃsāra*. It is the concept of self that everywhere and at all times, has most misled, deluded and divided mankind.

Although things around us give the impression of being solid and compact, they are in reality merely aggregates, combinations, and compositions of various elements that are constantly changing. If we remove the tiles, beams, bricks, stones, and other materials from a house that seems solid, then there will be no 'house' separate from these elements. No individual part is the whole that we call 'house'. When we refer to a 'house', we actually referring to an aggregate, a heap, and a combination of building elements that lasts only as long as these elements are arranged in a specific form. Should these very same elements be disconnected and rearranged as something else, we might perceive them differently.

Similarly, what we call 'I', 'self', or 'soul', which seems solid to us, is also merely an aggregate (*khandha*) of various elements, including:

1. the material body (*rūpa-khandha*),
2. feeling (pleasant, unpleasant, and neutral) (*vedanā-khandha*),
3. perception (*saññā-khandha*),
4. mental functions or formations (*saṅkhāra-khandha*), and
5. consciousness (*viññāna-khandha*).

These elements are constantly changing. They are in flux, like a river maintaining an apparent identity, although the water droplets that form it change every moment. Similarly, an individual maintains an apparent identity that they call 'self', 'I', 'ego', or 'soul', even though the body, feelings, perceptions, ideas, and consciousness that form it are subject to continuous change and differ every moment. In reality, only this self-consuming process of material and mental phenomena exists, continually arising and passing away, with no separate ego-entity existing within or outside this process.

The notion of 'self', 'I', or 'soul' is only an illusion created when one tries to identify with any one of the five aggregates or their entirety. It is a mental construct consisting of a series of momentary cognitions, each of which is a momentary point of consciousness (*cittakkhaṇa*) that focuses on whatever happens to occupy our attention at any given point in time. It is simply our human tendency to personify material and mental phenomena and identify ourselves with them, rather than objectively analysing them, breaking them down into their constituent elements and trying to understand them.

The stream of consciousness

Human consciousness can be described as a continuous stream (*viññāṇa-sota*)[32] in which people never experience the exact same thoughts twice. Consciousness is not a fixed spiritual substance, entity or soul. The concept of the 'stream of consciousness' was also recognised by William James, the father of modern psychology in America, in his work *The Principles of Psychology.*[33]

From one moment to the next, we experience a multitude of impressions, not only from the world around us but also from the mental activity inside us. While it might not be obvious at first, the truth is that we cannot perceive more than one impression at the same time. We may believe that we are seeing a visual object, hearing a sound, feeling a touch, and thinking a thought simultaneously, but this is an illusion caused by the rapid succession of 'moments' or snapshots in time. These impinge upon the fields of our sensory consciousness, with our attention turning to them successively or alternately. There is a

---

[32] The term 'stream of consciousness' (*viññāṇa-sota*) is found in D III.105, *Sampasādanīya-sutta,* in the sense of the uninterrupted flow of consciousness from life to life.
[33] William James (1890), *The Principles of Psychology*.

shift from one consciousness to another, but the process is so fast that we get the general impression that we see, hear, feel, and think at the same time and that there is an uninterrupted continuity in consciousness, giving us the sense of an entity behind the process.

However, what appears to be an entity—the total sum of feelings, perceptions, thoughts, opinions, views, desires, memories and so on, usually denoted by the word 'soul'—is nothing more than a process of 'becoming', namely the continuous movement and change of everything. It is this process that links one moment of consciousness to the next, each depending on previous factors of mental and material conditions as well as on external and internal stimuli.

External stimuli are sensory impressions and data received through the five sensory organs. Internal stimuli are those that arise in the mind from the memory of previous data or from the anticipation of future events. We tend to identify ourselves with individual states of our conscious experience, with our body, or with the complex of psychosomatic functions such as thought, will, memory, desire, and their concomitants. Like everything else, however, these phenomena, which are all conditioned and unstable, are states of the process of 'becoming' and have no permanent existence.[34] Once again, we can see our predisposition to personify material and mental phenomena come to the fore.

If we analyse these phenomena, we will see that just as in the field of physics, where the seemingly indivisible, inseparable, and solid atom is nothing more than fluctuating electrons, protons, neutrons, and other particles involved in dynamic activity and processes, the seemingly indivisible, solid 'self' in the field

---

[34] Paravahera Vajirañāṇa (1962), *Buddhist Meditation in Theory and Practice,* in the *Introduction* by Francis Story, Charleston Buddhist Fellowship edition, 2010.

of psychological activity is also nothing more than fluctuating and changing mental and material processes.

In both cases—physical and psychological activity—what we actually encounter is not a compact, solid phenomenon, but a series of events. In the ultimate reality, there are only the changing processes of material and mental phenomena that continually rise and fall according to causes and conditions (*hetu-paccaya*), which themselves are constantly shifting.

Conditionality and causality

Rise and fall are fundamental characteristics of the entire universe, which consist of conditioned—dependent on conditions—phenomena. Conditionality, like causality, is an integral part of existence.

All phenomena in the material, physical, and spiritual worlds are produced by a combination of causes and conditions. They are not absolute, self-existent, immutable, independent, and unrelated to other things. They are composed, formed, shaped, moulded, and created by conditions, on which they are both dependent and interdependent. This is an ever-changing cycle, as these causes and conditions also rise and fall according to other conditions and causes. Thus, the rising and falling reveals that the nature of conditions is transient, momentary, fleeting, impermanent, and not static.

In the final analysis, nothing can be found either inside or outside of mental and material phenomena that could be considered a self-sufficient, independent, or distinct ego, self, soul, or any other substance or entity that is unchanging, unalterable, permanent, continuous, perpetual, everlasting, stable, immovable, indivisible, indissoluble, self-existent, self-generated, eternal, ageless, immortal and indestructible.

What does exist is the changing process of conditions (*paccaya*) and their effects (*paccayupanna-dhamma*)—not a being, a person, a woman, a man, a self, something belonging to a 'self', an 'I' or 'mine', or 'someone', or something belonging to 'someone'.

Beings are composite and constantly changing, their existence not self-generated but dependent on causal factors. The terms 'self', 'soul', 'personality', 'ego', 'individual', 'man', 'woman', and so on are nothing but simple conventional expressions; they represent relative, customary, and conventional truths and realities (*sammuti*, *loka-vohāra*).[35]

The purpose of insight meditation

All knowledge of ultimate reality (*paramattha-sacca*) can be attained through the methodical and systematic observation in insight meditation (*vipassanā*), which eradicates ignorance (*avijjā*) or delusion (*moha*) regarding the three universal characteristics of existence. This delusion is considered the first link in the overall process of *saṃsāra*, where a being is subjected to repeated existences in an endless cycle of suffering. Therefore, the eradication of this delusion or ignorance through direct insight into the three universal characteristics puts an end to *saṃsāra* and, consequently, to existential suffering.

In reality, our minds are subject to perceptual and conceptual distortions, resulting in our tendency to interpret phenomena as permanent, pleasurable, and 'self'. Although these phenomena may seem evident, they are simply distortions of our perception, preventing us from seeing them as they really are. For instance, we perceive the sun as moving around the earth, rising, and setting, whereas the exact opposite is happening: the Earth rotates on its axis while orbiting the sun. The task of insight, therefore, is to correct perceptual and cognitive distortion through the

---

[35] S I.135, *Vajirā-sutta*; D I.201, *Poṭṭhapāda-sutta*.

study of phenomena 'as they really are', in other words, as impermanent, suffering, and non-self.

Thus, the essential purpose of insight meditation is to deepen one's understanding of the three universal characteristics of existence: 1) the impermanence of mental and material phenomena, which have the nature of rising and falling, 2) suffering or distress due to impermanence, and 3) the non-self, non-soul, non-ego nature of unstable and impermanent aggregates of material and mental phenomena.

Understanding of the three universal characteristics contributes to remaining independent (*anissito*) and not clinging to anything in the world (*na ca kiñci loke upādiyati*).

In this sense, 'independent' means not depending on cravings (*taṇhā*) or speculations or views (*diṭṭhi*) about any given phenomenon. 'Not clinging to anything in the world' in turn means not clinging to any body, feeling, thought, consciousness, or mind-objects with the belief that 'this is mine, this is me, this is my self, or this belongs to myself', since the body, feelings, and so forth are constantly changing.

In ultimate reality, there are only processes of material and mental phenomena that continually rise and fall according to causes and conditions (*hetu-paccaya*), not a being or a self.

In this way, the fundamental principle of insight meditation, through the observation of rise and fall, also reveals that the nature of causes and conditions is transient, fleeting, unstable, and impermanent.

This knowledge contributes to the purification (*visuddhi*) of the mind from passion and anything else that causes suffering and distress due to attachment to unstable phenomena. It therefore also leads to the overcoming of sorrow and lamentation, the disappearance of pain and grief, the attainment of the true method and the realization of Nibbāna, the supreme bliss, a perfect state of equilibrium that transcends the cycle of birth and death.

Regarding the characteristic of rising and falling, the Buddha says:

> Better to live one day
> seeing the rise and fall of phenomena
> than to live a hundred years
> without ever seeing their rise and fall
> (*udaya-vaya*).[36]

And the last words of the Buddha were:

> All conditioned phenomena have the nature to fall (*vaya-dhamma*). Strive to understand this diligently.[37]

Those who have attained the first stage of enlightenment and are called 'stream-enterers' (*sotāpanna*) are those who have understood the following fundamental principle:

> Whatever has the nature of arising, all that also has the nature of ceasing (fall).[38]

This understanding is called 'the eye or vision of the true nature of all phenomena' (*dhamma-cakkhu*), which perceives the nature of their continuous rise and fall, an integral natural law in all mental and material phenomena throughout the universe.

It is this understanding that severs the bond of the wrong view of self-identity or personality (*sakkāya-diṭṭhi*) and doubt (*vicikicchā*). It brings about the right view, which is excellent and liberating, leading to the complete cessation of existential suffering, namely the experience of Nibbāna. This cessation is

---

[36] Dhp, 113.

[37] *'Vayadhammā saṅkhārā, appamādena sampādetha.'* D II.120, *Mahāparinibbāna-sutta.*

[38] *'Yaṃ kiñci samudayadhammaṃ, sabbaṃ taṃ nirodhadhamman'ti.'* E.g. D I.148, *Kūṭadanta-sutta*; M I.379, *Upāli-sutta*; Ud.48, *Suppabuddhakuṭṭha-sutta.*

attained due to non-attachment and non-identification with the material body, feelings, perceptions, mental formations, and consciousness, by relinquishing the belief that 'these are mine, these I am, these are my self, or these belong to myself.'

Attachment

Attachment refers to intense desire and excessive dependence on, and devotion to, a person, idea, or emotions, or to a material or spiritual object. Attachment to mental, spiritual, and material phenomena occurs in two primary ways: ownership and identification.

Ownership

A sense of ownership arises when one has possessive tendencies, considering the above phenomena as one's own property. This leads to the perception that 'these are mine' (*etaṃ mama*), a perception that represents the act of ownership, which is a function of craving (*taṇhā*). Due to craving, attachment or clinging can arise and persist towards:

- existence (*bhavupādāna*),
- sensual pleasures (*kāmupādāna*),
- the meditative absorptions of the fine-material sphere (*rūpupādāna*), and
- the meditative absorptions of the immaterial sphere (*arūpupādāna*).

Identification

One identifies with mental or material phenomena, taking them as a basis for:

- pride, conceit, or arrogance (*māna*), or
- the view (*diṭṭhi*) that these are one's own 'true self'.

Thus, one is prone to think that:

- 'these I am' (*eso 'hamasmi*) or
- 'these are my self, my soul' (*eso me attā*).

Here, the notions 'these I am' and 'these are my self' represent two types of identification:

- the first ('these I am') expresses pride, conceit, or arrogance, and
- the second expresses the view 'these are my self, my soul'.

The notions of ownership and identification, along with the resulting attachments and illusions, are eliminated at the first stage of enlightenment, which is the initial experience of Nibbāna. This gradually leads to the abandonment of all attachments (*sabbūpadhi*). A detailed explanation about Nibbāna will be presented in Part III of the book, where its meaning will be made clearer.

The parts of this book

This book consists of five parts.

Part I will present meditations from the category of serenity meditation, which were taught by the historical Buddha Gotama and can significantly liberate the mind from the mental hindrances—sensual desire, anger, sloth and torpor, restlessness, and doubt—which all cause attachments. This liberation allows for the purification of the mind and the fruitful pursuit of wisdom. Meditations on breathing, friendliness, compassion and the four primary material elements of the body are all included in this part.

Part II will present insight meditation, which brings about the final liberation from all mental fetters and passions that cause existential suffering and anguish due to attachment to impermanent phenomena.

Part III will thoroughly analyse the Buddhist concept of Nibbāna as found in the Pāli Canon, the authentic texts of early Buddhism. In the same part, misunderstandings about Nibbāna, which prevail even in our times, will be addressed in the subsection titled 'Misconceptions and Fantasies about Nibbāna'.

Part IV will follow with questions and answers. In this section, clarifications can be found for those seeking answers to common questions relating to the meditations mentioned above. The questions were posed by students of the meditation seminars conducted by the author and have been answered by him.

Part V will feature an introduction and a translation of the Buddha's great discourse on the establishment of mindfulness (*mahā satipaṭṭhāna sutta*), where special emphasis is given to the development of insight meditation.

PART I

SERENITY MEDITATION

Meditation on Breathing

INTRODUCTION

Meditation with mindfulness on breathing (*ānāpāna-sati*), which belongs to the category of serenity meditation, was one of the meditations practiced by the Buddha before achieving enlightenment. It laid the foundation for the subsequent insight meditation through which he attained enlightenment.

Today, there are several types of meditation related to breathing, each offering different ways to observe the breath. However, none quite resemble the method explained by the Buddha. His explanation is unique because it not only induces relaxation, calmness, serenity, and stillness in the mind but also facilitates deep concentration, enabling one to attain the meditative absorptions known as *jhāna* (or *dhyāna*). This deep concentration can then be used for insight meditation.

We will explain this meditation as the Buddha himself taught and practiced it. We refer to the Buddha here precisely because he used this meditation on breathing as the basis for achieving deep concentration and serenity as well as for attaining enlightenment through insight meditation.

The Buddha praised meditation on breathing in many of his discourses, explaining how it can calm the mind and lead to a state of concentration, as well as how it can be used to bring immediate peace of mind. Here is an example of such praise from one of his discourses:

> This concentration (*samādhi*) by mindfulness of breathing, when developed and much practiced, is peaceful and sublime. It is an unadulterated blissful abiding that immediately dispels and quells evil and unwholesome thoughts, whenever they arise.[1]

The purpose of this meditation is to focus the mind, so that, over time, the meditator can realize the gradual unification and concentration of their previously scattered mind. The ordinary mind exists in an unstable and fickle state. Through breathing meditation, it can be brought to a stable and aligned state. The Buddha says about the fickle mind:

> This fickle, unsteady mind, difficult to guard, difficult to control the wise person straightens it as a fletcher straightens an arrow.[2]

Here, the Buddha gives us an example: the meditator who tries to straighten and align their unsteady and fickle mind. But what happens in the mind when it concentrates on a specific point, such as the breath, through continual repetition? It becomes unified, tamed, and prevented from engaging in any distracting thoughts. The Buddha has praised taming of the mind like this:

> Wonderful, indeed, is the taming of the unruly, swift, and wilful mind. A tamed mind brings happiness.[3]

---

[1] S V.321, *Vesālī-sutta*. – The Buddha's references to meditation on breathing are numerous, such as the following: D II.290, *Mahāsatipaṭṭhāna-sutta*; M I.56, *Satipaṭṭhāna-sutta*; M III.81, *Ānāpānassati-sutta*; M III.88, *Kāyagatāsati-sutta*; S V.322, *Kimila-sutta*; A V.111, *Girimānanda-sutta,* etc.
[2] Dhp, 33.
[3] Dhp, 35.

Conversely, an untamed, unruly, and fickle mind can only bring misery. This indicates that meditation also aims to improve our happiness by taming the mind.

The ordinary mind is unstable and fragmented by thoughts, ideas, and emotions. Concentration helps to unify it. This is exactly what we achieve by focusing on the natural rhythm of the in- and out-breath, which is continual and constant.

Fragmented mind

The Buddha speaks of the unification of the mind with the words *cittassa ekaggatā*. Here *citta* means 'mind', *eka* means 'one', and *agga* means 'point'; that is, concentration of the mind on one point. The mind is led to a point of unity and focus in order to achieve 'one-pointedness' or 'oneness'.[4]

Breathing is a vital part of our existence; even three minutes without it can be enough to end life. When someone uses breathing as an object of observation, it is quite easy to concentrate, since breathing is constantly repeated. This repetition provides the mind with a steady point to concentrate on, through which it can easily be tamed, achieving unity and focus in the process.

The Buddha refers to this form of concentration 'mindfulness on breathing', emphasizing the necessity for the meditator to remain mindful and consistently remember the breathing process. Consequently, observation of the breath is unattainable for someone who is unmindful, distracted, and forgetful. The Buddha asserts:

> I do not say that there is the development of mindfulness of breathing for one who is forgetful (*muṭṭhassati*) and not fully aware (*asampajāna*).[5]

---

[4] According to M I.301, 'Unification of mind is concentration' (*Yā ... cittassa ekaggatā ayaṃ samādhi*).

[5] M III.84, *Ānāpānassati-sutta*.

The Buddha also indicates that for an effective observation of the breath, in addition to being mindful (*satimā*), one needs to be ardent (*ātāpī*) and fully aware (*sampajāna*).

Conversely, being dull, sluggish, lethargic (*anātāpī*), unaware, and oblivious (*asampajāna*) are qualities that hinder the achievement of focused observation and concentration. This is relevant to other types of meditation as well. Particularly in cases of drowsiness, such as after a meal or due to fatigue, it is advisable to fully dispel it before engaging in meditation.[6]

Guarding the Concentration

Developing concentration may present challenges if not properly safeguarded. Guarding concentration involves avoiding unsuitable conditions (*asappāya*) and seeking suitable ones (*sappāya*). This principle applies to all types of meditation. The following conditions should be considered:[7]

1) *The dwelling*. A dwelling may be unsuitable if mindfulness and awareness cannot be practiced there, making it difficult for the unconcentrated mind to concentrate. Conversely, a dwelling is suitable when mindfulness, awareness, and concentration can be enhanced.

Such a dwelling could be a place free from disturbances by people and sounds, as well as visual, olfactory, or other stimuli that may distract attention. A quiet house, a room, even a space outside in nature—like in a forest or under the shade of a tree—are suitable dwellings.

2) *Speech*: When speech is aimless and distracting to meditation, it is unsuitable, as it leads to the disappearance of concentration. Conversely, speech that aims to increase energy,

---

[6] For the dispelling of drowsiness, see p. 262.

[7] These conditions are mentioned in Vism I.127, Ch. IV.

concentration, wisdom, and liberation from mental defilements is suitable, although it should be done in moderation.

3) *People*: Individuals who refrain from engaging in aimless talk, while preserving moral virtues, concentration and wisdom are deemed suitable. Through interaction with such people, the unconcentrated mind becomes concentrated, while an already concentrated mind may increase its focus further. Conversely, people overly concerned with their physical appearance and prone to aimless talk are unsuitable, as they tend to cause distractions.

4) *Food*: For some people, sweet food is suitable; for others, sour food is. Therefore, it is wise to know which foods are suitable for oneself to avoid indigestion and related problems. Moderation is also recommended in this context.

5) *Climate*: For some, a cool climate is suitable; for others, a warm one is. If one finds that in a particular climate one's mind becomes concentrated, or an already concentrated mind becomes more so, then that climate is suitable. Any other climate is unsuitable.

6) *Postures*: Although the ideal posture for meditation is sitting, one can try walking, standing, or lying down and determine which of these is suitable for oneself, so that an unconcentrated mind becomes concentrated or a concentrated mind becomes more so. Any other posture should be considered unsuitable.

We will now see how meditation on breathing is practiced.

The Practice of Meditation

The Sitting Posture

As the usual posture in meditation is sitting, the Buddha explains how the meditator should sit to practice this meditation, beginning his discourse as follows:

- Sitting down.
- Folding the legs crosswise.
- Keeping the body erect.[8]

These are the simplest instructions for a *yogi* (meditator) to take the correct posture, the one the Buddha himself is mostly depicted in. Indeed, if there were ever a true *yogi*, in the real sense of the word, it was the Buddha. Whatever he achieved, whatever truths he discovered, he accomplished it through meditation.

The ideal way of sitting is in full lotus posture, where the legs are folded so that both heels rest on the thighs. Because this is particularly difficult for Westerners, we will mention other options as well. The key is to keep the spine upright. [9]

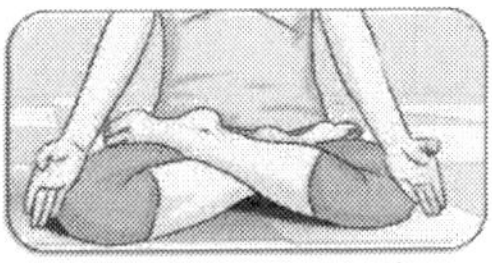

Full lotus posture*

Another option is the half-lotus posture, in which only one heel is placed on the thigh.

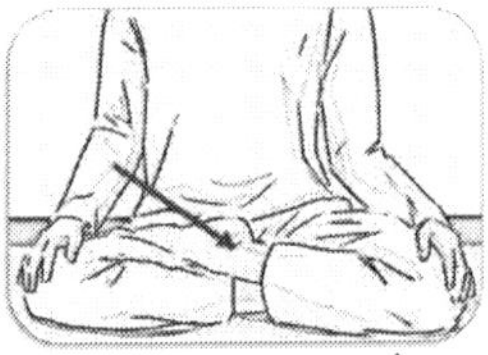

Half-lotus posture*

There is also the Burmese posture, in which both heels are placed on the floor, slightly away from the body. Many may find this posture more comfortable. It was named after the country in which it was exceptionally popular: Burma, now called Myanmar, where meditation practice is widespread and many meditation centres have been established. In Burmese posture the meditator can sit on a cushion, which can improve comfort. In any case, the back should be upright, as with lotus posture, so that the practitioner can

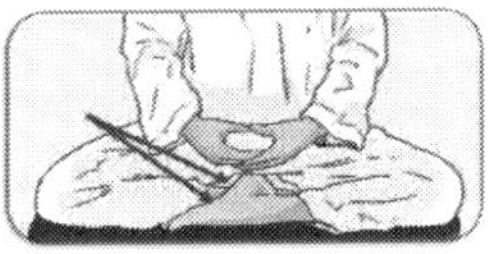

Burmese posture*

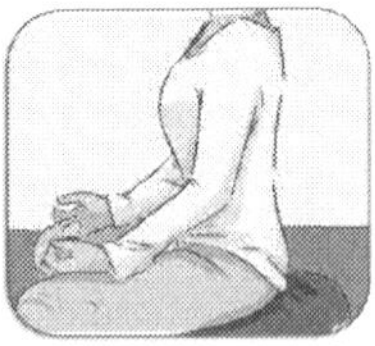

Sitting on a cushion*

[8] '*Nisīdati, pallaṅkaṃ ābhujitvā, ujuṃ kāyaṃ paṇidhāya*': M III.81.

[9] The images marked with an asterisk are courtesy of wiki-how.com.

easily concentrate on breathing. They can also relax the hands, with palms in a comfortable position, and place either the left or right foot in front.

Some believe that their hands must be in a certain position during meditation, as shown in the adjacent image. These hand positions, called *mudras*, are used in various types of meditation and are often attributed with symbolic and mystical meanings. They are unnecessary in breathing meditation, however. When one concentrates on the breath, the hands play no role; they should simply be in a relaxed position, so that their weight is not felt and attention is not diverted to them. By focusing attention on the breath, one can gradually lose the sense of the hands, and all concentration can shift to the sensation at the nostrils, where the air comes into contact with them.

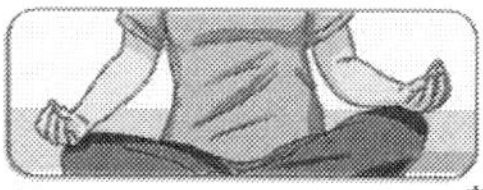

Unnecessary hand positions*

Below we see other meditation postures on a stool, cushion, and chair. In each of these, maintaining a straight and upright back is crucial, along with positioning the head so that the nose is parallel to the ground. This posture ensures that the vertebrae align vertically, counteracting gravity. When the body is aligned correctly, it avoids the imbalance that occurs when leaning slightly forward or backward, which can lead to a tendency to topple over.

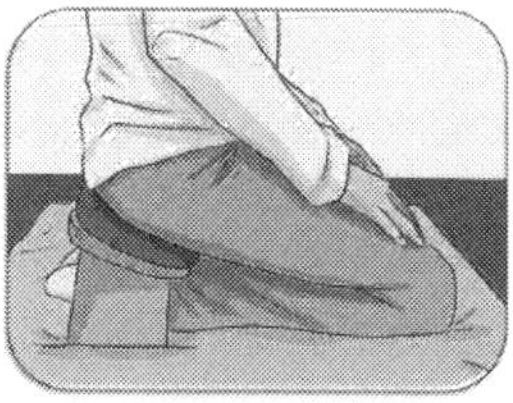

On a stool*

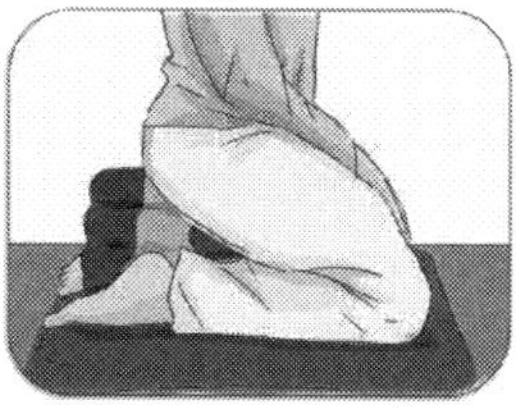

On a cushion*

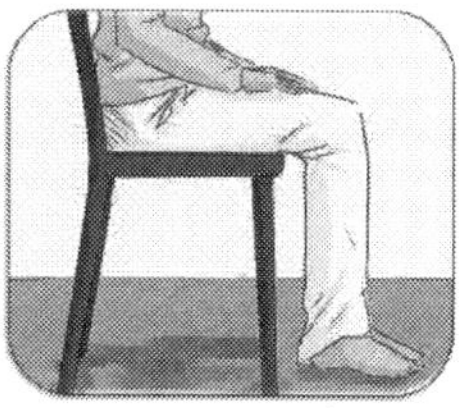

On a chair*

This covers the meditation postures one can adopt, depending on what is most comfortable for oneself.

The Place of Observing the Breath

Now, let us explain where one can observe their breath. After describing the physical posture of meditation, the Buddha continues by explaining the place where the observation of the breath should occur, saying in regards to the meditator:

> He establishes his mindfulness in *parimukha* (in front of or around the face).[10]

The Pāli word *parimukha* is composed of the prefix *pari*, meaning 'around' or 'in front', and the noun *mukha*, meaning 'face' or sometimes 'mouth'.[11] In this context, *parimukha* means 'in front of or around the face', as defined by official Pāli-English dictionaries.[12] What lies in front of our face? The nose, of course. That said, the Buddha did not specifically mention the nose because people with shorter or flatter noses may instead feel their breath on the upper lip. That is why he referred to the area 'in front of the face' (*parimukha*).

Let's now look at how one can observe the breath. Since the term *parimukha* is elucidated in the texts of the Pāli Canon, we can have a clear understanding of its meaning. The texts provide the following explanation:

> This mindfulness is established and well established at the nostrils or at the mark of the mouth (*mukha-nimitta*). Hence it is said: 'He establishes his mindfulness at *parimukha*.'[13]

---

[10] '*Parimukhaṃ satiṃ upaṭṭhapetvā*': M III.81, *Ānāpānassati-sutta.*

[11] See PED: *pari* - prefix, signifying (lit.) around, round about; (fig.) all round; *mukha* - face, mouth.

[12] See PED: *parimukha* - facing, in front (of the face).

[13] Vibh.252, *Jhāna-vibhaṅgo*, § 537: '*Ayaṃ sati upaṭṭhitā hoti, supaṭṭhitā nāsikagge vā mukhanimitte vā. Tena vuccati: "Parimukhaṃ satiṃ upaṭṭhapetvā".*'; Ps I.171, *Ānāpānassatikathā*: '*nāsik'agge vā mukhanimitte vā satiṃ upaṭṭhapetvā.*'

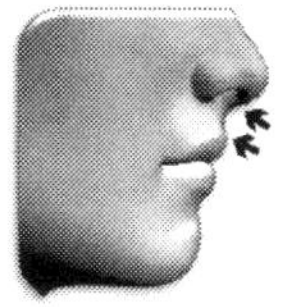

The phrase 'mark of the mouth' (*mukha-nimitta*) is explained by the commentary as 'the middle part of the upper lip where the nasal air strikes while breathing.'[14] *Parimukha* therefore indicates the region covering the nostrils and the upper lip. This is the area where one can feel the flow of the breath, especially on the upper lip for those with a shorter nose (*rassa-nāsika*) or at the nostrils for those with a longer nose (*dīgha-nāsika*).[15]

It should be noted that the nostrils serve as the primary gateway for air to enter and exit. Unless a person has a medical condition like asthma, which necessitates breathing through the mouth, normal breathing occurs through the nostrils, even during sleep. That is why, when we engage in breathing meditation, our attention is concentrated on this entry point, namely the nostrils.

Therefore, with respect to 'mindfulness of breathing', the Buddha advises that the observation at the *parimukha* should be as follows:

> Let your mindfulness of breathing be well established in one's own person at *parimukha*. ... When mindfulness of breathing is well established in one's own person at *parimukha*, any inclinations for outward and vexing thoughts cease to exist.[16]

---

[14] VbhA.368, *Jhānavibhaṅgo*: '*Mukhanimittan'ti cettha uttaroṭṭhassa vemajjhappadeso daṭṭhabbo, yattha nāsikavāto paṭihaññati.*'

[15] PsA II.479: '*Nāsikagge vā'ti dīghanāsiko nāsikagge. Mukhanimitte vā'ti rassanāsiko uttaroṭṭhe.*'

[16] It.80, *Asubhānupassī-sutta*: '*Ānāpānassati ca vo ajjhattaṃ parimukhaṃ sūpaṭṭhitā hotu. ... Ānāpānassatiyā ajjhattaṃ parimukhaṃ sūpaṭṭhititāya, ye bāhirā vitakkāsayā, vighātapakkhikā, te na honti.*'

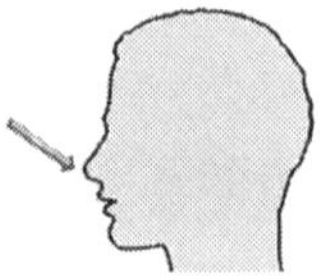

The expression 'well established' indicates the placing and fixing of one's mindfulness at *parimukha*, ensuring that it remains focused there without shifting from one place to another. The word 'established' contrasts with the notions of 'displacement', 'change', or 'movement', which are not relevant to the concentration achieved through mindfulness of breathing (*ānāpānassati-samādhi*).

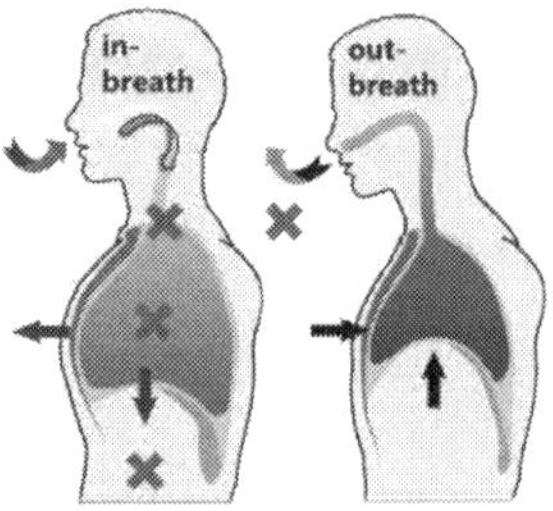

Therefore, place your mindfulness on the nostrils, where the air strikes them, or on the upper lip. Observe the natural flow of the in- breath and out-breath at that spot. Avoid paying attention to the in-breaths as they enter the body in the pharynx, lungs etc., or to the out-breaths as they leave the body.

The Method of Observing the Breath

The Buddha now explains how one can observe the breath. After telling us the place where we start observing the in- and out-breath, he continues with the method of observation, outlining four steps that the meditator can progressively follow to develop their concentration.

Step 1

Here, the Buddha says:

> Ever mindful he breathes in; ever mindful he breathes out.[17]

From the very first step, strong mindfulness, good memory, and awareness of the breath are needed. To achieve this, men-

---

[17] '*So, satova assasati, satova passasati*': M III.81, *Ānāpānassati-sutta*.

tally note 'in-breath' and 'out-breath' when you feel or understand them. This mental noting helps us remember whether we are breathing in or breathing out. That is, we remind ourselves what it is we need to remember. Therefore, always breathe in and out mindfully.

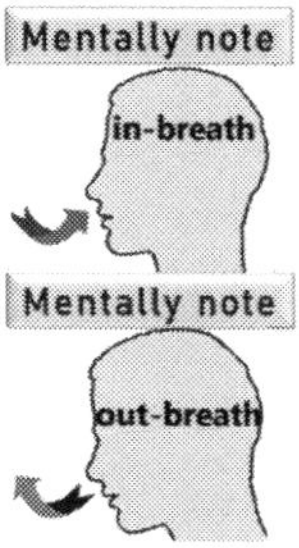

You can close your eyes; they are mostly unnecessary for this meditation, as the air we breathe in has neither colour nor shape to be seen. Pay attention to the sensation around the nostrils, or to the movement of air around them. When you do close your eyes, you will likely be able to feel, sense and perceive the in- and out-breath more clearly. The sensation helps you understand the motion of the air as it comes in and out.

Should you be distracted by other thoughts or emotions, ignore them. Do not try to push them away. Simply return to the nostrils, where you sense your breath, and mentally note: 'in-breath', 'out-breath'. These words prevent other thoughts from emerging within you, and the mind can focus more on the breath.

You can practice this first step for about five minutes, until you become aware of the process of the in- and out-breath.

Step 2

We now come to the second step, for which the Buddha says the following about the meditator:

> Breathing in a long breath, he understands: 'I breathe in a long breath'; or breathing out a long breath, he understands: 'I breathe out a long breath.'

> Breathing in a short breath, he understands: 'I breathe in a short breath'; or breathing out a short breath, he understands: 'I breathe out a short breath.'[18]

In this step, more attention should be directed towards the duration of the breath. We understand that once the breath reaches the nostrils, it does not stop immediately but continues to brush against them for a while. When we feel this brushing sensation lasting for a long time, we call it a 'long in-breath' or 'long out-breath'. However, if the breath stops almost immediately upon brushing the nostrils, we call it a 'short in-breath' or 'short out-breath'.

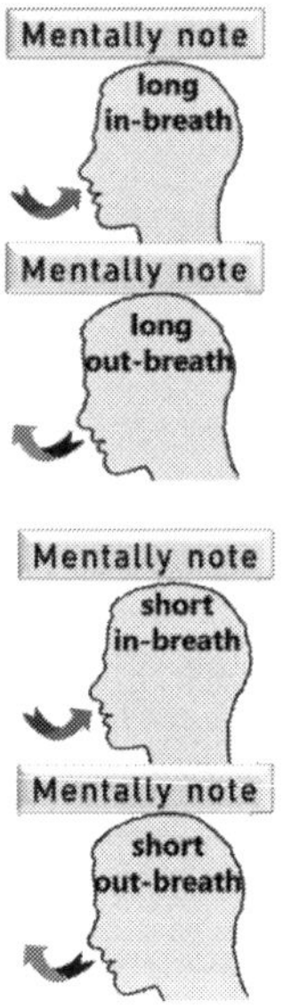

So, when you inhale or exhale a long, deep breath, try to understand it and mentally note: 'long in-breath', 'long out-breath'.

Conversely, when you inhale or exhale a short, shallow, brief breath, try to understand it and mentally note: 'short in-breath', 'short out-breath'.

In this second step, we endeavour not only to observe the in- and out-breath but also to become aware of their duration to enhance our concentration. That said, it is important that we do not try to control our breath by making it long or short; we only observe it in its natural rhythm.

Observing the breath is a mental, not physical, exercise, trying as we are to train our mind to concentrate on the very process of the in- and the out-breath. The duration is subjective and can be determined by understanding the difference between your own long and short in- and out-breaths.

---

[18] *'Dīghaṃ vā assasanto "dīghaṃ assasāmī"ti pajānāti. Dīghaṃ vā passasanto "dīghaṃ passasāmī"ti pajānāti. Rassaṃ vā assasanto "rassaṃ assasāmī"ti pajānāti. Rassaṃ vā passasanto "rassaṃ passasāmī"ti pajānāti.'* Ibid.

Practice this second step for about five minutes, until the mind gets used to it and you become aware of the state of your breathing in relation to its duration.

Step 3

The Buddha then describes the third step for a meditator:

> He trains thus: 'I shall breathe in experiencing the whole body (of the in-breath).'
>
> He trains thus: 'I shall breathe out experiencing the whole body (of the out-breath).'[19]

Here the emphasis is on the concept of the 'whole body' (*sabba-kāya*). This is a marked difference from the previous steps, in which we tried to understand the in- and out-breath superficially, without comprehending exactly when it began and when it ended. We only understood a part of it: sometimes the beginning, sometimes the end. In the third step, however, we try to understand what the Buddha calls 'the whole body' (*sabba-kāya*), which refers to the entire flow of the in-breath and out-breath, from beginning to end.

This phrase is sometimes misunderstood to refer to the whole physical body, including the hands, feet, chest, and abdomen, leading some to think they should observe the breath throughout the entire body. However, the word *kāya*, which literally means 'body', is used here in a metaphorical sense that requires clarification.

---

[19] '*Sabba-kāya-paṭisaṃvedī "assasissāmī"ti sikkhati. Sabba-kāya-paṭisaṃvedī "passasissāmī"ti sikkhati.*': M III.81, *Ānāpānassati-sutta.*

The meaning of the phrase 'the whole body'

The meaning of the word *kāya* in this context is given by the Buddha as follows:

> I say that this is a certain body (*kāya*) among the bodies, namely, the in-breaths and out-breaths (*assāsa-passāsā*).[20]

Therefore, 'body' (*kaya*) in this context is referring to 'the in- and out-breaths', not the physical body. The term *kāya* is employed here metaphorically in a collective, or functional sense to refer to the 'totality,' 'aggregation,' 'process,' or 'function' of breathing.

Other similar expressions by the Buddha where the 'body' (*kāya*) is used metaphorically are:

- the body of feeling (*vedanā-kāya*),
- the body of contact (*phassa-kāya*),
- the body of consciousness (*viññāṇa-kāya*),
- the body of wind element (*vāyo-kāya*), the body of water element (*āpo-kāya*)
- the military body (*bala-kāya*).[21]

In English, too, the word 'body' can have metaphorical, collective, or functional meanings, as demonstrated by the following examples: diplomatic body, legislative body, body of English literature, body of knowledge, and solid, liquid, and gaseous bodies. Here, 'body' is used metaphorically to represent the entirety of something, rather than its literal physical meaning.

[20] '*Kāyesu kāy'aññatar'āhaṃ evaṃ vadāmi, yadidaṃ assāsapassāsā*': M III.83, *Ānāpānassati-sutta*; S V.322, *Kimila-sutta*.

[21] E.g. M III.280, *Chachakka-sutta;* M I.513, *Sandaka-sutta;* A I.109, *Cakkavatti-sutta*.

Hence, *sabba-kāya* in this context is used to mean the entire or whole function and process of the in- and out-breaths (*assāsapassāsā*). It is so called because, at this step, the meditator begins to lose perception of the physical body and instead perceives the entire breath as a 'body'—that is, as a mass or collection of air.

In the adjacent illustration we see that, as the meditator concentrates on their breath at *parimukha*, it gradually becomes so clear and evident that they lose the sensation of the physical body itself. What remains in front of them is their awareness of the in-breath and out-breath as a 'whole'.

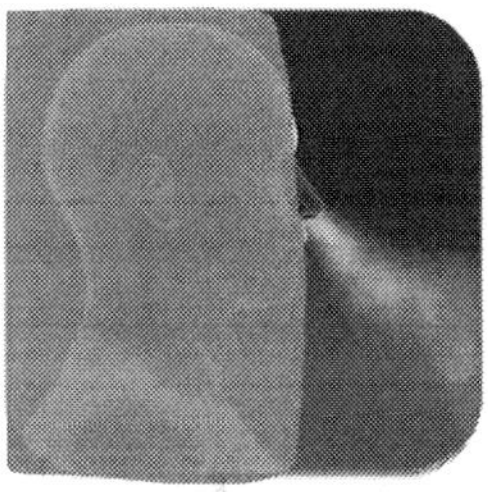

To remove any doubt that attention should not be diverted to other parts of the body, a text from the Pāli Canon makes it clear that the meditator should not follow the breath's movement inside or outside the body. It states:

> He sits down, establishing mindfulness at the nostrils (*nāsikagge*) or at the mark of the mouth (*mukhanimitte*, i.e. the upper lip). He does not pay attention to the in-breaths coming inside [the body] or the out-breaths going outside [the body].[22]

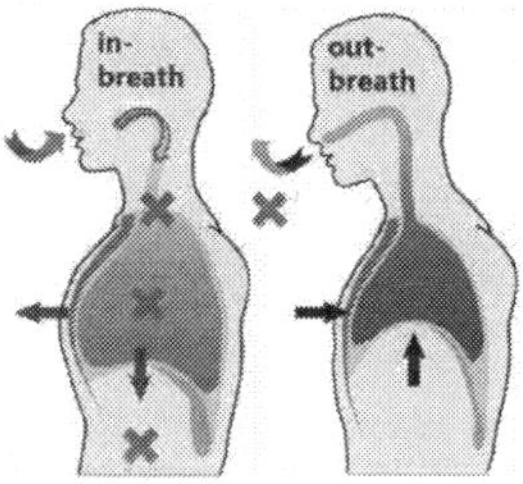

The rationale is that if someone followed the air of the in-breath inwards as it traveled to various parts of the body, then they would be practicing elements meditation (*dhātu-manasi-*

---

[22] Ps I.171, *Ānāpānassatikathā*: '*Evamevaṃ bhikkhu nāsik'agge vā mukhanimitte vā satiṃ upaṭṭhapetvā nisinno hoti. Na āgate vā gate vā assāsa-passāse manasi karoti.*'; PsA II.478: '*phuṭṭhaṭṭhānato abbhantaraṃ āgate, bahiddhā gate.*'

kāra) in relation to the air element (*vāyo-dhātu*), but not mindfulness of breathing meditation.

Even so, by meditating solely on the air element, someone is not fully practising elements meditation, as it also necessitates meditation on the other three elements (solid, liquid, and heat) in order to understand their interrelation.

In the body, we have the air element, along with the solid, liquid, and heat elements, for which there is a different meditation. We will explain this later. For now, the point is that focusing exclusively on the air element within the body cannot be regarded as successful practice, either as a mindfulness of breathing meditation or as an elements meditation.

In this third step, then, try to experience the whole in-breath at the nostrils and mentally note 'whole in-breath'. Do likewise for the 'whole out-breath'.

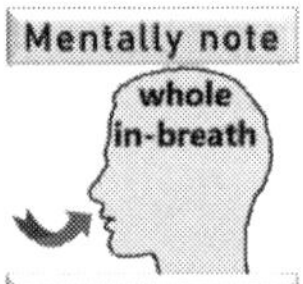

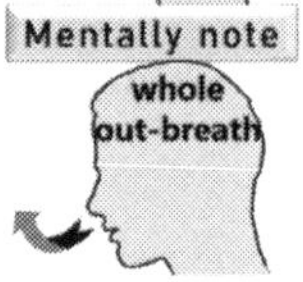

To clarify this process, we will give examples of how to observe the whole in- and out-breath from beginning to end. Since most people in the West have a longer nose, the explanation will focus on the nostrils, where *the place of contact* (*phuṭṭhaṭṭhāna*) for the inhaled and exhaled air is located, rather than on the upper lip. Here, 'whole' means to discern at the place of contact the beginning, middle, and end of the breath, and not just a part of it.

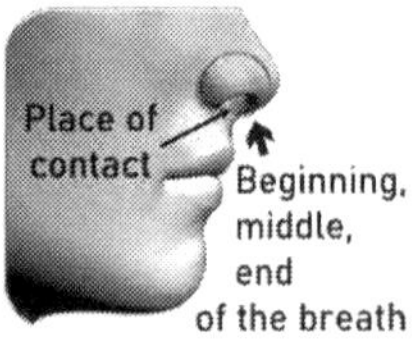

In the first example, a violinist focuses their attention on the place where the bow touches the strings of the violin. It is from that point that the notes and the melody emerge. The violinist does not pay attention to either the upper or lower end of the bow, but instead concentrates on the *place of contact* of the bow with the strings. It is here that the violinist can discern the beginning of the bow's movement on the strings, the middle (in other words, the duration of the movement), and the end of the movement.

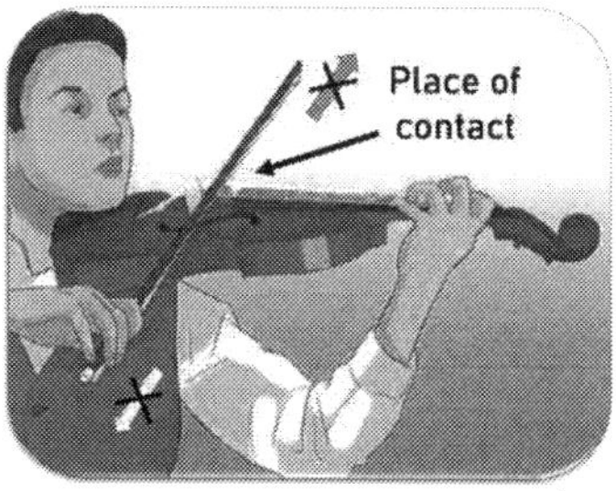

*

Something similar occurs with the meditator, who does not pay attention to the breath entering or exiting their body but concentrates on the area where the air touches their nostrils, at the *place of contact*. The effort is to experience or feel the beginning of the air's movement, the middle (the duration) of the movement, and the end of the movement.

In the case of the in-breath, the beginning occurs when the air first enters and touches the nostrils, the middle as it continues touching them, and the end when it stops doing so. The same applies to the out-breath: the beginning is when the air first exits and touches the nostrils, the middle as it continues, and the end when it stops.

When the meditator can observe this beginning, the middle, and the end, it can be said that they have experienced the whole process of the in-breath and the whole process of the out-breath.

The opposite is to experience only a part of the breath. Sometimes, for instance, the meditator may only focus on the beginning. That is, they understand when the air first touches the nostrils but do not understand when it stops. The same applies if they were to experience only the middle, or the end, or even the beginning and the middle, and nothing else. Likewise for the middle and the end, or the beginning and the end. All these facets are parts of the breath, though not the breath in its entirety. It is only when experiencing the beginning, middle and end that one can say they have experienced the process in its entirety.

Therefore, to reach the point of experiencing the whole process of the in-breath from beginning to end, start by observing at the place of contact just the beginning of the in-breath, when the air begins touching the nostrils. When you feel it, mentally note ‘beginning’. Then observe the end of it, when the air has stopped touching the nostrils. When you feel it, mentally note ‘end’. These are the two reference points: beginning and end. In this way, you can see the process clearly and accurately, gain better concentration, and observe more details.

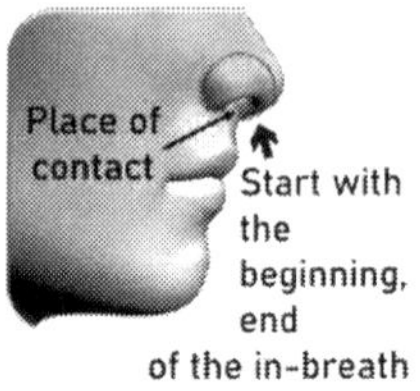

You can do something similar with the out-breath. Start by observing the beginning and end of the out-breath. When you feel them, mentally note: ‘beginning’, ‘end’. The beginning is when the air exits and touches the nostrils, and the end is when it stops touching them.

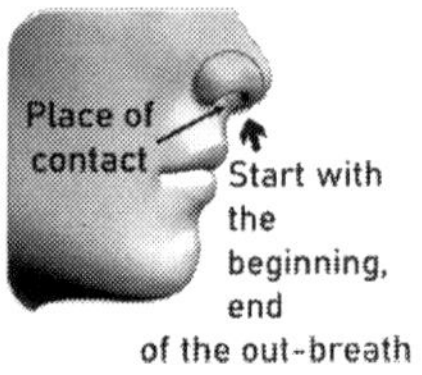

Then, try to discern the ‘middle’ of the in-breath. This refers to the intermediate period between the beginning and the end, during which the air continues to move, touching the nostrils at the place of contact before it stops. When you feel it, mentally note ‘middle’.

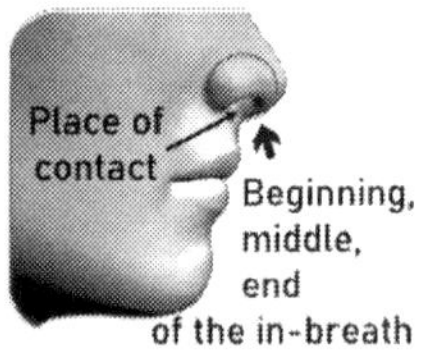

Repeat the process for the out-breath. When the air exits and you feel the intermediate duration between the beginning and the end of the out-breath, mentally note ‘middle’.

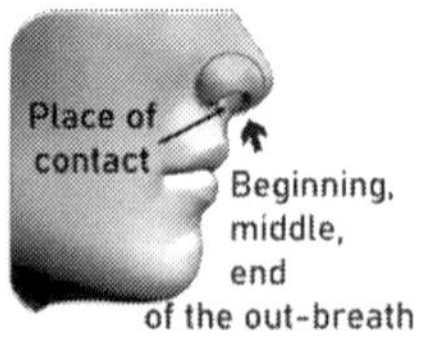

Doing this, you complete the observation from beginning to end by mentally noting for each in- and out-breath, 'beginning, middle, end'.

These are the words that help you realize the entire process of the in- and out-breath. Later, of course, when the mind becomes accustomed to this process, you may eventually omit the words. There is no need to continuously repeat 'beginning, middle, end, beginning, middle, end,' because the mind now knows what to focus on. If distracting thoughts appear or the mind begins to wander, however, you can repeat the words in order to refocus. This third step brings us closer to understanding not just a part of the breath but the whole body of the in-breath and out-breath.

This concludes the third step, and we move on to the fourth.

Step 4

The Buddha continues, stating the following regarding the meditator:

> He trains thus: 'I shall breathe in, even though the bodily process (of the in-breath) is calming down'; he trains thus: 'I shall breathe out, even though the bodily process (of the out-breath) is calming down.'[23]

Here the bodily process of breathing (*kāyasaṅkhāra*) is mentioned. These words mean that, although the breath can become calm, quiet, peaceful, and relaxing, the meditator should not stop observing them but continue paying attention to the in- and out-breaths. This is important because, as the mind attains some calmness, the meditator may begin to enjoy

---

[23] '*Passambhayaṃ kāyasaṅkhāraṃ assasissāmī'ti sikkhati, 'passambhayaṃ kāyasaṅkhāraṃ passasissāmī'ti sikkhati*'': M III.81, *Ānāpānassati-sutta.*

it and forget to observe the breaths. In this case, the Buddha advises the meditator to train in observing the breaths and not to rest in the calmness and tranquillity that can arise, as the purpose here is to train more deeply in concentration.

Therefore, the fourth step is an encouragement to urge the meditator not to be satisfied with the brief calmness and tranquillity but to continue observing the breaths.

The meaning of the phrase 'bodily process'

Here the word *kāya* (body) appears again and may cause confusion for some if they perceive *kāya* as a body with hands, feet, and other limbs. Its meaning is clarified in two discourses as follows:

> In-breaths and out-breaths ... are a bodily process (*kāya-saṅkhāro*); ... these states are bodily, are connected with the body; that is why in-breaths and out-breaths are a bodily process.[24]

From this explanation, we understand that the 'bodily process' refers to the in-breaths and out-breaths. Therefore, we should not confuse the word *kāya* with the physical body itself, as here too it has a metaphorical meaning; it is simply the entirety or the process of the in- and out-breaths. There is another related text in the Pāli Canon that provides a similar explanation:

> What is the bodily process (*kāya-saṅkhāro*)? Long in-breaths/out-breaths ... [and] short in-breaths/out-breaths, are

[24] M I.301, *Cūḷavedalla-sutta*; S IV.292, *Dutiya-kāmabhū-sutta*: '*Assāsa-passāsā ... kāya-saṅkhāro ... Kāyikā ete dhammā, kāya-ppaṭibaddhā, tasmā assāsapassāsā kāya-saṅkhāro.*'

bodily. These states are connected with the body and are bodily processes (*kāya-saṅkhārā*).[25]

Just as before, we see that this 'body' refers to the entirety of the in- and out-breaths. The meditator tries to understand just this: the wholeness and the process or function (*saṅkhāra*) of the in- and out-breaths. Therefore, they should continue to observe the natural process of the in- and out-breath at the *parimukha*, even though it may become calm, quiet, peaceful, and relaxing.

This fourth step, as mentioned earlier, is an encouragement, or exhortation to continue observing the process, without merely being content with attaining a little calmness and enjoying the tranquillity. To achieve deep concentration, we need to continue to focus on the process of the in- and out-breath. If we go deeper into concentration, we will see that much more can happen. This will be explained in detail below.

Here we complete the fourth step.

Overcoming distracting thoughts

Distracting thoughts or emotions often pose difficulties that most meditators will encounter, as they may intervene and impede concentration. The thoughts that arise can be repetitive and might not fade as the meditator tries to concentrate. Or it might seem as though more thoughts than ever spring to mind. Of course, this is not actually the case. Our thoughts are always with us, passing rapidly, one after another, in fractions of a second. In our normal state, we do not necessarily perceive

---

[25] Ps I.184, *Satokāriñāṇaniddeso*, § 171: '*Katamo kāyasaṅkhāro; Dīghaṃ assāsā/dīghaṃ passāsā ... rassaṃ assāsā/rassaṃ passāsā kāyikā. Ete dhammā kāyapaṭibaddhā, kaya-saṅkhārā. ...*'

each one, but when the mind begins to concentrate, it becomes much clearer and starts to be aware of these thoughts.

In meditation, we must ignore all these thoughts, because the mind does not stop; it constantly jumps from one thought to another. Just as a monkey jumps from branch to branch, grabbing one and letting go to grab another, the mind moves from one thought to another, endlessly.

It is wise to stop paying attention to the monkey-like mind and try to tame it, to fix it on a point of focus, which is none other than the place where we feel the air entering and leaving the nostrils. If we notice the mind beginning to wander, we should repeatedly bring it back to the same point, using the words 'beginning, middle, end' mentally. In this way, we are in a position to locate and observe the in- and out-breath, and to concentrate on the details, continuing meditation in this manner. Through this, we can achieve deeper concentration. Our minds become very calm and can achieve profound tranquillity, to such an extent that we can sit motionless for half an hour or an hour with our mind undisturbed.

The results for both physical and mental health are beneficial. A calm mind is far more perceptive and clear than a confused one. We know that a confused mind clouds judgment, making otherwise solvable problems seem difficult. It also adversely affects our nervous system, intensifying anxieties, which impacts the heart and other bodily organs. A clear mind, on the other hand, can solve everyday issues much more easily. Likewise, the stress, anxiety, and worry that burden us gradually diminish. All the tension in our nervous system relaxes.

Nonetheless, if, during meditation, you encounter difficulties due to intense and persistent distracting thoughts and emotions, potentially caused by life events that have unsettled your mind, you can try the following methods of counting the breath to easily focus your mind. Similar methods are mentioned in the commentaries of the Pāli Canon, but the two described below are the simplest. You can use them if there is an urgent need.

First method of counting

This method involves counting from one to five, placing the number at the end of the out-breath. That is, you inhale and exhale normally, and at the end of each out-breath, you mentally count: 'one' after the first, 'two' after the second, 'three' after the third, 'four' after the fourth, and 'five' after the fifth.

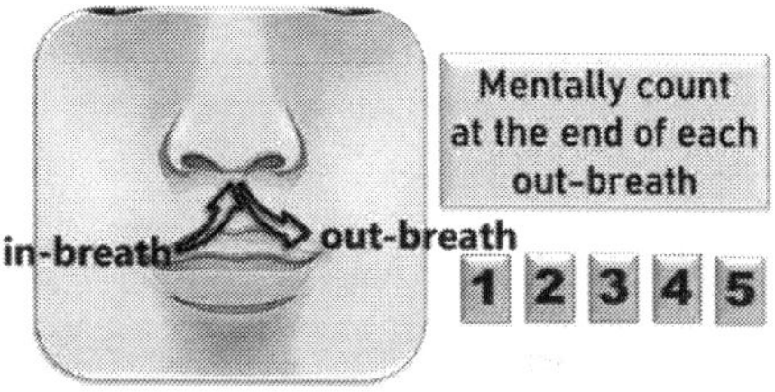

Each in-breath-out-breath cycle is one round. Once you reach 'five', you start again from 'one'. Do the same if you happen to forget the number you're on or to skip one.

Since there is a specific sequence to the numbers one through five, you need to remember it. This way, the mind is preoccupied with the numbers, pushing away any distracting thoughts. If you forget a number, it means that your mind has wandered and is thinking of other things. You can effectively catch it and bring it back by making it remember the breaths and the numbers. This is a method of calming intense and distracting thoughts.

If these thoughts and emotions persist, however, you can try the next dynamic counting method, which repeats the same number for both the in-breath and the out-breath.

2nd method of counting

This method again involves counting from one to five, but with the same number for both the in-breath and the out-breath. Repeating the same number twice helps you remember the number, and limits the potential that the mind will wander.

Inhale and exhale normally. For the in-breath, mentally count 'one'. Then for the out-breath mentally count 'one' again. For the next in-breath, out-breath, mentally count 'two' for the in-breath and again for the out-breath. Mentally count 'three' for the next in-breath and again 'three' for the out-breath breath, and so on, until you reach five.

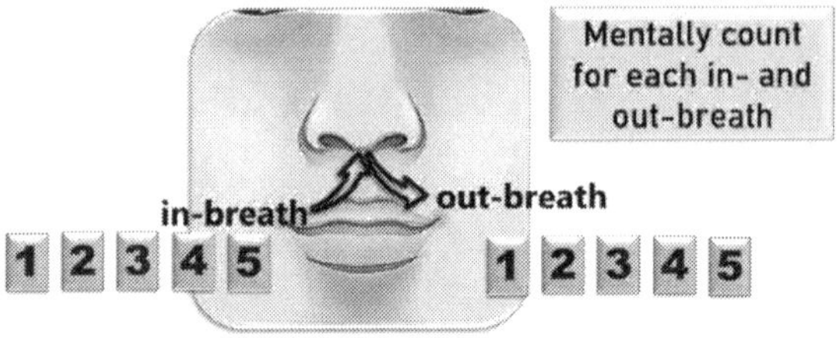

It will look like this: |in-breath 'one' – out-breath 'one'|| in-breath 'two' – out-breath 'two'|| in-breath 'three' – out-breath 'three'|| in-breath 'four' – out-breath 'four'|| in-breath 'five' – out-breath 'five'|. After 'five', start again from the beginning. Do the same if you forget a number in between.

With repetition, the mind withdraws from various distracting thoughts and attention returns to the in- and out-breath.

Both the first and the second counting methods are for emergency situations. You can use them when, after ten or fifteen minutes, you are unable to concentrate because your mind is distracted.

Once the mind calms down with these methods, you can return to the experience of the whole breath as mentioned in the third step (beginning-middle-end of the breath). The method of concentrating on the whole breath aids in achieving deeper focus, while the counting method is more shallow. If one wants to deepen their level of concentration, it is beneficial to use the experiential method in which they can feel the breath from the beginning to the end.

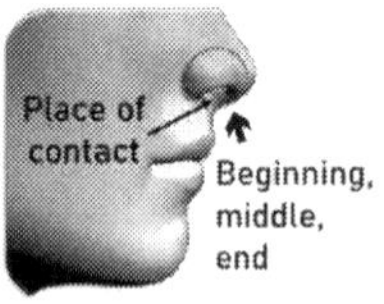

We will now see the potential results of concentration. The deeper one delves into breathing meditation, the clearer the sign of progress becomes. This is referred to as the 'sign of concentration' (*samādhi nimitta*).

The sign of concentration

The sign of concentration is a mental luminosity that appears in the meditator's mind. It is simply a by-product of the dynamic concentration achieved by the meditator. Some dispute that the Buddha spoke about this, but we will see that there are many relevant references in his discourses that are often overlooked. To dispel any doubts, let us first talk about the word *nimitta.*

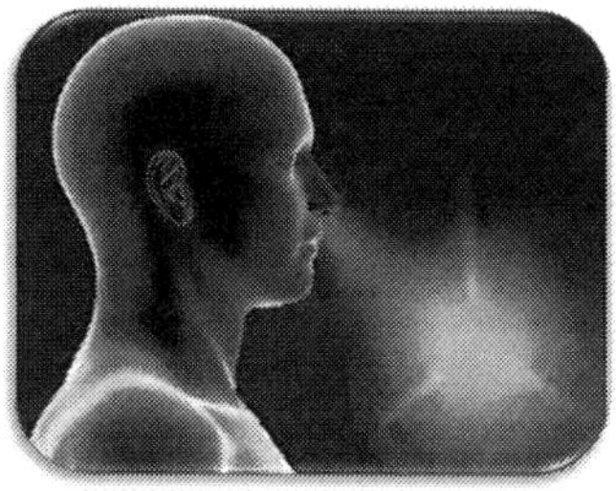

Nimitta (Sign)

Words used by the Buddha in connection with *nimitta* are *samādhi-nimitta* (the sign of concentration) and *samatha-nimitta* (the sign of serenity meditation).

The term *samādhi-nimitta* occurs about 25 times in the *Sutta-piṭaka* (Canon of Buddha's Discourses) and is mentioned in relation to serenity meditation (*samatha*) and insight meditation (*vipassana*), depending on the context. Here is an example of how the Buddha uses the term *samādhi-nimitta* in relation to the light mentioned above. He says:

> When one is devoted to the higher mind (*adhicitta*) ... and gives attention to the sign of concentration (*samādhi-nimitta*) ... one's mind (*citta*) becomes malleable, wieldy, and luminous (*pabhassara*).[26]

[26] A I.256, *Nimitta-sutta.*

The word 'luminous' (*pabhassara*), as related to the sign of concentration, is used to describe a mind that has achieved higher and elevated concentration (*samādhi*). It seems, then, that luminosity emerges in deep concentration, as is stated: 'When one is devoted to the higher mind (*adhicitta*)', meaning the higher levels of the meditative mind. Here we see the correlation between the sign of concentration and the luminosity that appears during deep concentration.

Next, we have another term used by the Buddha, namely *samatha-nimitta* (sign of serenity meditation). This term occurs 11 times in the *Sutta-piṭaka* and refers exclusively to the serenity meditation (*samatha*). Let us look, for example, at the following passage, where the Buddha says:

> There is the sign of serenity (*samatha-nimitta*) ...: frequently giving careful attention to it is the nutriment for the arising of the unarisen enlightenment factor of concentration (*samādhi*).[27]

Regarding this sign, a Pāli commentary and subcommentary explain its meaning thus:

> The sign of serenity meditation is a) serenity itself (*samatha*), as well as b) its object (*ārammaṇa*), that is, the 'counterpart sign' (*paṭibhāga-nimitta*).[28]

Let us take a moment to explain what 'counterpart sign' means. In doing so, we will see that the sign of concentration is divided into three parts. This will also help us understand how this sign of concentration can gradually appear during the practice of meditation.

---

[27] S V.66, *Kāya-sutta.*

[28] SA III.141, *Kāyasuttavaṇṇanā;* Sṭ II, Mahāvaggaṭīkā, *Kāyasuttavaṇṇanā.*

The three types of signs

According to the Pāli commentaries, there are three types of signs:

1) The preliminary sign – *parikamma-nimitta*
2) The acquired sign – *uggaha-nimitta*
3) The counterpart sign – *paṭibhāga-nimitta*

The preliminary sign

The preliminary sign is the *parimukha*, which we encountered earlier, about which the Buddha says: 'He establishes his mindfulness in *parimukha* (around the face or mouth).'

Initially, the meditator needs to have a sign or a focus point on which to direct their attention. This is the nostrils or the upper lip, where the breath touches and becomes noticeable. From there, they begin to understand the movement of the breath entering and exiting.

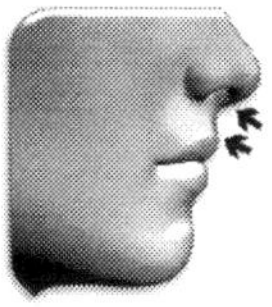

This is considered the preliminary sign because, without it, the meditator would not be able to start concentrating on anything. When they concentrate on the place where the air touches the nostrils or the upper lip, however, then they experience the sensation that something is moving there. It serves as a sign to recognize when the in-breath enters and the out-breath exits.

The acquired sign

This is the luminous, but not yet stable, sign that arises when the mind has reached a relatively high degree of concentration. The mental luminosity we previously mentioned appears, representing the first sign or indication that the mind has acquired

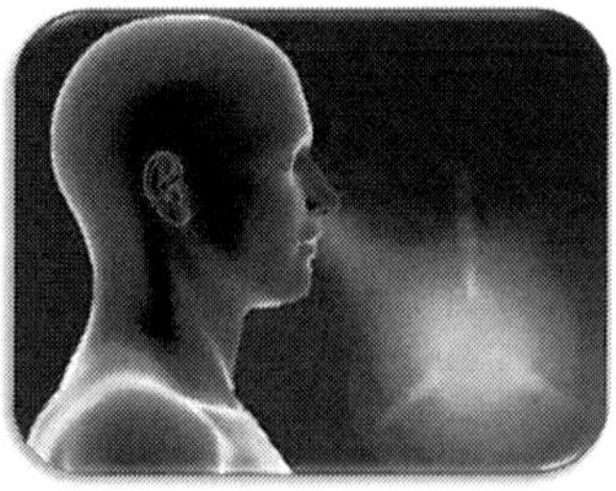

quite good concentration. At first, the luminosity appears diffused. But as concentration increases, it gradually condenses and becomes one with the breath. This luminosity is produced due to concentration, through which the mind acquires clarity and purity. It presents itself like a friend, we might say, to help the meditator see more details in the in- and out-breaths clearly. The more it comes to the forefront, the more one can discern every part of the in- and out-breaths. The meditator, though, must continue to pay attention primarily to the in- and out-breaths rather than the luminosity, which is still unstable and can disappear if concentration on the breath decreases. The more the meditator concentrates on the breath, the more intense and stable the luminosity becomes.

The counterpart sign

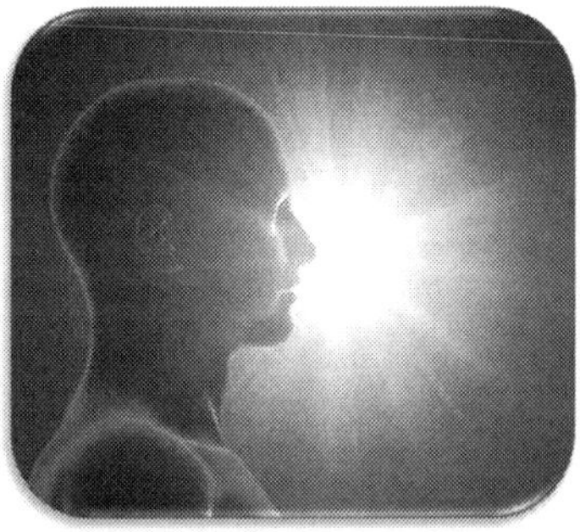

This is a clear, stable, and transparent luminous sign resulting from a higher degree of concentration. When the concentration increases significantly, the luminosity of the acquired sign begins to grow until it covers the meditator's entire face. In this situation, there are moments when the breathing stops, because the mind has achieved such a deep calm and tranquillity that the body does not need as much oxygen as before.

Sometimes, the meditator may stop breathing in and out for half a minute or more. However, instead of leaving the mind without an object of attention and thereby losing their concentration, they can concentrate on the luminosity as an object because it remains still and facilitates the stabilization of the mind. When the in- and out-breaths resume, the meditator can refocus on them.

The meditator, who started out with two objects of attention—the in-breath and the out-breath—now has a third object, the luminosity of the counterpart sign. This sign indicates that the meditator has reached the stage of 'access concentration' (*upacāra-samādhi*), which comes closer to the first meditative absorption (*jhāna*). It is the degree of concentration just prior to the attainment or full absorption of any of the meditative absorptions (*jhānas*), but still belongs to the consciousness of the sensuous sphere (*kāmāvacara*).

Attainment of the first meditative absorption

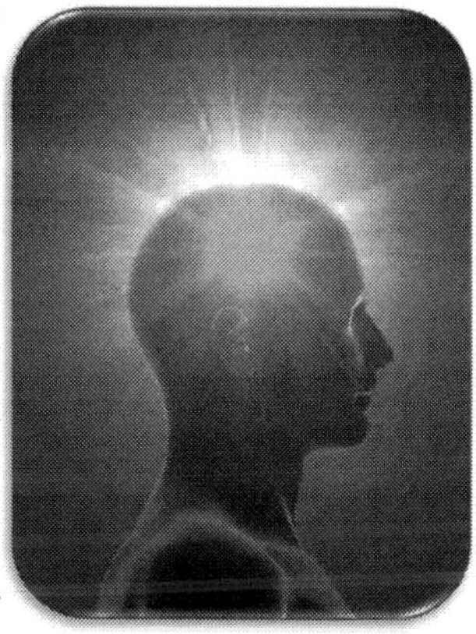

The first meditative absorption is attained through the full 'immersion' of the mind into the luminosity, or in other words, the counterpart sign, which becomes the object of the consciousness of the meditative absorption. The mind's familiarization with the luminosity leads to absorption into it. This specific stage is called 'attainment concentration' or 'full concentration' (*appanā-samādhi*).

The counterpart sign is considered a conceptual object (*paññatti*), but generally arises as a luminous form of matter. Therefore, the meditative absorption (*jhāna*) belongs to the consciousness of the fine-material sphere (*rūpāvacara*), which transcends the consciousness of the sensuous sphere. *Jhāna* is a mental state beyond the faculties of the five senses, and can be attained in isolation and silence through persistent dedication to the practice of concentration. During its attainment, all activities of the five senses are suspended. External visual, auditory, or bodily impressions are not perceived. Yet the mind remains active, fully alert, awake, and lucid, with total awareness of the object of concentration and the blissful feelings that result from it, such as rapture and bliss.

While immersed in *jhāna*, the mediator's mind is not empty or inert, as some believe, but active and filled with five significant mental factors, known as the 'five factors of meditative absorption' (*jhānaṅga*). These are:

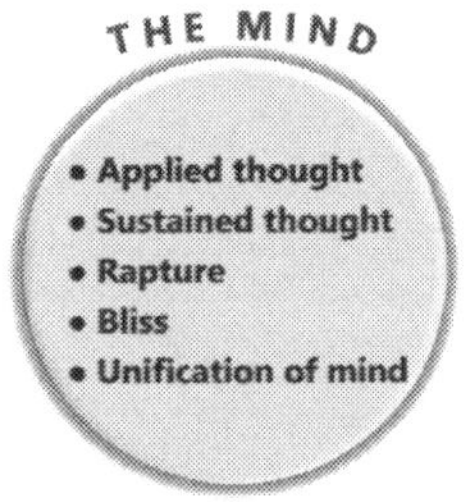

1) Applied thought (*vitakka*), which applies the relevant mental factors to the object of concentration,
2) Sustained thought (*vicāra*), which keeps them there,
3) Rapture (*pīti*), which brings about joy regarding the object,
4) Bliss (*sukha*), the feeling of experiencing happiness within the *jhāna*, and
5) Unification of the mind (*ekaggatā*), which has the ability to unify the other mental factors on the object of concentration. The mind is so unified that it does not turn to any other object, meaning it does not think about the past or the future but remains only in the present moment.

This is the description of the first *jhāna*.

Attainment of the other meditative absorptions

The meditator can further progress to the second, third, and fourth *jhānas*, which are deeper absorptions than the first.

Upon repeated attainment of and entry into the first *jhāna*, applied thought (*vitakka*) and sustained thought (*vicāra*) begin to seem gross, and the mind inclines more towards rapture (*pīti*) and bliss (*sukha*), which appear more refined and pleasant. Over time, the mind detaches from applied and sustained thought, resulting in the attainment of the second *jhāna*. This state has the counterpart sign as the object of attention and includes only rapture (*pīti*), bliss (*sukha*), and unification of the mind (*ekaggatā*) as its mental factors.

When the meditator repeatedly attains and enters into the second *jhāna*, rapture (*pīti*) begins to seem gross and the mind inclines more towards bliss (*sukha*), which appears more refined and pleasant. Over time, the mind detaches from rapture, resulting in the attainment of the third *jhāna*. This state has the counterpart sign as the object of attention and includes only bliss (*sukha*) and unification of the mind (*ekaggatā*) as its mental factors.

Should the meditator continue to attain the third *jhāna* and enter into it repeatedly, bliss (*sukha*) also begins to seem gross and the mind inclines more towards unification of the mind (*ekaggatā*), which appears more refined and pleasant. Eventually, the mind detaches from bliss, leading to the attainment of the fourth *jhāna*. This state has the counterpart sign as the object of attention and includes only unification of the mind (*ekaggatā*) and equanimity (*upekkhā*) as its mental factors.

As discussed in the general introduction, rapture, bliss, and equanimity differ as follows: rapture is the joy one feels in the anticipation of obtaining a desired object, like the joy a thirsty person in the desert would feel upon seeing a lake at the edge of an oasis. Bliss is the satisfaction of the actual experience of obtaining the desired object, like when that person drinks and enjoys the cool water of the lake. Equanimity is the spiritual calm that follows, such as when, having quenched their thirst, the person sits in the shade of the trees of the oasis and rests. Usually, where there is rapture, there can also be bliss, as when someone sees the cool water of the lake from a distance. However, where there is bliss, there is not necessarily rapture, as in the case of the third *jhāna*, where one fully enjoys bliss.

During a *jhāna*, the meditator can remain motionless for hours, even days, immersed in it and enjoying the ensuing bliss or equanimity, without feeling the need to get up due to discomfort. *Jhānas* offer a bliss that cannot be found in everyday life, which is why meditators who attain them often see the other joys of the world as insignificant. For them, the bliss that stems from *jhānas* constitutes their main source of satisfaction and they often enjoy it in solitude.

This, however, can lead to attachment and dependence. In our subsequent discussions of insight meditation, we will examine how one can overcome such states of attachment by recognizing the transient nature of even these intense feelings of bliss and equanimity.

The nature of meditative absorptions

Although the meditative absorptions (*jhānas*) are blissful experiences, they lack the wisdom of insight. They are therefore insufficient for achieving final liberation and enlightenment, remaining merely transient attainments. However, the high degree of concentration, which calms the five mental hindrances (*nīvaraṇa*)[29] while also producing feelings of deep tranquillity, serenity, and stillness, can be used for insight meditation (*vipassanā*).

[29] The five mental hindrances are: 1) sensuous desire (*kāmacchanda*), 2) ill-will, hate or anger (*vyāpada*), 3) sloth and torpor (*thina-middha*), 4) restlessness and remorse (*uddhacca-kukkucca*), and 5) sceptical doubt (*vicikiccha*). These five are considered obstacles to any kind of clear understanding or wisdom and, in fact, to any kind of progress. See M I.60, *Satipaṭṭhāna-sutta*.

The luminosity during meditation

We will now explain some of the peculiarities regarding the luminosity we mentioned, which varies depending on the meditator. For some, it is a bright light, like the morning star. For others, it resembles a luminous gemstone, or a radiant pearl. There are meditators, for instance, to whom the luminosity appears like a distant moon which, as concentration increases, comes closer and brightens, making the observation of the in- and out-breath very clear. For others, the luminosity is like the sun, a golden disc, or simply a white light.

The type of the luminosity depends on human perception, which varies. This can be compared to a prism that refracts a ray of light into the colours of the rainbow. The angle from which one observes these colours also plays a role. From one angle, blue might be more prominent; from another, red. Something similar happens with meditators. How they see the luminosity during meditation depends on their perception. Regardless of its specific appearance, though, this luminosity brings such great brightness to the mind that it facilitates the observation of in- and out-breath.

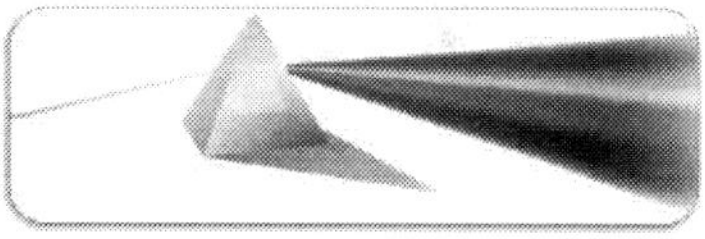

The nature of luminosity

We should know that the luminosity is a product of intense concentration, and does not appear from somewhere external. Instead, it is simply biophotons—light particles generated within the human body—appearing in the mediator's mind due to the condensation of electromagnetic waves when concentration is increased.

*

Biophotons are photons with weak electromagnetic waves, either in the ultraviolet or low-visibility spectrum of light, produced by a biological organism. In a way, they could be called the glow or radiance of life.

The biochemical reactions in our cells are what produce electromagnetism or bio-electromagnetism, which in turn generates light.[30] Our body emits electrical signals, which are measurable with devices such as a galvanometer. For instance, placing a finger on such a device might show a measurement of about 1.5 volts, comparable to the voltage of a small battery.

Our electromagnetic waves, present in the heart and brain, are what enable us to undergo electrocardiograms or electroencephalograms. An interesting fact: there are 60 times more electromagnetic waves in our heart than in our brain. These electromagnetic waves produce biophotons in other parts of the body as well.

In examining the electromagnetic spectrum, we see that wavelengths produce visible light only when condensed into a narrow area between infrared and ultraviolet radiation. When these wavelengths are shorter or longer than those in this limited range, the light emitted becomes invisible to our eyes. A similar phenomenon occurs during meditation, where there is a condensation of electromagnetic waves due to concentration. The more one concentrates, the more electromagnetic waves condense, resulting in the appearance of the light spectrum.

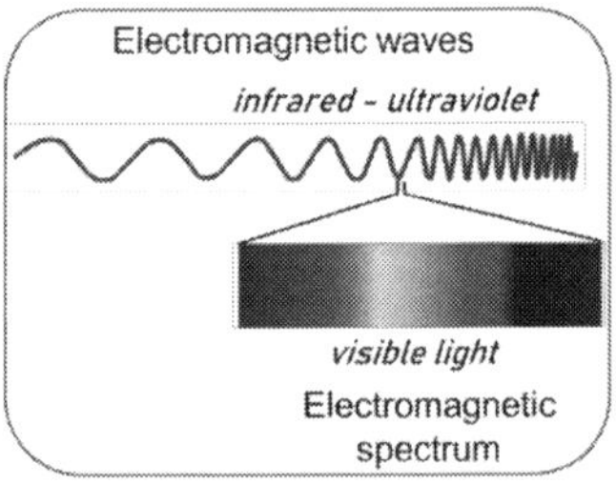

[30] For further information on biophotons see: Balasigamani Devaraj, Masashi Usa, Humio Inaba (1997): *Biophotons: ultraweak light emission from living systems,* and Marco Bischof (2005): *Biophotons - The Light in Our Cells*, Institute for Future Science & Medicine, Journal of Optometric Photography.

One of the changes that meditation can bring over time is the emission of more gamma brain waves, which are essentially bio-electromagnetic waves related to biophotons. These can be detected by electroencephalography or magnetoencephalography.

Gamma waves have a much higher frequency than delta waves and other types of brainwaves. These are the waves that produce the luminosity we mentioned earlier. They are associated with large-scale activities of the brain network and with high-intelligence cognitive processes such as active memory, attention, and perceptual organization. They can be significantly increased through neuro-stimulation or meditation, and appear in states of highly developed intelligence or when there is a need to remember an object or pay intense attention to it.

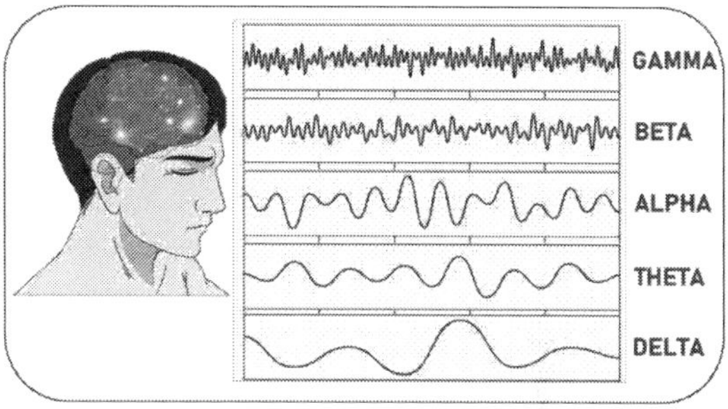

Especially during meditation, when there is an effort to concentrate for a prolonged period, gamma waves exhibit a very intense frequency, generating electromagnetism within the meditator and leading to the emergence of biophotons. These biophotons become visible to the meditator's mind.

Gamma waves at 40 Hz are the fastest of our brain waves. They propagate 40 times per second, producing increased focus, concentration, calmness, and even happiness. This means that high gamma wave activity has beneficial effects such as enhanced intelligence, improved self-control, natural optimism, better memory, and a higher level of perception.

High gamma wave activity can also generate biophotons in the brain or other organs of the body, such as the heart, whose electrical field is about 60 times greater in amplitude than the electrical activity generated by the brain.[31] This results in the appearance of rays of light, which a meditator in deep concentration and with a clear, pure mind can see, not with the consciousness of the physical eye, but with the developed consciousness of the mind through a higher level of perception, which is purified, elevated, clear and unobstructed by the dark veil of everyday worldly thoughts. There are thousands of testimonials from meditators who have experienced this.

It should be pointed out that the mind itself does not have light, photons, colours, or shapes, but it can produce electromagnetic waves and light fluctuations in the body through advanced concentration and the intense emotions of rapture and bliss it induces.

The mind is also a form of energy. As living beings, we utilize it in our daily lives to move our hands, feet or head, to hear, see, smell, taste, and touch, and to feel, perceive, and think. In contrast, a dead body, which lacks mental function and energy, lies inert and inactive.

When, during meditation, we concentrate our mental energy within us and do not let it dissipate outward, we see that a light is lit within us. This light is none other than the condensation of electromagnetic waves and biophotons caused by the concentrated mind. This should not be considered a mystery.

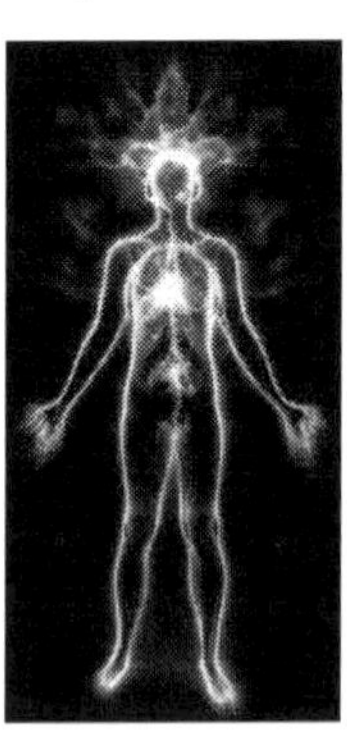

In the adjacent Kirlian photograph, we can see that our body emits electromagnetic waves. All biochemical organisms, including plants, have this capability. Our hearts beat, for example, because of this electromagnetism. What Kirlian photography actually captures are natu-

[31] McCraty, Rollin (2015): *Science of the Heart - Exploring the Role of the Heart in Human Performance* (Vol. 2), HeartMath Institute, USA, p. 36.

ral phenomena in our body, such as pressure, electrical grounding, humidity, and temperature. Changes in humidity (sometimes reflecting changes in emotions), barometric pressure, and electrical voltage, among others, produce different 'auras'. Thus, when our emotions change, these auras in our body also begin to shift. In a state of deep concentration, the emotions of bliss particularly, as mentioned above, generate various auras, which the meditator can perceive as shades of light.

Misinterpretations of the luminosity

It is easy to misinterpret the luminosity or light during meditation. People who have experienced it, not knowing what it is and how it is created, have often given it a mystical dimension, personified it, or even deified it by attributing metaphysical or supernatural properties to it. Hence, we hear them speak of the immortal pure light of infinite consciousness, cosmic light, cosmic consciousness, cosmic energy, God, divine grace, union of man with the divine, enlightenment, infinite ego or spirit, infinite soul, the *Brahma* or His Grace, a *Bodhisattva* or His Grace—each interpretation varying according to the individual's religious or philosophical background.

But when we analyse this light through the lens of insight meditation, which we will discuss below, we understand that it is nothing more than particles or waves of light that arise and fall in every moment, having no inherent, permanent essence. Similarly, the consciousness that perceives this light arises and falls like waves, lacking permanent substance. This is how, the meditator can overcome attachment to the material phenomenon of light, as well as to the mental phenomenon of consciousness, and surpass the tendency for mysticism, personification, or deification of material and mental phenomena.

Nevertheless, in serenity meditation, this light or luminosity is a good sign that the meditator has reached a high degree of concentration. We call it a 'sign' because it gives us a signal to which we can say, 'Yes, I have made good progress in concentration!' Therefore, when a teacher wants to know what stage of concentration the student has reached, they ask, 'What did you experience? How did you experience it?' If the student refers to such a luminosity, the teacher can recognize from the descriptions whether it is the acquired or the counterpart sign in order to give further instructions for progressing to the next stage. There are also gradations in the hue, distance, intensity, clarity, and duration of this luminosity, through which the level of concentration can be determined.

It should be noted that this luminosity can also be experienced through other methods of meditation, not just through meditation on breathing. This occurs as long as the mind attains deep concentration, which generates rapture, bliss, unification of the mind, and equanimity.

SUMMARY

Below are the key points of this meditation summarized.

1) The meditator chooses a suitable environment, where there are neither disturbances from people nor noise, nor any other distractions.
2) They sit with the spine erect and the hands comfortably placed on the thighs.
3) With eyes and mouth closed, they direct attention to the nostrils, specifically, to the place of contact where the air touches them as it enters and exits, observing the natural rhythm of breathing without strain, force, or modification.
4) *1st Step*: With attention focused on this point, the meditator observes the in-breath, mentally noting 'in-breath' when they feel it, and observe the out-breath, mentally noting 'out-breath' when they feel it. They continue in the same

way for a while, repeating the mental noting to remind their mind of what to watch out for.

5) *2nd Step*: They become aware of the duration of the in- and out-breath. When inhaling a long in-breath, the meditator mentally notes 'long in-breath'. When exhaling a long out-breath, they mentally note 'long out-breath'. When inhaling in a short, shallow, or brief manner, they mentally note 'short in-breath'. When exhaling a short out-breath, they mentally note 'short out-breath'. They continue in the same way for a while.

   The meditator does not repeat the mental noting mechanically like a *mantra* but in line with the natural in- and out-breath, and with full awareness of it. Later, when the meditator's mind becomes familiar with the process, the words can be omitted.

6) *3rd Step*: Gradually, the meditator can start to observe the whole in-breath from beginning to end, mentally noting 'beginning, middle, end (of the in-breath)', and observe the whole out-breath from beginning to end, mentally noting 'beginning, middle, end (of the out-breath)'.

   This helps to perceive the sensation of the in- and out-breath as a whole rather than in parts, contributing to deeper concentration. If the meditator cannot discern the middle, they at least try to discern the beginning and end. If they cannot discern the end, they at least try to discern the beginning, and so on. Eventually, they are trained to discern not only the beginning and the end but also the middle. If confused, they can return to the first step and gradually progress to the third step.

7) *4th Step:* This step is simply a reminder that the meditator should continue to observe the breaths in order to deepen their concentration, and not just enjoy the calm, peace and tranquillity that arises, as this may cause distraction.

8) If, during meditation, the meditator encounters difficulties due to intense and persistent distracting thoughts and emotions, they can start counting their breaths from one to five. This allows them to refocus their mind on the in- and out-breath. When the mind is calm, they can return to the experience of the whole breath, as in the third step.
9) The meditation duration can gradually increase day by day, from 10 minutes at the start, to 20, 30, 40, 45, 60 minutes and so on for beginners, and can last for hours for more advanced practitioners. Good concentration typically begins after about 45 minutes.

As the meditator practices daily for extended periods, in a suitable environment and under appropriate conditions, they will start to mentally perceive a luminosity in front of their nose, related to the breath, which is the first sign of concentration (*samādhi-nimitta*). This is called the 'acquired sign' (*uggaha-nimitta*) and is still unstable. With continuous concentration on the in- and out-breath, the luminosity becomes completely clear, stable, and transparent. This results from a higher degree of concentration and is known as the 'counterpart sign' (*paṭibhāga-nimitta*). Once this sign appears, the mind reaches the stage of 'access concentration' (*upacāra-samādhi*), which is remarkably close to *jhāna*. Continuing with concentration on the in- and out-breath, the mind becomes absorbed in the luminosity, now unified with the breath, and immerses itself in it. This is the moment of attaining the first meditative absorption (*jhāna*). The object of *jhāna* consciousness is essentially the mental image of the counterpart sign (*patibhāga-nimitta*).

As the meditator continues practising concentration, they can attain the other three *jhānas*.

This concludes the analysis of the serenity meditation on the breath. Next follows the meditation on friendliness.

Meditation on Friendliness

INTRODUCTION

Meditation on friendliness (*mettā*) is a form of meditation that allows us to eliminate hostile or negative dispositions towards ourselves and others, helping us develop good, positive, or friendly dispositions.

The word *mettā* in the ancient Indian Pāli language is derived from the noun *mitta* (Sanskrit: *mitra*), which means 'friend'. Its true meaning is a 'friendly disposition', that is, 'friendliness'. It denotes the 'disposition of a friend' (*mittassa bhāvo*): friendly attitude, friendly feeling, or friendly behaviour. In a word, it means friendliness, as opposed to hostility, and hostile dispositions, attitudes, and behaviours.

This form of meditation provides an escape and a means to liberate the mind from negative emotions such as enmity, malice, resentment, bitterness, antipathy, anger, hate, ill-will, fear, sadness, jealousy, depression, and stress. Accordingly, the Buddha states in his discourses:

> This is the escape from ill-will, anger, hate (*vyāpāda*), namely, the liberation of mind by friendliness (*mettā cetovimutti*).

> Cultivate meditation on friendliness; for by cultivating it, ill-will, anger, hate (*vyāpāda*) disappear.[1]
>
> There is the liberation of mind by friendliness. Frequently giving wise attention to it is the denourishment of ill-will, anger, hate (*vyāpāda*).[2]
>
> Friendliness (*mettā*) should be developed to abandon ill-will, anger, hate (*vyāpāda*).[3]

The dimension of the word *vyāpāda*, as found in these discourses, can be understood by looking at its synonyms, such as:

> *paṭigha* (aversion), *rosa* (wrath), *āghāta* (abhorrence, annoyance), *dosa* (hate), *vera* (enmity, hatred), *virodha* (resentment), *viddesa* (malevolence), *kodha* (rage), *kopa* (grudge), *caṇḍikka* (aggression), and *anabhiraddhi* (fury).[4]

According to Buddhist psychology, *vyāpāda* belongs to the group of mental factors rooted in hate (*dosa*), including jealousy (*issā*) and remorse or guilt (*kukkucca*). Such negative emotions are the foundation for the emergence of grief and anxiety, leading to feelings of distress, fear, and insecurity. Generally, they form the basis for the disturbance of mental peace and tranquillity. These emotions stem from dissatisfaction (*domanassa*) regarding the object of experience, considered undesirable, inappropriate, or annoying. The more intense the dissatisfaction becomes, the more it manifests as resentment, mental strain, and anxiety or hate, which is to say emotions detrimental to the mental and physical health of an individual or a society.

---

[1] A III.390, *Nissāraṇīya-sutta*; M I.424, *Mahārāhulovāda-sutta*.
[2] S V.105, *Āhāra-sutta*.
[3] A IV. 352, *Sambodhi-sutta*.
[4] *Abhidhānappadīpikā-ṭīkā*; Vbh.252, § 542.

Many of us have high ideals, often relating to notions of goodness, justice, peace, tranquillity, happiness, equality, solidarity, love, moral perfection, human rights, freedom, and quality of life, whether on an individual or societal level. However, as long as we fail to rid ourselves of hate, anger, and enmity, such ideals will always remain distant and fragile. Meditation on friendliness is designed to eradicate these harmful emotions at the root, paving the way for noble ideals like peace and tranquillity to flourish naturally. This then makes it more straightforward to nurture and maintain these ideals.

Suppose a farmer aims for a bountiful harvest but overlooks the crucial step of eradicating the weeds from his field. Regardless of the quality of the seeds he plants, his negligence in removing weeds will hinder his chances of achieving yield he desires. However, when he diligently uproots the weeds, the crop that emerges is not only abundant but also can be sustained more easily over time. In a similar vein, cultivating an attitude of friendliness helps to clear the mind's landscape of disruptive emotions and fosters a fertile ground for peaceful qualities and experiences to take root and thrive.

Meditation on friendliness can also arouse positive feelings of happiness, goodwill, and well-being within us by wishing happiness for oneself or for others, as advised by the Buddha:

> May all beings be happy and secure;
> may they be inwardly happy![5]

In fact, what all beings have in common is a desire for happiness and an aversion to pain and suffering. Therefore, our concern should be focused on wishing for all beings to be happy and free from pain, suffering, or harm.

---

[5] Sn.25, *Mettā-sutta*: '*Sukhino'va khemino hontu, sabbe sattā bhavantu sukhitattā.*'

Of course, this applies to us as well, since as beings we desire happiness and are much closer to ourselves than to others. So, we can start with ourselves, wishing ‘may I be happy’. Then, we can extend that friendliness to other beings.

When friendliness is extended to all beings in the world, it acquires an altruistic, universal dimension. As the Buddha said:

> Let one develop a boundless mind of friendliness (*mettā*)
> for the entire world—-above, below, and across—
> unconfined, without enmity, and without hatred.[6]

Various types of meditation focus on different objects and scopes, but the object of meditation on friendliness is beings (*satta*), encompassing all beings without exception. Instead of friendliness directed solely towards one individual or any specific group of beings, in one area or certain areas, the above lines explicitly express the importance of universal friendliness towards all beings.

This impersonal method of meditation on friendliness truly broadens the mind, making it boundless, and thus liberates it from the prison-like walls of egocentrism, individualism, narcissism, ill-will, anger, hate, aversion, hostility, jealousy, and pettiness.

As long as the mind is imprisoned within these walls, it remains confined, obstructed, and bound. By breaking down these walls, friendliness frees the mind, which then easily becomes boundless. This is why the Buddha speaks of ‘liberation of the mind by friendliness’ (*mettā ceto-vimutti*).

Friendliness also denotes less obvious qualities such as patience, tolerance, forbearance, and non-violence. It also expresses acceptance, appreciation, liberality, open-mindedness, and benevolence.

---

[6] Ibid. ‘*Mettañca sabbalokasmiṃ, mānasaṃ bhāvaye aparimāṇaṃ. Uddhaṃ, adho ca tiriyañca, asambādhaṃ, averaṃ, asapattaṃ.*’

The concept of friendliness can be analysed through its characteristics, function, manifestation, and proximate cause. Its characteristic can be defined as the perception of the well-being (*hitākāra*) of beings, while its function is to promote their well-being. Its manifestation, then, is the disappearance of annoyance (*āghāta*). Its proximate cause is that it sees the pleasant or positive side (*manāpa-bhāva*) of all beings. Friendliness succeeds when it causes anger and ill-will to recede and fails when it produces affectionate love (*sineha*),[7] which leads to attachment.

Moreover, meditation on friendliness pacifies and calms the mind, and its frequent practice allows the meditator to:

- eliminate negativity towards oneself and others,
- create positivity towards oneself and towards others,
- eliminate bad habits,
- improve one's character,
- feel peaceful, calm, and relaxed, and
- understand oneself and those around oneself.

In addition, the meditator will be able to experience the following benefits:

- sleep happily,
- awaken happily,
- not have bad dreams,
- be pleasing to human beings,
- be pleasing to non-human beings,
- concentrate one's mind quickly,
- have a serene facial expression.[8]

---

[7] Vism.318, *Brahmavihāra-niddeso, Pakiṇṇakakathā*, or *The Path of Purification*, p. 311.
[8] A V. 341, *Mettā-sutta*.

In other discourses the Buddha also says:

> It is difficult for human or non-human beings (animals or evil spirits) to assail someone who has developed and cultivated the liberation of mind by friendliness (*mettā*). ... If they think they can overthrow his mind, they will only experience fatigue and vexation.[9]

The word *mettā* has been translated into English mainly as 'love' or 'loving-kindness', which is essentially based on, or arises from, love. This translation, however, is in contrast with Pāli, Sanskrit and Hindi, where the word 'love' is *pema/prem* or *piya/pyār/priya*, and implies strong feelings of affection, tenderness, attraction, and attachment, which, in turn, can bring sadness, sorrow, fear, or jealousy if there is no response from its object. That's why the Buddha says:

> From love (*piya/pema*) springs sorrow,
> from love springs fear.
> For him who is wholly free from love
> there is no sorrow; whence then fear?[10]

He says the same about craving (*taṇhā*), making it clear that love is a form of craving, passion, and attachment. He states the following:

> From craving (*taṇhā*) springs sorrow,
> from craving springs fear.
> For him who is wholly free from craving
> there is no sorrow; whence then fear?[11]

To many this may sound paradoxical, but even the supreme love, that of a mother for her child, becomes hatred towards

---

[9] S II.263, 264, *Kula-sutta & Satti-sutta.*
[10] Dhp, 212, 213.
[11] Dhp, 216.

others if she feels that they threaten it. If her own child shows her indifference, then her love can turn into bitterness, sorrow, and sadness. From this we understand that love can create negative emotions within us, even going so far as to result in hate and sorrow. In other words, people who love can easily hate when their love is not reciprocated.

Therefore, instead of 'love', the Buddha urged his disciples to develop other noble emotions towards themselves and others, such as friendliness (*mettā*), compassion (*karuṇa*) and altruistic joy (*mudita*).

Here we see a distinction among these terms, which in the West are usually confused with love. All of them are very beneficial emotions that do not bring about attachment or craving and are helpful to us and to others.

To start with, the meditator should develop friendliness in order to eliminate hostility. This will make it easier to develop compassion and altruistic joy. Let us now see how this meditation on friendliness is practised.

The Practice of Meditation

THE POSTURE OF THE BODY

Typically, one begins meditation on friendliness by assuming a comfortable seated position. Later, when sufficient awareness and concentration have been gained, one can meditate in any position. As the Buddha suggests:

> Whether one stands, walks, sits
> or lies down, as long as one is awake,
> one should sustain this mindfulness (of friendliness).[12]

There are some specific procedures you should follow when preparing for meditation on friendliness. First of all, ensure

---

[12] Sn. 26, *Mettā-sutta.*

that you aren't feeling drowsy, as can happen as after a big meal or a busy day. Identify a specific time slot in which you'll be free and abide by the guidelines below.

1) Sit in a quiet place that ensures privacy and silence. It is essential to plan your schedule so that there are no distractions from responsibilities or issues that do not allow you to concentrate all your attention on the effort of meditation.
2) Place a mat or pillow on the floor and sit comfortably in a cross-legged or half cross-legged position. If this is difficult, you can also sit on a bed, a low chair, or a bench, as illustrated on pp. 52, 53.
3) Keep your spine and neck upright and your shoulders down and relaxed, without leaning against a wall or chair.
4) Keep your hands relaxed on your thighs.
5) Close your eyes and turn your attention inwards.

The period of meditation can be gradually increased from day to day, from 10 minutes in the beginning, to 20, 30, 45, 45, 60 and so on for beginners, and can last for hours for the more advanced meditators.

The Attitude of the Mind

Meditation on friendliness can be developed gradually in four steps.

Step 1 - *Dispelling negative emotions towards ourselves*

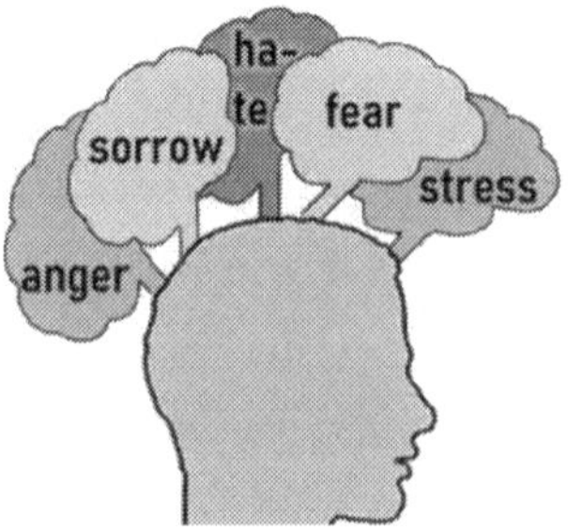

If you are feeling anger, hate, fear, sadness, jealousy, anxiety, stress, or other negative emotions, it is time to begin this meditation to dispel them.

To start, you can pay attention to your whole body and bring to mind an image of yourself as you are at the present moment. This is because negativity affects the entire nervous system. For example, when someone is angry, tension flows through the nervous system, resulting in the feeling of agitation.

At the same time, take a moment for positive thinking, which can help you dispel negativity. As the Buddha says, it is through positivity that we can best overcome negativity: 'Conquer anger by non-anger, and evil by good.'[13] Should we need to clean up a mess, we cannot do so with another mess. To clean a dirty garment, we need clean water, not more dirt. Likewise, to remove negativity within us, we must employ the opposite energy of positivity.

We encounter many negative emotions, such as those we discussed earlier, in our daily lives. If we allow them to multiply and fester, they become habitual and manifest automatically at the slightest provocation. Those who dwell on these emotions, therefore, become angry instantly and misunderstand others easily. This tendency can also manifest as self-blame and self-hatred.

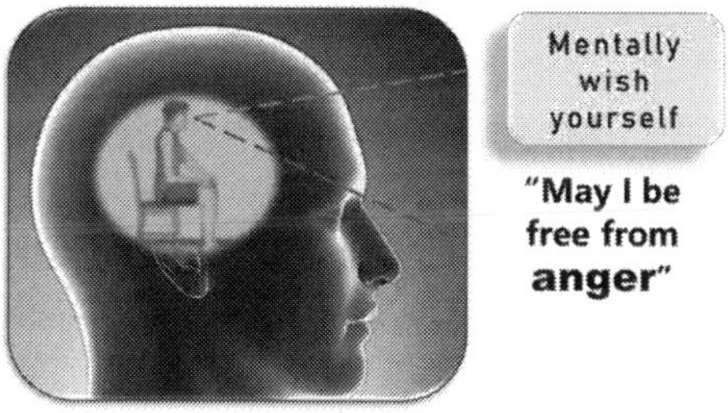

But there is a way to overcome this negativity. Start by bringing to mind the image of yourself, and then mentally express the wish with the following words: 'May I be free from anger', 'May I be free from hate', or 'May I be free from fear', depending on what is the most common, pronounced, and obvious negative emotion you are feeling.

[13] Dhp, 223: '*Akkodhena jine kodhaṃ, asādhuṃ sādhunā jine.*'

This is not a command, but a wish. Alternatively, you can use the words 'May I be *without* …' instead of 'May I be *free from* …' You are not trying to push away these negative emotions from within yourself; you are not trying to fight them, suppress them, or smother them. You are simply trying to withdraw your mind from them.

In this way, you detach your mind so that it does not get swept away by the tide of these emotions or become entangled in them. It's akin to removing fuel from a fire, whereas allowing oneself to be consumed by anger is like pouring fuel on the fire. Therefore, withdraw your mind by repeating 'May I be free from anger' again and again. During this practice, if you notice areas of your body that are particularly tense, direct your focus there while continuing to mentally repeat 'May I be free from anger'.

If there is hate within you, which is simply a higher and more intense degree of anger, then you mentally repeat 'May I be free from hate'. If it's fear, then you mentally repeat 'May I be free from fear'. If the emotion is more like stress than anger, you can mentally repeat 'May I be free from stress'. Repeat it—not too slowly, not too quickly—many times.

It's not merely about reciting words, however. You must at the same time understand their meaning and direct your attention inward to yourself, while saying mentally, 'May I be free from anger', or whatever your chosen phrase is.

If, during this meditation, you have memories of incidents in the past where you were under the influence of anger, hate, or fear, you can again consider yourself as the object of attention and wish to be free from anger, hate, and so on, depending on the negative emotion.

Negative feelings do not arise by chance, but because unpleasant and undesirable incidents have occurred in our lives. With this meditation, one can delve deep into the past and discover such emotions, even from childhood, which have influenced, and in many cases continue to influence, our characters and personalities. When they appear in our mind during meditation, either from the past or the present, and we start remembering them, we simply wish to be 'free from them'.

These negative emotions can appear at any moment in our lives and are not something strange. What we need to realize is how much they consume us from the inside, rob us of happiness, serenity, and peace, and how much they hurt us. It is good, therefore, to take the time to dispel them and purify the mind, especially as they sometimes accumulate over days, weeks, months, or even years.

Eventually, you will find out that, if you are carried away by these emotions, they will only become stronger. But by practicing this meditation, repeatedly wishing to be free from them and learning to withdraw and detach your mind, they will disappear, bringing deep relief, calm, and serenity within you. You can achieve this; it is not impossible.

This meditation also contributes to your self-awareness, as it helps you understand not only your weaknesses but also the strength you possess to overcome them. For instance, when you feel anger, you will immediately become aware and able to dispel it on the spot before it overwhelms you. The same applies to hate, fear, and anxiety. It is a way to be aware of yourself, know what is happening inside you, and overcome any negativity.

Step 2 - *Increasing positive emotions towards ourselves*

With this meditation, we can not only dispel negativity but also increase feelings of positivity within ourselves. When the negative emotions have been appeased, you can move to the second step: developing positive emotions about yourself. This approach helps to foster a great deal of positivity, ensuring that negative emotions like anger, hate, anxiety, and fear cannot easily overwhelm you when you are enriched and empowered with positive ones.

A significantly positive emotion that you can cultivate is happiness. This is a state of deep and lasting contentment and satisfaction. After all, a happy person is one who feels good, is safe, does not experience suffering and stress, and is free from hardship, misery, and pain. It is a state that all humans, or rather, all living beings, desire. As the Buddha says, 'Beings long for happiness.'[14] It is rare to find someone who wishes to be unhappy!

'Happiness' is a charming word. We may not consciously say it every day, but subconsciously, it is what we aspire to. That is, we long to be happy, even though it often seems like an elusive dream. Even if we have experienced some happy moments in our lives, we tend to forget them when negative emotions stir within us, and we remember only the dark side of life.

However, when we remove negative emotions and develop the positive emotion of happiness through meditation, we are able to maintain the joy and euphoria that it brings within ourselves.

To do this, focus your attention on yourself and repeatedly wish 'May I be happy'. If memories of happy moments you experienced with friends or relatives come to your mind, take yourself as the object of attention as you remember yourself, and mentally wish 'May I be happy'. You will find that your mind will become stronger and that

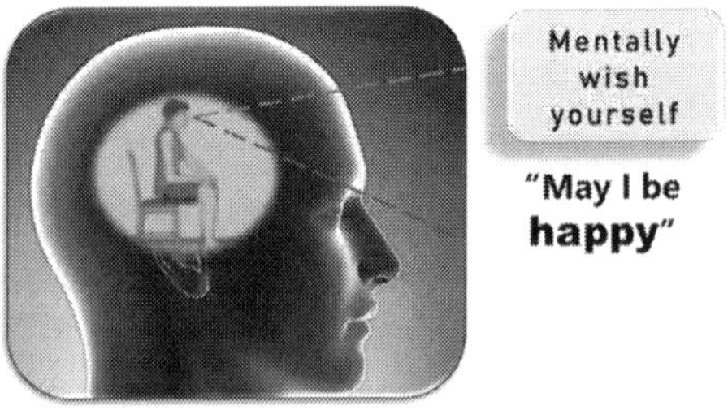

[14] Dhp, 131: '*sukhakāmāni bhūtāni.*'

you will become more optimistic, with a bright outlook and self-confidence, freed from unpleasant emotional states such as sadness, melancholy, and jealousy.

Step 3- *Increasing positive emotions towards acquaintances*

When you feel happiness flooding in, you can share it with acquaintances, too. That is, you can take another step in wishing for others to be happy.

Therefore, if you remember other people, whether one, two, or many, keep their image in your mind as you know it and wish for them to be happy, mentally saying 'May he/she be happy' or 'May they be happy'.

Repeat the phrase—neither too slowly, nor too quickly—many times. Over time, you will feel the impact of this positivity grow and grow. This is because our happiness does not depend solely on how we view ourselves, but also on how we think, act, and react towards our fellow human beings. Therefore, it is good to cultivate positive thoughts for people we interact with, whether they are friends, relatives, parents, neighbours, partners, colleagues, or even just our fellow citizens. A significantly positive thought is to wish for them to be happy as well.

By doing so, especially in cases where misunderstandings have occurred, we can easily forgive them and live harmoniously with people. Harmony does not mean only a good relationship with ourselves but also with our neighbours. We do not live alone but coexist and live with others in our society. Consequently, it is good to cultivate positive thoughts about others and wish for them to be happy in order to preserve balance in terms of both internal and general harmony.

The effects of this kind of thinking are greatly beneficial. The more you wish for others' happiness, the greater happiness you will feel. It's like throwing a ball against a wall; it bounces back and returns to you. Similarly, when you wish for others to be happy, happiness returns to you, allowing you to feel it.

We must possess the source of happiness to be able to offer happiness to others. That's why we start this meditation by focusing on ourselves first. Usually, we expect happiness from others, but life often operates on a principle of give and take. If we don't give, we can't expect to receive. By giving happiness, we receive happiness in return; if we give misery or negativity, that is what we will receive in return. For example, if we smile at someone, it's natural for them to smile back at us. And if we frown at them, it's natural for them to respond in kind. How we act and are reacted to depends on us.

Furthermore, in this meditation, if you remember someone who was angry with you, bring their image to mind and repeatedly wish 'May he/she be free from anger' or 'be free from hate'.[15] Over time, you will find that their hostile attitude will change to become more friendly.

When we reach the point of wishing for others to be free from anger or hate, we will gradually understand that, just as we suffer when anger is ignited within us, others suffer also when they experience anger. We will see others as victims of the distress and pain caused by anger, and thus be able to forgive them. It is a way to dispel negativity from within us, both for ourselves and others. Only when we wish all this can we increase our feelings of positivity so much that old angers, enmities, and hatreds gradually diminish until they are forgotten. At this point, we are able to forgive our fellow human beings for any mistakes they may have made.

---

[15] In his discourses, the Buddha advised on how one should abide by pervading hostile people with a mind imbued with friendliness (*mettā*), without inner hate (*dosantarā*), wishing them to be free from hatred (*avera*) and anger/ill will (*abyābajjha*). See M I.129, *Kakacūpama-sutta*; M I.128, *Sāleyyaka-sutta*.

Step 4 - *Increasing positive emotions towards all beings*

The Buddha calls this meditation *appamaññā*, which means 'boundless', because one can extend their friendliness to limitless beings, the whole world, without any discrimination. So, another step to friendliness meditation is to wish happiness upon all beings by mentally saying 'May all beings be happy'. You can do this gradually as follows:

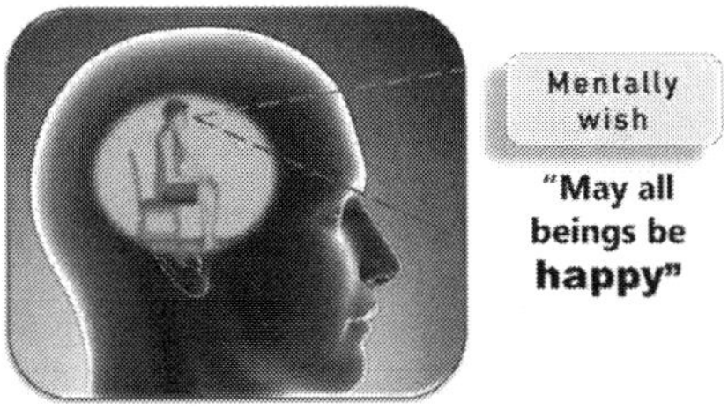
Mentally wish
"May all beings be happy"

1) Remember people you have seen in small groups indoors or outdoors and repeatedly make the wish 'May all be happy'.
2) After some practice, you can recall people you have seen in a large gathering in indoor or outdoor spaces (on the street, at a bus stop, at the beach, and so on). Again, wish repeatedly, 'May all be happy'.
3) After more practice, you can extend your friendliness to people you have not seen (*adiṭṭha*) but know exist in nearby or distant neighbourhoods. Make a wish for them many times: 'May all be happy.'
4) You can do the same for people beyond your neighbourhood, gradually extending your friendliness to an entire community, village, town, city, or country, and even to other countries. You can continue by wishing happiness for people on an entire continent or multiple continents, and generally in the whole world, as follows: 'May all beings be happy.'[16]

---

[16] 'Beings' can refer not only to human beings but also to any living beings, whether they are weak or strong, long, large, middle-sized, short, small, or bulky, including those already born and those seeking rebirth. (Sn.65).

This kind of mind is elevated, boundless, and free from hate and hostility. With continuous practice, it can achieve the first meditative absorption (*jhāna*), as we explained in the meditation on breathing, with the difference that here the object is living beings and not the breath. The luminosity we mentioned on p. 73ff. will also appear with the same intensity.

By cultivating, developing, and repeating the same wish, 'May all beings be happy', one can then attain the second and third meditative absorptions, which have bliss (*sukha*) and unity of mind (*ekaggatā*) as their factors. Because the bliss is so intense, however, the meditator cannot transcend it and progress to the fourth absorption unless they switch from the meditation on friendliness to, for example, the meditation on equanimity (*upekkhā*) or the meditation on the breath (*ānapāna*).

These absorptions are called *mettā-jhānas* (absorptions through friendliness). To understand their transient nature, see p. 29.

The Divine Abiding

Describing the sublime experience of spreading friendliness throughout the world, the Buddha refers to it as 'Divine Abiding' (*Brahma-vihāra*), with the following advise for the meditator:

> Let him develop a boundless mind
> of friendliness for the entire world.
> Let him keep this mindfulness (of friendliness).
> This is called here the 'Divine Abiding'.[17]

'Divine Abiding' refers to the absorptions (*jhāna*) through friendliness. They are so called because they are sublime and exquisite as means for achieving a friendly attitude towards all

[17] Sn.26, *Mettā-sutta*.

beings. And just as the Brahma gods live with an immaculate, pure mind, free from the stain of malice, hate and hostility, so too does the meditator who achieves these attainments live on their same level. The term 'Brahma' here signifies the highest and most sacred entity.

The meditator can also see that all beings are victims of negative emotions. Everyone suffers from them, and, when afflicted by them, do not know how to react. Experiencing such emotions, they usually react negatively, hurting themselves and others and creating a hostile environment. Seeing them as victims, the meditator feels friendliness towards them, free from the stain of enmity, and views them with a pure mind, like that of the Brahma gods.

SUMMARY

Meditation on friendliness can be developed using the following four steps:

First, we dispel negative emotions by wishing to be free from them ourselves. Second, we cultivate positive emotions by wishing for our own happiness. Third, we share this happiness with others—relatives, friends, companions—wishing for them to be happy as well. Fourth, we extend friendliness to all beings, wishing for everyone to be happy.

We can practice this meditation even when walking on the street, or while standing, sitting, or performing various activities of daily life, as negative emotions can appear at any moment. For instance, if anger arises, we mentally say, 'May I be free from anger'. If we want to cultivate positive emotions within us, we say, 'May I be happy'.

Aid in meditation

Finally, here are seven important pieces of advice that act as aids to overcoming negative emotions:

1) Learn the meditation on friendliness.
2) Dedicate yourself to the meditation on friendliness.
3) Frequently remind yourself that we are the owners and heirs of our actions (karma). Whatever actions we perform, whether good or evil, we will inherit their consequences.
4) Frequently remind yourself that the same applies to all beings regarding the ownership and inheritance of their actions.
5) Associate with kind-hearted friends.
6) Engage in suitable conversations with others about abandoning anger, hate, and generally negative emotions.
7) Undertake and observe the moral precepts that contribute to internal and external harmony, namely refraining from: 1. killing living beings, 2. stealing, 3. engaging sexual misconduct,[18] 4. lying, 5. using intoxicating and addictive substances that cause heedlessness, 6. divisive speech, 7. harsh speech, 8. idle chatter, and 9. anger or ill-will.

   These rules are based on the principle of non-harm, non-violence, and non-cruelty (*ahiṃsā*). They aim to restraint the mind and, consequently, speech and the body, from harmful actions. They also support other meditations as a basis for purifying the mind from evil thoughts and actions.

This concludes the analysis of the serenity meditation on friendliness. Meditation on compassion follows next.

[18] This includes infidelity, adultery, violation of mutual trust in a relationship, sexual intercourse without the consent of the parties involved and their guardians, and rape.

Meditation on Compassion

INTRODUCTION

The method of meditation on compassion is similar to the meditation on friendliness. However, meditation on compassion is more inclusive and comprehensive. It allows us to realize that we can experience pain, stress, anxiety, and distress even due to small things, and suffer as a result.

Generally, compassion is the awareness of someone's suffering and the willingness to help. Its characteristic is that it promotes the removal of suffering, distress, misery, or pain from us and others. Its function is that it cannot endure the suffering or pain of ourselves and others. Its manifestation is non-cruelty. The Buddha says in this regard: 'This is the escape from cruelty or harming (*vihesā*), namely, the liberation of mind by compassion (*karuṇā cetovimutti*).' [1] Its proximate cause is that it sees the helplessness, incapacity, weakness, and wretchedness of those who are overwhelmed by suffering or pain.[2]

---

[1] A III.290, *Nissāraṇīya-sutta.*

[2] Vism.318, *Brahmavihāra-niddeso, Pakiṇṇakakathā*, or *The Path of Purification*, p. 312.

Pain, distress, and suffering can manifest in various forms. From the moment we are born, we experience some kind of pain in our lives, the remnants of which can remain in our subconscious, sometimes evolving into minor mental traumas, phobias, neuroses, and anxiety.

In light of this, it is beneficial to clear our minds of such remnants. Meditation on compassion offers a broader understanding of how pain can easily enter our lives, disturb our peace of mind, and how we can overcome it. It soothes like a balm on a wound; one can truly feel its comforting effect on the mind and body.

Any thoughts of cruelty we may have towards ourselves, or others disappear. When we see suffering, we find that our heart softens, losing its hardness, harshness, and coldness. We cannot be harsh with those we see in pain, nor with ourselves in such situations. This has a very soothing effect on our entire nervous system as the harshness and tension disappear.

The Practice of Meditation

The Posture of the Body

The posture of the body is the same as in the meditation on friendliness.

The Attitude of the Mind

The meditation on compassion can be developed gradually in three steps.

Step 1 - *Increasing compassion towards ourselves*

This involves dispelling the sense of suffering and pain from within us. You should pay attention to your entire body and bring to your mind an image of yourself as you are in the present moment. At the same time, you should mentally wish 'May I be free from suffering' or, if you prefer, 'May I be free from pain'.

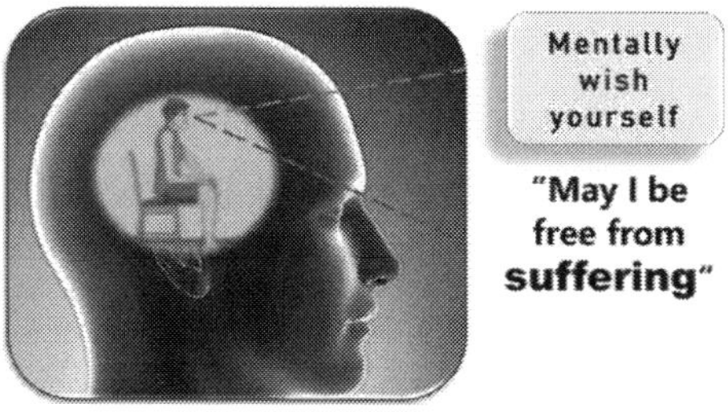

If, during this exercise, you identify areas in your body where there is great tension, focus your attention there, continuing to mentally repeat 'May I be free from suffering'. Repeat this—not too slowly, not too quickly—many times.

However, it is not enough to just say the words. You should understand their meaning and direct your attention inward, towards yourself, not towards anything external.

If, during this meditation, memories of past episodes in which you experienced unpleasant or stressful situations come to mind, you can again wish for yourself: 'May I be free from suffering.'

Step 2- *Increasing compassion towards acquaintances*

When you feel deeply relaxed from following the first step of this meditation, you can wish for others to be without suffering or pain. Should you remember other people—friends, relatives, parents, neighbours, companions, colleagues, fellow citizens—whether one, two, or many, bring to mind their image as you know it and mentally wish for them: 'May he/she (or they) be free from suffering.'

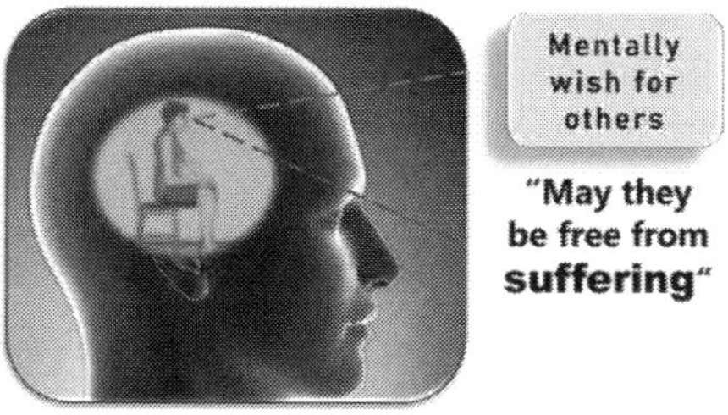

You will realize that other people have their anxieties, hardships, and pains, and you will be able to feel greater empathy and compassion for them.

Step 3 - *Increasing compassion towards all beings*

The Buddha also calls this meditation *appamaññā*, meaning 'boundless', because one can extend one's compassion to limitless beings, to the entire world, without exception. Thus, another step you can incorporate into the process is to express compassion for all beings, by mentally saying 'May all beings be free from suffering'.[3]

You can do this gradually, as with the meditation on friendliness. The method is the same, except that instead of wishing 'may they be happy' you wish 'may they be free of suffering or pain'.

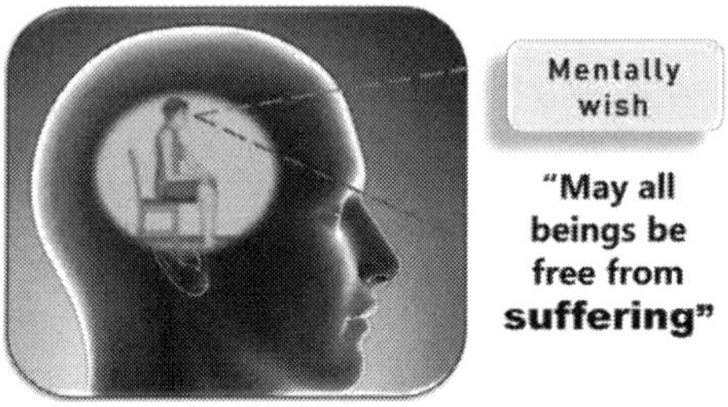
Mentally wish
"May all beings be free from suffering"

This concludes the analysis of the serenity meditation on compassion. Next follows 'four elements meditation' regarding the material body.

[3] Here too, 'beings' can refer not only to human beings but also to any living beings, whether they are weak or strong, long, large, middle-sized, short, small, or bulky, including those already born and those seeking rebirth. (Sn.65).

Four Elements Meditation

INTRODUCTION

Four elements meditation was taught by the Buddha in various discourses, both briefly and in detail. Specifically, he explains how the four primary elements—solid, liquid, heat, and air[1]—and their derivatives constitute matter, and how, through this meditation one can understand the material dimension of existence and, with wisdom, see it as it really is.

Meditation on these elements serves as a path to self-knowledge, aiding in the realization that our existence is not solely composed of thoughts and emotions. It also encompasses material elements that permeate and affect our lives. Through this meditation, we come to understand:

1) how we are internally, with our material body, and externally surrounded by and immersed in material objects;

[1] *Paṭhavī-, āpo, tejo, vāyo-dhātu.*

2) how our attachment to matter, which is unstable, and our identification with it, lead to instability and imbalance in our psychological world and form the basis for our existential pain, suffering, and unhappiness; and
3) how by meditating on the material elements we can acquire the liberating knowledge that leads to detachment, disidentification, deep tranquillity of our psychological world and, consequently, to liberation from existential suffering.

Our existence is defined not only by our psychological world but also the material world that surrounds us. People grow attached to it, identify themselves with it, are affected by it, and ultimately suffer emotionally from their relationship with it. Many narcissistic tendencies or mental disorders arise from attachment and identification with matter or material form.

However, when one wisely perceives the material elements of which one is composed, realizing that *these are not mine, these are not me, these are not my self*, one is freed from illusion, becomes disenchanted, detaches from them, and liberates one's mind. Thus, neither pleasant nor unpleasant stimuli invade or remain within us.

We will now analyse what these elements are, discuss how one can become aware of them, and provide a general theoretical overview of how they are categorized and interrelated, as well as their primary importance. This applies not only to us but also to the universe, as we are also part of it.

We will begin by explaining these elements, and then offer practical guidance on how to meditate on them.

The information we present is mainly based on a lengthy discourse of the Buddha called *Dhātu Vibhaṅga Sutta* (*The Discourse on the Analysis of the Material Elements*).[2] In this

[2] M III.237, *Dhātuvibhaṅga-sutta*.

discourse, the Buddha gives a detailed exposition about recognizing these elements in our body and in the bodies of others, as well as meditating on them. As the term 'element' is something abstract for most people, the Buddha gives specific explanations about its meaning.

The four primary elements

Solid, liquid, heat and air are the four primary elements (*mahābhūta*) because they are the basic and fundamental constituents of matter. They are inseparable and, through their various combinations, participate in the composition of all material substances, from the tiniest particle to the tallest mountain or the vastest galaxy. In physics, they are also called the 'four fundamental states of matter'.

Although these elements can appear into various forms, they exist in everything, even within our bodies or within atoms and subatomic particles, as we will see below. Being part of nature, we too try to understand the composition of our material bodies, which are not fundamentally different from other material bodies, such as plants or rocks, that are also composed of solid, liquid, heat, and air elements.

Regarding the meditation, the Buddha explains how one can observe these elements at any time. Merely hearing about them gives us an abstract idea, but if we begin to observe them systematically, we gain empirical and clear knowledge of the crucial role they play in our material and mental existence. First, let us explain the concept of matter on a theoretical level.

The concept of matter

The word 'matter' the Pāli is *rūpa*, which also means 'material form', 'material shape', 'material body'. It is derived from the verb *ruppati*, which means to 'transform', 'deform', or 'reshape'. The Buddha himself, explaining the terms 'matter', 'material form', and 'material body', states the following:

> And why is it called 'matter'(*rūpa*)? It is transformed (*ruppati*), therefore it is called 'matter'. Transformed by what? Transformed by cold and by heat.[3]

Regarding the material body, he states:

> It is transformed by cold, heat, hunger, and thirst; transformed by contact with flies, mosquitoes, wind, sunlight, and reptiles [reptile venom], and so on.[4]

The Pāli commentators explain:

> Matter is so called because it undergoes transformation, but also because it imposes transformation due to adverse natural conditions such as cold, heat, and so on.

In modern physics, there is also talk of the transformation of matter. There are three types of transformation: physical, chemical, and nuclear. An example of the physical transformation of matter is as follows: A piece of ice, which is a solid element, when it absorbs heat, melts and is transformed into a liquid. If it loses its heat, it condenses and is transformed back into a solid. If the temperature rises too high, the ice evaporates and becomes a gas (air). Should the temperature drop again, the gas condenses and freezes, becoming solid again. If, again, as a liquid, it then reabsorbs heat, it evaporates and becomes a gas once more. If it loses heat, it condenses and becomes liquid again. This is the

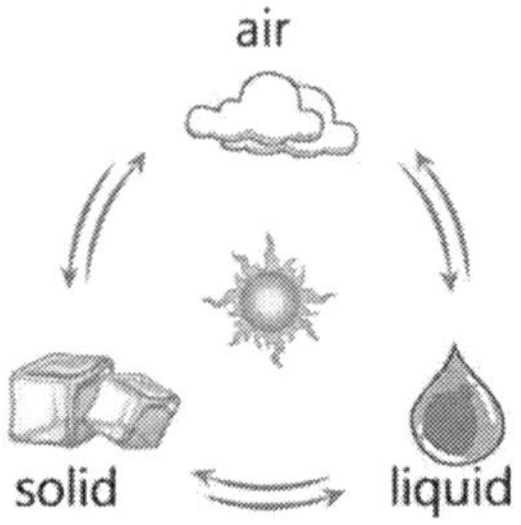

[3] S III.86, *Khajjanīya-sutta*.

[4] Ibid.

physical transformation of matter, where a solid can become a liquid and vice versa, a solid can become a gas and vice versa, and a liquid can become a gas and vice versa.

This cycle is continually repeated in all physical phenomena, including our bodies. For example, we drink water, it evaporates, and the remainder must be expelled through urination. Then we rehydrate our body with water, which evaporates and is expelled through urination, and so on.

There is, however, a common denominator that contributes to the transformation of matter, and that is heat. Material bodies, including our own, are transformed by heat and the pressure created by it. That is, the physical state of a material body can be solid, liquid, or air (gas), depending on heat and pressure.

So, due to transformation, matter can be hard like steel, soft like clay, fluid like water, warm like fire, or invisible like air. In our own bodies, for instance, there are hard parts, like bones; soft parts, like flesh; fluids like blood; warm parts like the heart; and invisible elements such as the air we breathe.

The terminology 'solid, liquid, air' is still used in modern physics and chemistry, for example, in the Periodic Table of Elements, part of which is shown in the adjacent image.

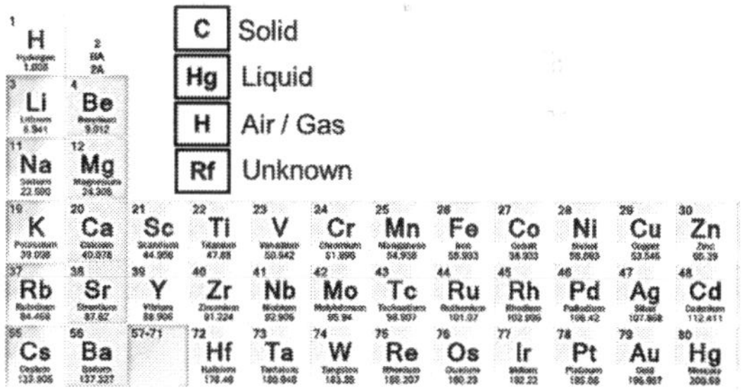

Looking at the table, we see that hydrogen is a gas (air), while magnesium and calcium are solids. All 118 elements in the table can be classified into these three categories: solids, liquids, and gases. This terminology is used for the three phases of matter, depending on the composition and density of the molecules.

The molecules of material bodies are in constant motion. Depending on the intensity of the motion of the molecules and the distance between them, the bodies are solid, liquid, or gaseous.

In solid bodies, molecules move very close to one another. Their positions and distances are fixed and do not change easily.

The three phases of matter

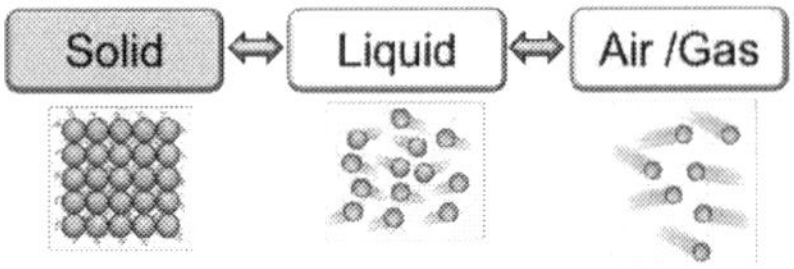

In liquid bodies, molecules move and change position but remain close to one another, maintaining consistent distances. They cannot move closer or farther apart.

In gases, molecules move freely, changing position and distance among one another. They can move apart but not too close together. All these characteristics are due to the density ratio of the material bodies.

As for the element of heat, it appears as heat and temperature. Heat is a form of energy of the total molecular motion of a material body. Temperature is the property and magnitude of heat. For example, the transfer of thermal energy when we touch something gives us the sensation of hot or cold. An increase in energy corresponds to hot or warm when we receive energy, and a decrease in energy corresponds to cold when we lose energy. Thus, the property and magnitude or degree of warm or cold is measured as temperature.

Percentage of Liquid & Solid in our Body

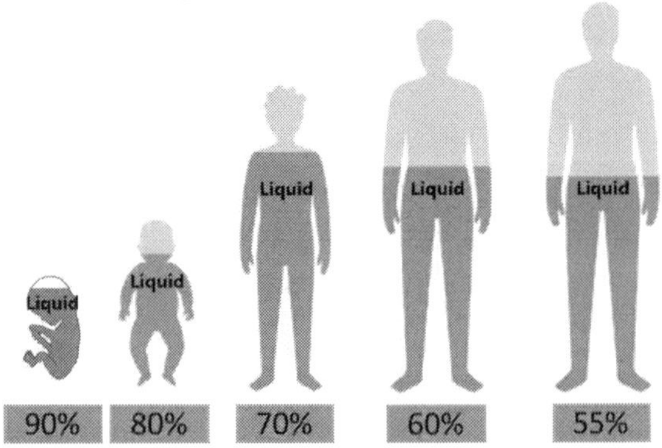

In our bodies, liquid is the most dominant among the four elements. As embryos we are 90% liquid and only 10%

solid; as children, we are 80% liquid; as teenagers, 70%; and as adults, 60%. In the elderly, the percentage of the liquid element drops to 55%, and the solid element increases to 45%. We see that, in the life cycle of a human, the liquid element is dominant for the most part of their existence.

An adult weighing 70 kilograms has about 45 litres of liquid in their body. This means that there are 25 kilograms of the solid element. What we see on the scales when we weigh ourselves, then, is mostly the liquid element.

Examining our body more deeply, we find that the liquid element is not only in our blood (50%). It is present in many systems, such as the lymphatic system, and in various organs, including the heart (75-80%), brain (80-85%), lungs (75-80%), liver (70-75%), kidneys (80-85%), muscles (70-75%), teeth (8-10%), bones (20-25%), and skin (70-75%).

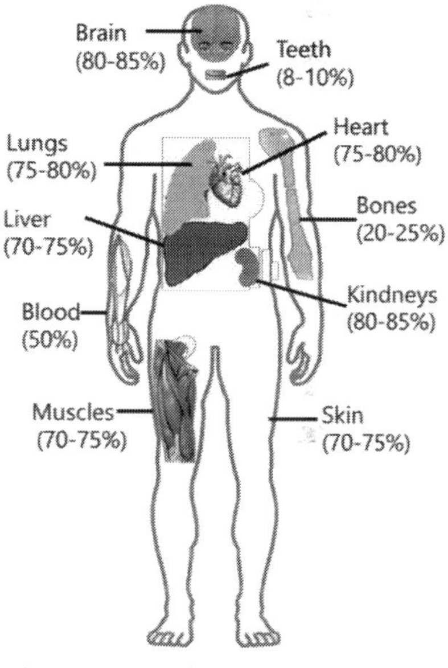

Studying the subject even further, we will see that our cells are also mostly composed of 80-85% liquid, while the solid and gaseous elements are less prevalent. This is true for plant cells as well.

Our bodies also consist of trillions of cells that relate to the liquid element, which has the property of connecting material bodies with one another. If the liquid element within us is reduced, the cells cannot exist.

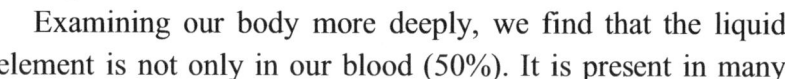

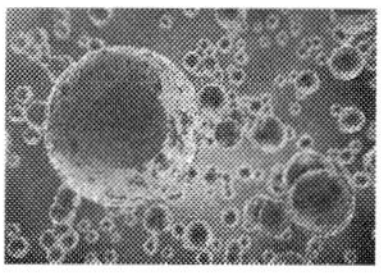

In fact, because the liquid element is so changeable, every hour a billion cells die in our body and a billion are born. Every second, 15 million blood cells are destroyed and produced. In a day, a human loses 10 billion skin cells, amounting to nearly two kilograms in a year. Also, every 27 days, our outer skin changes, producing new cells. Essentially, we have new skin every month.

Humans need to provide their bodies with a constant supply of water (1.5 to 2 litres per day) in order to fuel the continuous production and healthy function of cells. The liquid element contained in the cells cannot last forever, so it must be replenished with a new one; otherwise, we become dehydrated.

Our bodies are not static as we often think, but instead undergo constant change and transformation. Cells are produced, grow, and decompose quickly. They are continuously born and die rapidly, like bubbles of foam that last briefly and almost immediately burst. The Buddha himself likens the body to foam, saying:

> One should realize that this body is like foam (*pheṇa*) and understand its mirage-like nature.[5]

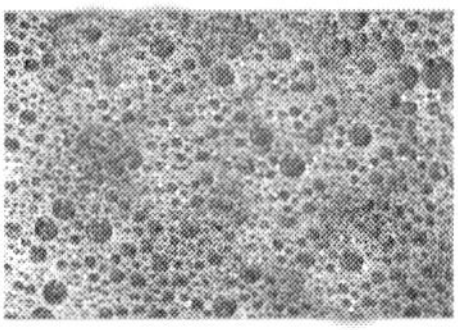

That is, although a lump of foam may seem compact and solid at first glance and is pleasant to look at, upon closer examination, it is revealed to be internally hollow and void. Something similar happens with our body. Hence, the Buddha says:

> When one investigates a lump of foam carefully, it would appear to them to be hollow (*rittaka*), void (*tucchaka*), and lacking any permanent substance (*asāra*). For what permanent substance could there be in a lump of foam? Similarly, when one investigates the body carefully, it would appear to them to be hollow, void, and lacking any perma-

[5] Dhp, 46.

nent substance. For what permanent substance could there be in the body?[6]

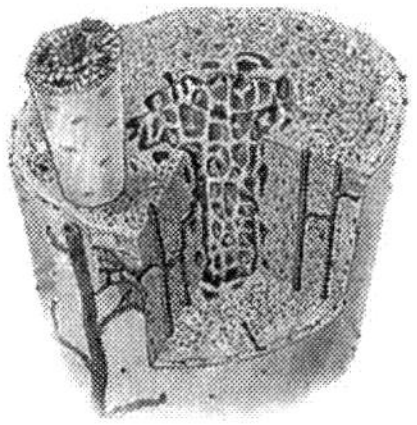

We should also know that our bones, which appear to be sta-ble, solid, compact, and strong from the outside, are actually made up of spongy bone tissue, which is a porous network of different types of cells.

In order to see the true nature of the body, to fully understand it and to acquire superior empirical knowledge, one must not be fooled by outside appearances but investigate it carefully and see it as it really is through meditation and concentration. Indeed, when it is viewed at a microscopic level, one will immediately realise that, like every material body in the environment, our own bodies are also made up of particles bonded with the liquid element.

We will now examine how the four primary elements are interrelated and combined to give us the impression of compactness, or 'cohesiveness' and density, not only in our bodies but also in external bodies. We will start with an examination of the solid element.

1. *The solid element*

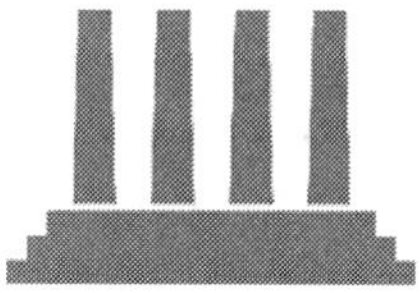

The solid element is so named because it serves as a support or foundation for the coexisting material elements. Generally, it has the following macroscopic properties:

1) Its characteristic is hardness.
2) Its function is to provide a foundation for the other primary elements and for the 'derived matter', such as

[6] S III.140, *Pheṇapiṇḍūpama-sutta.*

colour, smell, taste, and nutritive essence.

3) Its manifestation is the reception of the other elements.
4) Its proximate cause is the coexistence of the other three primary elements.[7]

Besides hardness, softness is also a way in which the solid element can be experienced through the sense of touch. We usually understand if an object is solid through touch because some objects, when viewed from a distance, cannot always be discerned as solid or not. For example, foam from a distance looks solid. By touching it, we realize that it is not.

Furthermore, because the solid element has opposite properties, it is divided into two categories: heavy and light solidity. Each category has three sub-categories, each of which has its opposite in the other category, as shown in the following table.

Opposite Properties in the Solid Element

Category of Heavy Solidity		*Category of Light Solidity*
1) Hardness	←→	1) Softness
2) Roughness	←→	2) Smoothness
3) Heaviness	←→	3) Lightness

For example, a stone (which is hard, rough, and heavy) and cotton (which is soft, smooth, and light) are both solid elements. But the stone belongs to the heavy solidity category while cotton belongs to the light solidity category. The same applies by analogy to the objects of the other categories. Thus, we discern the opposite properties that exist in the solid element. Therefore, in meditation, when we observe the solid element in our body, we should not consider only the bones as solid. The solid

[7] Vism.365, 443.

element also includes our skin and flesh, our tongues, and many other soft, smooth, or light material elements of the body.

2. The liquid element

The liquid element is the material agent that causes various particles of matter to unite, bond, condense, and stick together, preventing them from dispersing.

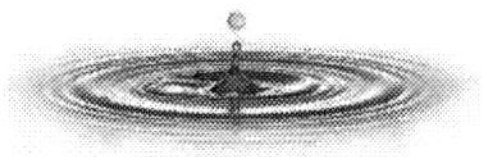

For example, if someone blows on flour, which is a solid element, all of its grains and particles disperse because there is no cohesive element to hold them together. If water is added to the flour, however, the grains unite and stick together, resulting in dough.

Flour

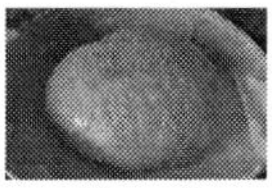

Dough

The liquid element, therefore, has the property of gluing and bonding together various particles of solid bodies. Our body can also be likened to dough because it is composed of many particles united by the liquid element. Our cells, for instance, are united with each other through the liquid element. Without it, they could not come together and reproduce.

Generally, the liquid element has the following macroscopic properties:

1) Its characteristic is flow or fluidity.
2) Its function is to intensify or enhance coexisting material states.
3) Its manifestation is the coagulation, retention, or cohesion of material phenomena.
4) Its proximate cause is the coexistence of the other three primary elements.[8]

---

[8] Vism.365, 443.

Due to its fluidity, however, the liquid element also has the property of erosion. In the image, we see how, with its fluidity, a river has eroded and destroyed everything in its path: proof of the destructive aspect of the liquid element. We find that the liquid element, like the solid, has opposite properties, namely:

River flow erosion

Fluidity ←→ Cohesion

For example, when it rains lightly, dry soil becomes mud (cohesion) while when it rains heavily, the fluidity is intense and possibly causes erosion.

The non-tangible element

We can refer to the liquid element as 'non-tangible' since it has a specific peculiarity: unlike the other three primary elements, one cannot directly perceive it by touching it. Instead, it can only be inferred inductively from the cohesion or density of the other three primary elements. That is why it is not included among the tangible objects.

For example, we know that water is composed of hydrogen and oxygen, with two hydrogen atoms and one oxygen atom giving us one molecule of water. But what are hydrogen and oxygen? Both are gases and instances of the air element. Since water is the compound of two gases—hydrogen and oxygen—we could say that water is essentially a gaseous element. However, due to its density, when we put our hand in the water, what we feel is nothing but the condensation of the gaseous element, giving us

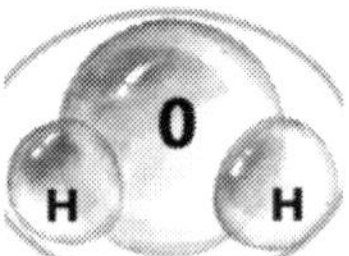

air element

air + heat + solid

the sensation of solidity and temperature.

If we look at it practically, we will see that, if we were to put our hand in the water with our eyes closed, the first thing we would feel is its temperature (cold or warm). Then, we would feel the minimal and gentle resistance of the solid element, caused by the density of the gaseous element. Finally, we would feel that we could move our hand in the water, which happens because of the abundance of the gaseous element allows for movement. On the contrary, in sand, we would find it harder to move our hand so easily due to the significant resistance caused by the abundant solid element. Therefore, what we perceive as the liquid element, or water, is the coexistence of the other three elements. The liquid element itself can only be perceived and felt conceptually or by inference, but not tangibly as a datum of touch.

3. *The heat element*

The heat element generally has the following macroscopic properties:

1) Its characteristic is temperature.
2) Its function is to heat, mature, or cool other material bodies.
3) It manifests itself as warm or cold.
4) Its proximate cause is the coexistence of the other three primary elements.[9]

The heat element has two opposite properties:

Heat ←→ Cold

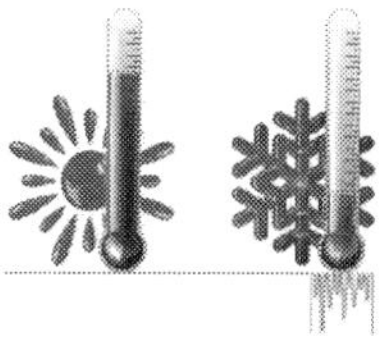

[9] Vism.365, 443.

In the winter, for example, when the heat element decreases, we wear warm clothes, and turn on heaters or other heating devices, while in the summer, when the heat element increases, we wear light clothes and use air conditioning and fans. When our internal temperature drops, we can cool to the point of hypothermia; when it rises, we burn with fever.

As for the function of maturing, it is related to any organism that depends on temperature, as in the case of plants for germination and the ripening of fruits, or in the case of animals for the growth of offspring. When the temperature is moderate, it supports the growth of life, but when it is extreme, it becomes destructive.

The heat element also produces phenomena in inorganic matter, like climatic and geological transformations. Life on Earth is possible thanks to the moderate temperature of the Sun. Without it, life would not exist as we know it, as is the case on other planets where temperatures are extreme.

Generally, our life depends on the bearable temperatures of the seasons, which are determined by the Earth's distance from the Sun and its axial tilt. Atmospheric phenomena such as

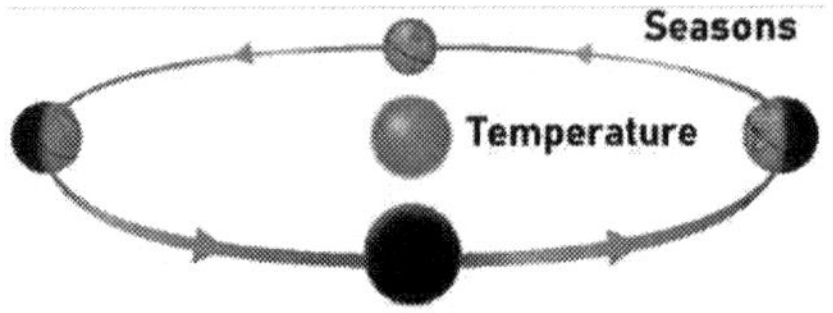

heat	←→	cold
humidity	←→	dryness
breeze	←→	storm

are due to the effect of solar heat, causing barometric pressure. This contributes to the formation of air masses, vapour, and rain, as well as the manifestation of other phenomena.

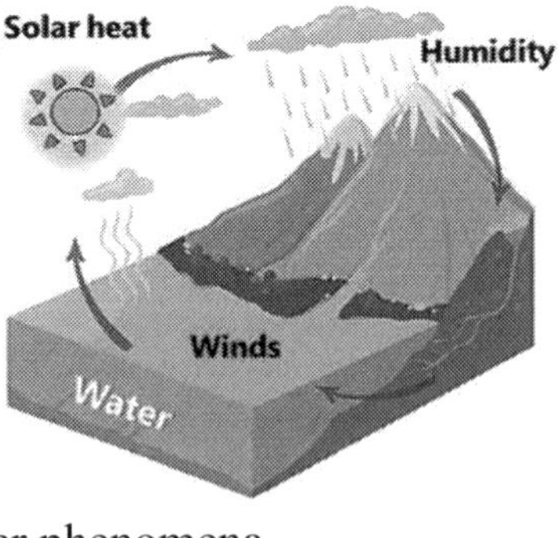

We also have geological transformations. We know that the Earth's core is composed of very hot molten iron. We walk on Earth's crust, but we also depend on the temperature of its core. Life would be very difficult were the core to cool and solidify. The Earth would resemble Mars, with a very thin atmosphere and inactive volcanoes.

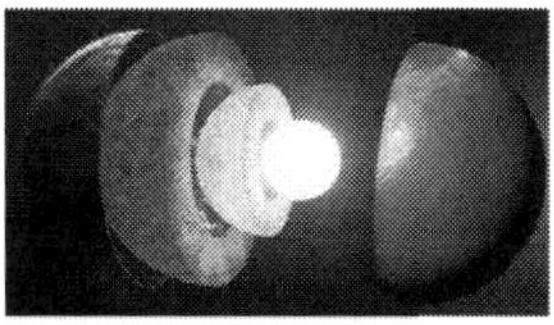

The fiery magma located in the Earth's interior, with a temperature above 1000°C, and the volcanoes through which it flows to the surface, contribute to the movement of the Earth's tectonic plates. This movement shapes the land and sea by creating mountains and plains, thereby affecting our lives on Earth.

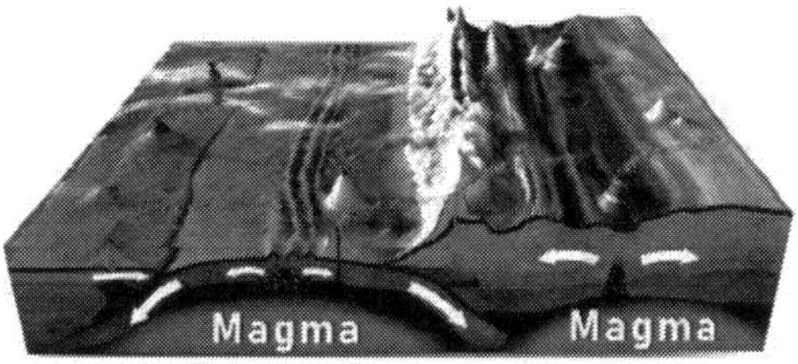

4. *The air element*

The air element is the basic principle of motion and pressure of material elements. Generally, it has the following macroscopic properties:

1) Its characteristic is expansion, swelling, and inflation.
2) Its function is to cause movement in the other material elements.
3) It manifests as a transfer or transmission to other parts.
4) Its proximate cause is the other three primary elements.[10]

[10] Vism.365, 443.

It has two opposite properties:

Motion ←→ Pressure or pushing

Our body moves because of the air element within us. This can be likened to a balloon which, when deflated, lies motionless on the ground. But when it is inflated with air, it moves and rises from the ground.

Because most air or gas is colourless and shapeless, and therefore invisible, it is difficult to observe directly. We can experience it, however, through our sense of touch, as movement or push and as pressure or support, specifically:

1) as *movement*, when we breath in and out or when we perform various movements like walking, giving a *push* or *thrust* to our body;

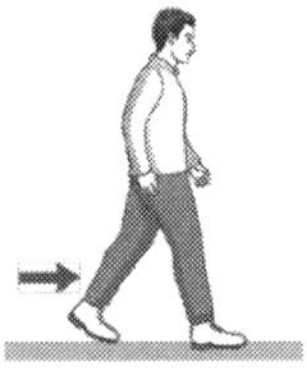

-Movement-
Push

2) as *pressure*, when our body expands and contracts while breathing in and out, which provides *support* to the body to maintain an upright or sitting posture.

-Pressure-
Support

General properties

The four primary elements, as a whole, possess the following general properties:

- They are based on the solid element.
- They are cohered together by the liquid element.
- They are maintained in their duration by the heat element.
- They are expanded by the air element.

Derivatives of the primary elements

The four primary elements also have four derivatives. These are:

- colour
- smell
- taste
- nutritive essence.

Together, the four primary elements and their four derivatives form a material group (*kalāpa*) called the 'simple or pure octad' (*suddhaṭṭhaka*), which is inseparable (*avinibbhogarūpa*). This is because these eight components are always interconnected and present in all material objects, from the simplest to the most complex. That is, wherever the four primary elements exist macroscopically, colour, smell, taste, and nutritive essence are also found.

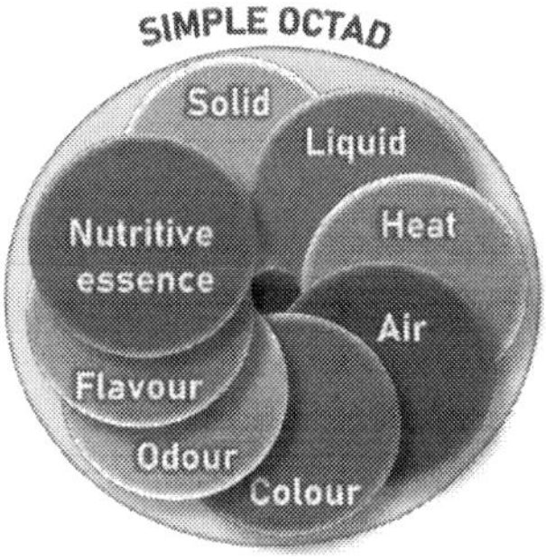

An example is food we eat. We find that without the solid and liquid elements and so on, the colour, smell, taste, and nutritive essence of the food cannot exist. Every day we consume the four primary elements and their derivatives to sustain life. Our survival depends on them. We need to continually supply our body with fluids, solids, and gases, as well as heat (calories), in the right proportions. The slightest changes can affect our physical and mental health, including our moods, emotions, and thoughts.

The primary elements can be compared to the earth and their derivatives to the plants, shrubs, and trees that grow in dependence on it.

The space element

The space element (*ākāsa-dhātu*) is also a derivative of the four primary elements, but it is separable. Space is not merely a geometric extension. It is also an empty area that delineates and separates objects and groups of material phenomena, allowing them to be perceived as separate and distinct. It demarcates the point where one object begins and another ends. Without space, it would not be possible to distinguish one object from another. It is, therefore, the boundary or limit between local points where there is an empty interval, as shown in the adjacent image. Thus, space is called the 'limiting material phenomenon'.

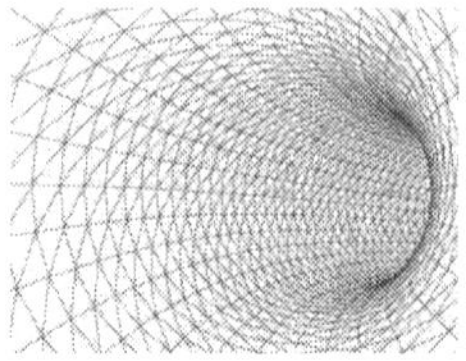

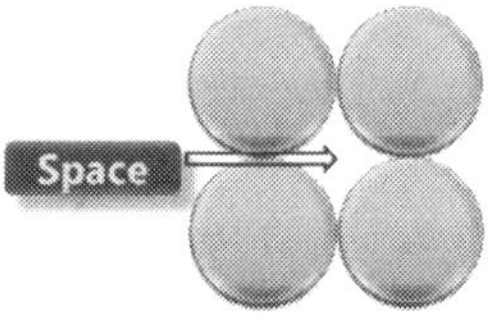

Generally, space has the following macroscopic properties:

1) Its characteristic is the delimitation of matter.
2) Its function is to display the boundaries of matter.
3) It manifests as the confines of matter or as the gaps and apertures in matter, 'untouched' by anything.
4) Its proximate cause is the matter delimited.[11]

Accordingly, it is not the material world that delimits space, but space that delimits the material world through the 'relative absence' of matter. We say 'relative absence' because, in fact, there is no 'absolute' absence of matter, as space is not entirely empty.

[11] Vism.448; cf. Dhs.143, §637.

Space is not empty

Space appears empty to us because we cannot see most things in it and because there is much less air than we are accustomed to.

However, at the microscopic level, space is not empty or void. A point in space is filled with gases, dust, stellar wind from charged particles, light from stars, cosmic rays, radiation left over from the Big Bang, gravity, electric and magnetic fields, and neutrinos from nuclear reactions. As described in Dr. Henning Genz's book *Nothingness: The Science of Empty Space,* space is also filled with two things that we cannot directly detect: dark matter and dark energy. Even if all these things could be removed and excluded from a particular region of space, there would still be three things that, according to Dr. Genz, we could never remove: vacuum energy, the Higgs field, and the curvature of space-time.[12]

Even atoms, which in classical physics were once considered to be about 99.9% empty space, are not empty according to the latest discoveries in quantum mechanics. They are mostly filled with clouds of electrons, all bound by the quantum rules that govern the entire universe. The same applies to our material body. It is not empty, but largely composed of a series of such electron clouds.

According to quantum mechanics, the space around a particle is filled with countless 'virtual' particles that quickly pop into and out of existence.

---

[12] Dr. Christopher S. Baird (2012), *What keeps space empty?* www.wtamu.edu/~cbaird/sq/2012/12/20/what-keeps-space-empty/.
The picture above is an artistic rendering and belongs to the *public domain.*

This is what is referred to as quantum fields of energy or a vacuum space filled with fluctuations of quark and gluon fields. It turns out that all this empty space around us is actually matter, a fluid-like material of invisible virtual particles that constantly appear and disappear rapidly, and in which we are immersed.

To understand this better, let's think of a fish living deep in the ocean. From the fish's perspective, all the water around it is like empty space, a medium in which everything else exists. It takes water for granted and sees only the other things in the water, such as fish, plants, and rocks, as the material world. But for us, who see the water of the ocean from the outside, the reality is that water itself is matter and not empty space.

The internal and external primary elements

So far, we have discussed the four primary elements and some of their derivatives as they are found mainly in the external environment. Next, we will examine them as they are found in the internal environment, that is to say, inside our bodies, in comparison to other external bodies.

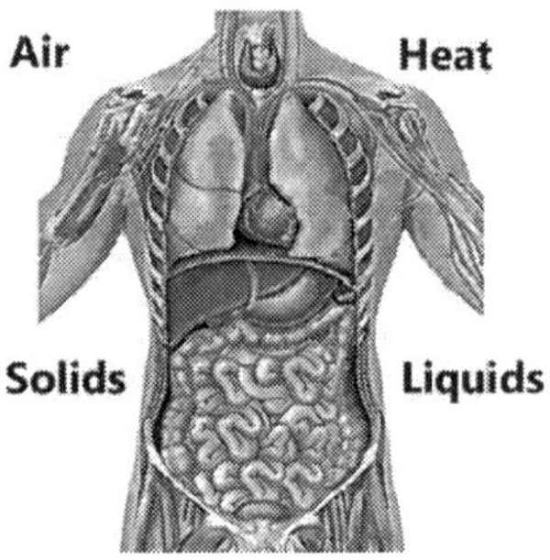

The internal solid element

The internal solid element in our body includes hair, nails, skin, teeth, and so on. Although the liquid, heat, and air elements exist within these, they are called solid because the solid element predominates.

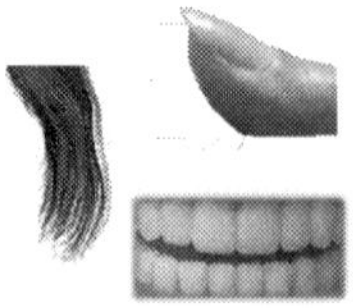

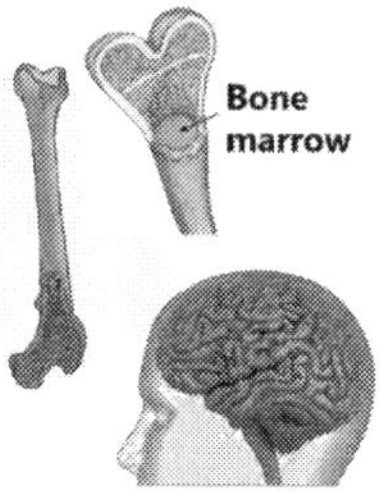

Other parts of the body include bones, bone marrow, and the brain. The brain contains about 80% liquid. If we touch it, we perceive the solid element, but in the form of softness, not fluidity like water.

The internal solid element also includes other parts of the body, such as:

> flesh, tendons, kidneys, heart, liver, diaphragm, spleen, lungs, small intestine, large intestine, stomach, and faeces.

The external solid element

The external solid element includes the bodies of other humans and beings. When we investigate them, we realize that they have the same organs that we have. If we compare them, we will not find any significant differences elementally speaking; we will identify essentially the same things that can be seen in our own bodies, such as the solid element.

This similarity can also be discerned in any inanimate things that are solid, such as soil, trees, rocks, mountains, and metals.

The internal liquid element

The internal liquid element in our body includes bile, phlegm, pus, blood, sweat, fat, tears, grease, saliva, mucus, oil of the joints, and urine.

The external liquid element

The external liquid element includes the bodies of other humans and beings. Just as we discern blood, mucus, and oil in our own bodies, we can discern that the bodies of other humans and beings contain blood, mucus, oil, and other similar liquid substances.

Any other liquid bodies or quantities of water that form seas, rivers, lakes, and so on through evaporation, condensation, and precipitation are also part of the external liquid element.

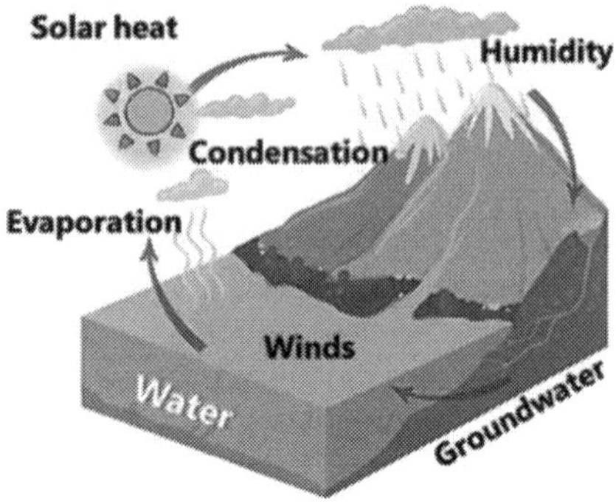

The internal heat element

The internal heat element in our body is the temperature of the warmth and cold that we can feel in various parts of the body. In some areas, the temperature is more intense, and in others, it is more subdued.

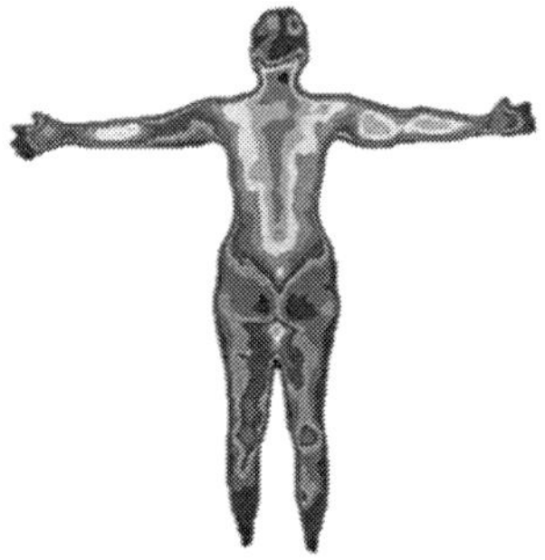

Thermography
The warm parts of the body with light shades are distinguished from cooler parts with very dark shades.

Our body generates heat and maintains it at a safe level, even when external temperatures vary greatly, by regulating excess heat. When we feel very hot, the blood vessels in our skin dilate in order to transfer excess heat to the surface of the skin. We might start to sweat, and as the sweat evaporates, it helps cool our bodies. On the other hand, when we feel very cold, our blood vessels constrict, reducing blood flow to our skin in order to conserve body heat. Our muscles start to tremble, enhancing heat production.

Particularly when we go outside in the cold, our bodies direct blood flow towards essential and vital organs to keep them warm. This can alter the amount of blood flow to our hands and feet, making them feel cold. The blood vessels in our hands and feet then constrict, preventing heat loss from vital organs.

In this way, we can detect the fluctuation of the heat element within ourselves.

The external heat element

The external heat element includes the bodies of other humans and beings, or any other external heat sources such as solar radiation and fire.

The internal air element

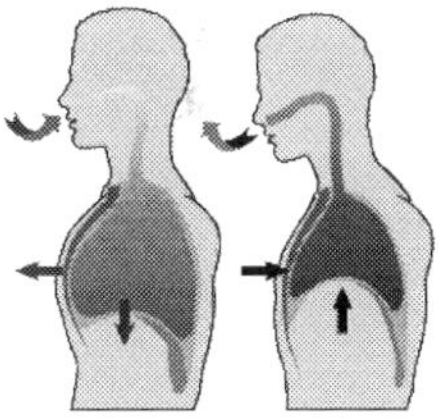

The internal air element in our bodies is the air we breathe. An adult body requires about 40 litres of oxygen daily, which means an average of 23,040 breaths each day. Without oxygen, a person can die within two to three minutes.

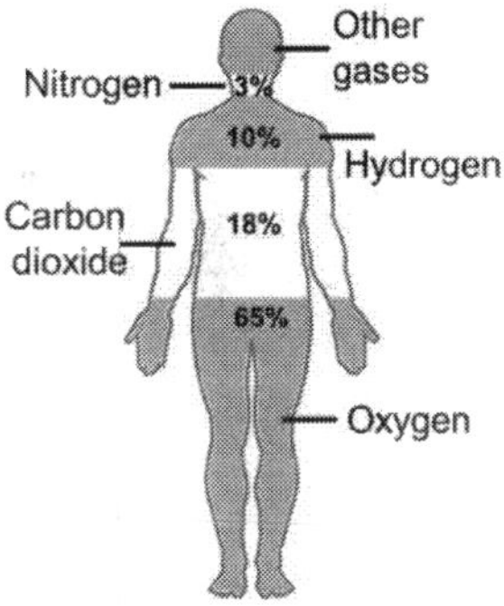

However, it's not only oxygen that is important. Our bodies and lives also depend on balanced amounts of hydrogen, carbon dioxide, nitrogen, and other gases.

The external air element

The external air element is found in the bodies of other humans and beings, or any other form of external air.

The derivatives

The derivatives of the four primary elements—colour, smell, taste, nutritive essence, and space—are all present in every part of our body. Space, for example, exists in our nostrils, which allow for the entry of air into the pharynx, enabling air to pass to the lungs; in the oesophagus, which allows food to go down; and in the stomach, intestines, and other organs.

The practice of meditation

At this point, we can examine the practical aspect of four elements meditation: how we can identify the four primary elements in our body and understand their true nature.

The Posture of the Body

As with the other meditations explained previously, we usually begin four elements meditation in a comfortable sitting posture. Later, when we have gained sufficient awareness and concentration, we can meditate in any posture.

The duration of the meditation, like in the previous meditations, can gradually increase day to day, starting from 10 minutes and then progressing to 20, 30, 45, 60 minutes, and so on for beginners. For more advanced practitioners, it can last for hours.

The Attitude of the Mind

Initially, we must identify the solid element in our body and understand what it is. Speaking vaguely about the solid element without knowing it directly and empirically leads us into theories and speculation. We need to be more specific and identify which parts of the body belong to the solid element. Given that the liquid element also exists within us, it is necessary to distinguish one from the other.

1. *The solid element*

Starting from the outside and moving inward, passing through the skin,, the solid element in the body includes:

1) head-hair, 2) body-hair, 3) nails, 4) teeth, 5) skin,	*1st pentad*
6) flesh, 7) sinews, 8) bones, 9) bone marrow, 10) kidneys,	*2nd pentad*
11) heart, 12) liver, 13) diaphragm, 14) spleen, 15) lungs,	*3rd pentad*
16) small intestine, 17) large intestine, 18) stomach, 19) faeces, 20) brain.	*4th pentad*

Start with the first pentad, memorizing its five body parts first, so that you remember their sequence. Then, close your eyes, focus your attention on each separately, and try to form a mental image. For example, focus your attention on the head-hair by mentally saying 'hair..., hair..., hair...', and try to form a mental image of the hair. Then say mentally, 'solid element..., solid element..., solid element..., solid element...'.

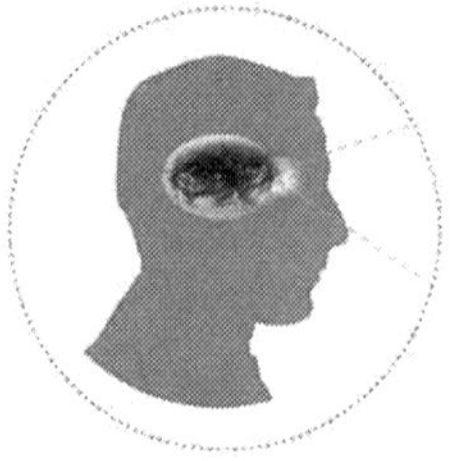

Continue in the same way with the other body parts—body-hair, nails, teeth, and skin—which are external and which you see every day in front of you. You know them very well and can form a mental image with your eyes closed.

Then memorize the second pentad and continue in the same way, mentally saying 'flesh..., flesh..., flesh...', 'solid element..., solid element..., solid element...' or 'bones..., bones..., bones...', 'solid element..., solid element..., solid element...'. In this way, the mind becomes so perceptive that, in the end, the flesh, bones, and so on appear mentally as if you were seeing them with open eyes.

Continue this mental 'scanning' with the other parts of the body, gradually memorizing the remaining pentads and becoming familiar with the solid element. If some parts are not clear, consider using an anatomy book as a reference, where the position, shape, and colour of these parts are depicted. Then, try to form a mental image of the corresponding parts.

2. The liquid element

Next, examine the liquid element in your body, which includes:

1. bile, 2. phlegm, 3. pus, 4. blood, 5. sweat,	*5th pentad*
6. fat, 7. tears, 8. grease, 9. saliva, 10. mucus,	*6th pentad*
11. oil-of-the-joints, 12. urine.	

As before, begin by memorizing them so that you remember their sequence. Then, close your eyes, focus your attention on each one separately, and try to form a mental image, saying at the same time, for example, 'bile..., bile..., bile...', 'liquid element..., liquid element..., liquid element...'.

3. *The heat element*

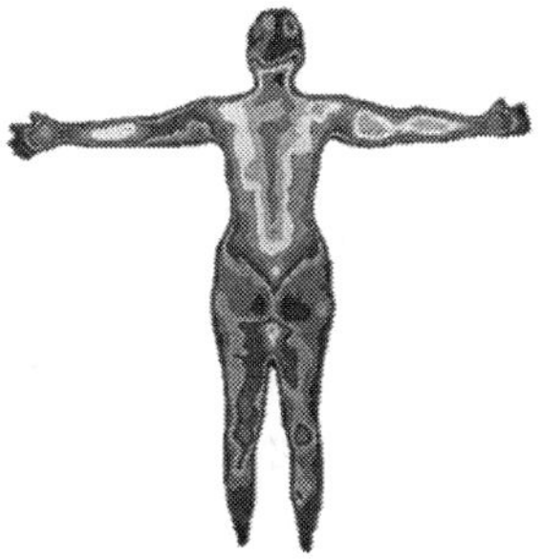

The heat element in the body is the temperature of warmth and cold that we can feel in various parts of the body. In some places, the temperature is more intense, and in others, more mild. Try to locate it by turning your attention to the body and, wherever you feel warmth, mentally note 'warmth'; wherever you feel cold, mentally note 'cold'. Observe the fluctuations in temperature from moment to moment.

4. *The air element*

As mentioned earlier, since the air element is colourless and shapeless, and therefore invisible, it is difficult to observe directly. However, we can experience it through sensation as tangible motion—thrust or pushing—and as pressure or support. Thus, we experience it:

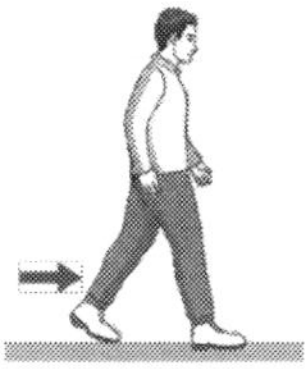

1) as *motion*, when we breathe in and out or when we perform various movements by walking and moving parts of our body, a movement that gives *thrust* or *push to* our body; and

2) as *pressure*, when our body expands and contracts while breathing in and out, which pro-

vides support to our body so that we can maintain an upright or sitting posture.

An easy way to start observing the air element is through breathing. With this meditation you can observe it wherever it is most evident and obvious in your experience. If you feel the in-breath at your nose, you can observe it there; if you feel it in your chest or abdomen, observe it there and mentally note 'in-breath, air element'. Do the same with the out-breath. Mentally note 'out-breath, air element'. Observe it repeatedly, emphasizing the 'air element'.

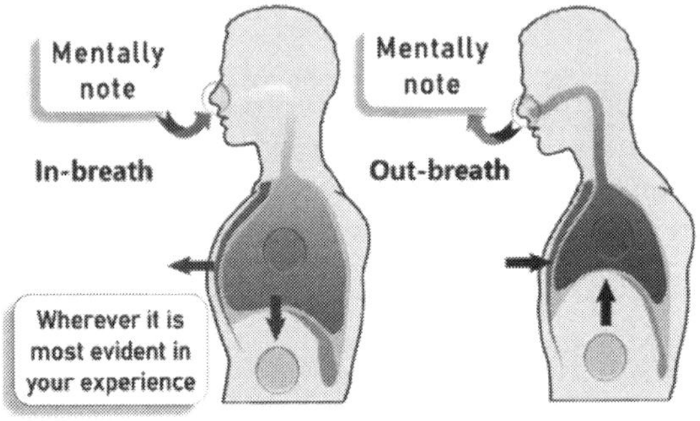

Then you can feel the in- and out-breath as a movement that gives a push when entering and exiting, and you mentally note 'push, air element'. Observing the push, you will later be able to feel the pressure created in your body, which supports it in maintaining an upright posture. Mentally note 'support, air element' in order to be aware of what you are observing.

The derivatives

When you identify the derivatives of the four primary elements—such as colour, smell, taste, and nutritive essence—whether they are pleasant or unpleasant, you can name them by mentally noting 'colour', 'smell', 'taste' or 'nutritive essence', as appropriate.

As for space, it is in the nostrils, pharynx, oesophagus, stomach, intestines, and generally wherever there are cavities and passages in the body. Identify it, mentally noting 'space' and try to comprehend its dimension.

SUMMARY

The solid element serves as the foundation for the existence of the other elements in our body. If, for example, the lungs, which are a solid element, did not exist, we would not be able to retain the air element within us, and without breathing, we could not live. If the heart, which is a solid element, did not exist, the blood, which is a liquid element, would not circulate. However, the solid element cannot exist on its own; it, too, depends on the other elements. Examining each element, we realize that none can exist without the presence of the others. The elements are inseparable and interdependent. Through this meditation, we can understand that every millimetre of the body is composed of the four primary elements.

This concludes the analysis of serenity meditation on the four material elements of the body. Insight meditation follows next.

PART II

INSIGHT MEDITATION

Insight Meditation

INTRODUCTION

Insight meditation (*vipassanā*) was first taught by the historical Buddha Gotama and is unique in its kind. It was actually through this form of meditation that he achieved enlightenment and became a Buddha.

Insight meditation plays a central role in his teachings. The Buddha himself was the greatest meditator (*yogi*) the world has ever known, and his usual posture, as depicted in statues, among other things, is the cross-legged meditative posture. He realized the truths he discovered through deep insight meditation, namely the analytical and systematic observation and contemplation of mind and matter—especially the mind, with all its illusions and the suffering that it creates—and the transcendence of these illusions and suffering through non-attachment and liberation, something no one had dared to do until then.

Insight meditation exists today in its original form in Theravāda Buddhism, which has preserved the authentic teachings of the Buddha. The word Buddha used for this meditation is *vipassanā*, which means 'special or refined (*vi*)' + 'seeing or vision (*passana*)'. In a sense, it means the ability to be aware of things that are not perceptible in ordinary ways.

Indeed, insight meditation does not use the usual methods of meditation but employs systematic and methodical observation of material and mental phenomena to penetrate their true nature, which includes:

1) Impermanence or transience (*anicca*),
2) Suffering, unhappiness, or pain (*dukkha*), and
3) Non-self or absence of a permanent self (*anattā*).

Insight meditation involves training in memory, mindfulness, and awareness (*sati-sampajaññā*), which are employed for observing and understanding the impermanent, transient, unstable, ephemeral, and temporary nature of all material and mental phenomena, attachment to which creates existential suffering, unhappiness, and pain.

The fundamental principle of insight meditation is the observation of the rise (*samudaya*) and fall (*vaya*) of every material and mental phenomenon, such as the material body, feelings, thoughts, and mind-objects, which constitute our entire existence.

If one observes these phenomena, one will see that they have the nature of rise and fall. 'Rise and fall' is the characteristic of a phenomenon that is impermanent, transient, momentary, fleeting, and unstable. Through insight meditation, it can be confirmed and verified that this characteristic prevails and is omnipresent in all phenomena of mind and matter. This knowledge leads to insight of the three universal characteristics of our existence:

1) Impermanence (*anicca*),
2) Existential suffering, unhappiness, anxiety, or pain (*dukkha*) caused by our attachment to impermanent phenomena, and
3) Non-self (*anattā*) within the impermanence of phenomena.

This dispels the delusion that there is a permanent, individual self or an 'absolute' universal self, being, existence, or substance that is the fundamental unchanging basis or background of the world. This delusion arises from a metaphysical error in not correctly understanding the transient nature of our world through systematic and methodical observation of the 'rise and fall' that occurs in all phenomena without exception. Failure to understand this results in our attachment to and identification with phenomena that are, in fact, unstable. This attachment causes instability and imbalance in our psychological world.

The aim of observation through insight meditation is not to deactivate, suppress, or stop something, or to criticize, alter, prolong, repel, imagine, or visualize something. Without succumbing to the power of suggestion or auto-suggestion, and without arbitrary views, prejudices, or fixations, we simply observe empirical phenomena objectively and with detachment, just as they occur in reality—not trying to influence them, but to understand them.

The Buddha's Discourse

A detailed explanation of insight meditation is given in *The Discourse on the Establishment of Mindfulness* (*Satipaṭṭhāna Sutta*). In it, the Buddha mentions that in order to acquire true knowledge, we must develop our mindfulness and remember the phenomena we observe objectively. People who do not do this easily lose touch with the true nature of phenomena. This discourse is one of the most important and comprehensive of the Buddha's teachings on meditation and gives particular emphasis on the development of insight meditation. It is the most widely studied and practically applied discourse of the Buddha, rightly called 'the heart of Buddhist meditation' and forms the basis for the development of insight meditation. It contains the most thorough, direct, and straightforward way of achieving the Buddhist goal of Nibbāna or Nirvāna—as the Buddha calls it, it is 'the direct path for the realisation of Nibbāna'. It presents a complete system, aiming to train the mind to see with microscopic precision the true nature of the body, feelings, thoughts, and mental objects, and to overcome attachment to them.

The purpose of Satipaṭṭhāna

The Buddha begins this discourse with the following statement, indicating the purpose of *Satipaṭṭhāna*:

This is the direct path
  for the purification (*visuddhi*) of beings,
  for overcoming sorrow and lamentation,
  for the disappearance of pain and grief,
  for the attainment of the true method, and
  for the realization of Nibbāna —
  namely, the four establishments of mindfulness.

But why does he call it 'the direct path'? It is in order to distinguish it from other meditations belonging to different categories. While other meditations may lead to a certain degree of concentration and serenity, they do not lead to Nibbāna. Indeed, they may even lead to deviations from that path.

Therefore, the aim of this meditation is the direct purification of the mind of beings, the overcoming of sorrow, and so on. Here 'purification' means cleansing the mind of the mental defilements of lust, hatred, and delusion. The establishment of mindfulness is the way for the purification and cleansing of the mind that leads to Nibbāna. As the Buddha says:

> For a long time this mind has been defiled by lust, hatred, and delusion. Through the defilements of the mind beings are defiled; with the cleansing of the mind (*citta-vodānā*) beings are purified (*visujjhanti*).[1]

The four establishments of mindfulness

In this discourse, the Buddha refers to four ways of establishing mindfulness, accompanied by awareness and observation, as follows:

1) observation of the body (*kāyānupassanā*),
2) observation of feelings (*vedanānupassanā*),
3) observation of thoughts (*cittānupassanā*),[2] and
4) observation of mind-objects (*dhammānupassanā*).

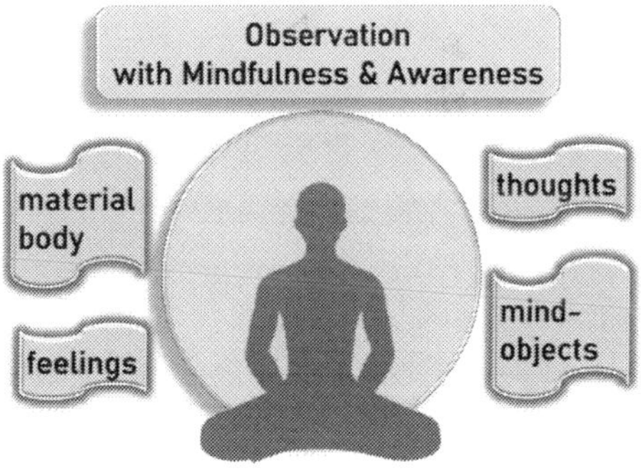

Observation (*anupassanā*) is the process of careful examination, analysis, and contemplation of a phenomenon, during which a person is able to pay close attention and observe much more than most people, with the main goal of self-knowledge.

[1] S III.151, *Dutiyagaddulabaddha-sutta*.
[2] ***Citta***, derived from the verb *cinteti* (to think), can mean 'thought' or, more broadly, 'mind'. Please see PED.

To make this observation, one needs, as the Buddha says, to be ardent (*ātāpī*), fully aware (*sampajāno*), and mindful (*satimā*). Here, 'ardent' means not being sluggish, sleepy, or tired, so that we have enough energy for observation. 'Fully aware' means being able to be fully conscious of the object one observes, which is the opposite of unawareness. 'Mindful' means not forgetting what is being observed.

Now, we will examine the practical aspect, namely, how we can apply observation in this meditation with awareness and mindfulness.

The practice of insight meditation

Observation can begin with the body or the feelings that may arise within it. It can also start with thoughts or mind-objects; depending on what is most obvious to one's own experience at a certain moment. The purpose is to develop mindfulness and acquire knowledge of the true nature of these phenomena, which is to say their rise and fall.

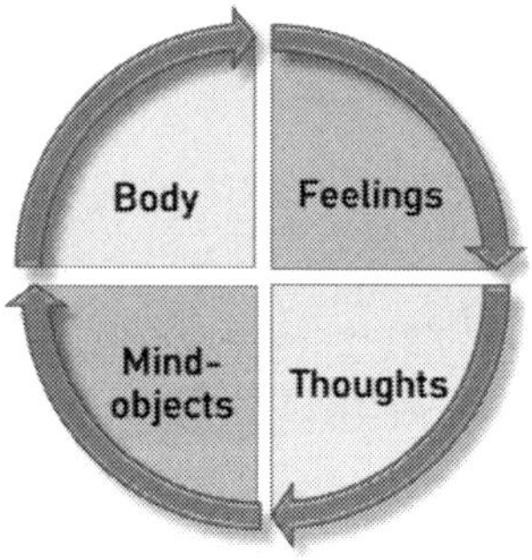

Therefore, you can start by observing what is most distinct or most evident. If the body is more evident, begin with observing the body. If feelings, thoughts, or the mind-objects are more evident, start with those.

Observation of the Body

The breath

Since the body is the most evident aspect for many people, the Buddha begins his explanation first with the observation of the body, specifically highlighting a phenomenon that can be easi-

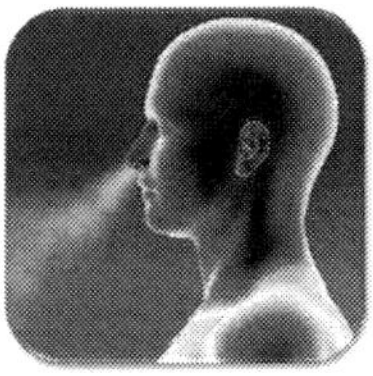

ly perceived in our bodies: the breath. Our breathing causes our bodies to both expand and contract. For this reason, when we close our eyes and start observing our bodies, the first thing we will notice is this movement of expansion and contraction.

Thus, the first observation one can make about the body relates to the breath, which can be observed in order to develop mindfulness of it. This mindfulness, as mentioned, can be used as serenity meditation (*samatha*) by concentrating only on the breath, for example, at the tip of the nose, without paying attention to any other point or phenomenon. However, in insight meditation, mindfulness can be used in a broader way to observe the breath in any part of the body where it is most apparent, evident, or perceptible—such as in the chest, abdomen, or nose—in order to realize its nature, which is none other than the continuous rise and fall. Let's look at how this can be done.

If you feel the in-breath in the nose, you can observe it there; if you feel it in your chest or abdomen, you can observe it there, mentally noting 'in-breath'. The same applies to the out-breath. Observe it wherever it is most evident in your experience, mentally noting 'out-breath'. This is the first part of the observation.

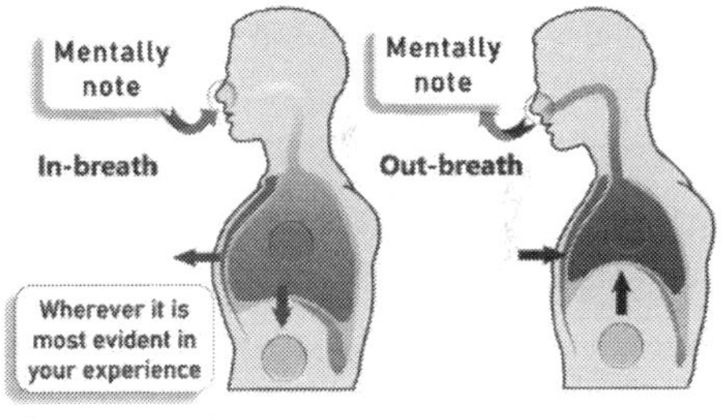

Insight meditation

We now come to the second part, where insight meditation actually begins. Remember to note that the fundamental principle here, as previously mentioned, is observing the rise and fall of every material and mental phenomenon.

For instance, if we observe our breath, we will see that it rises and falls. When we breathe in, we do not do so continuously; there is a limit. After that, the in-breath stops. The beginning of the in-breath is its rise, and the cessation of the in-breath is its fall. The same happens with the out-breath. When we breathe out, we do not do so continuously; there is also a limit. After that, the out-breath stops. The beginning of the out-breath is the rise, and the cessation of the out-breath is its fall. As we shall see below, something similar, in terms of rise and fall, applies to other phenomena as well.

The Buddha says the following about a meditator who observes the breath in the body:

> He abides observing in the body:
> its nature of rise,
> its nature of fall, or
> its nature of both rise and fall.[3]

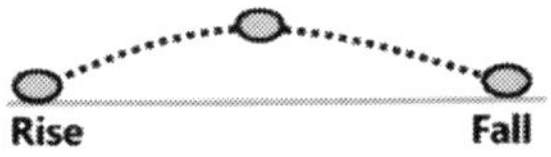

Therefore, this mindful observation of the body has the following two parts:

1st Part	2nd Part
Knowledge of the Object of Observation	*—Insight—* Observation of the Rise & Fall
BODY	✓

When we breathe in, our body expands; this is the rise of the body. When we breathe out, our body contracts; this is the fall. In this way, we try to recognize the in-breath and the out-

---

[3] M I.56, *Satipaṭṭhāna-sutta*: '*Samudaya-dhammānupassī vā kāyasmiṃ viharati. Vaya-dhammānupassī vā kāyasmiṃ viharati. Samudaya-vaya-dhammānupassī vā kāyasmiṃ viharati.*'

breath, which cause expansion and contraction, as rise and fall. This process, in fact, occurs continually, whether we observe our breathing or not. Our task is to become aware of it in its entirety.

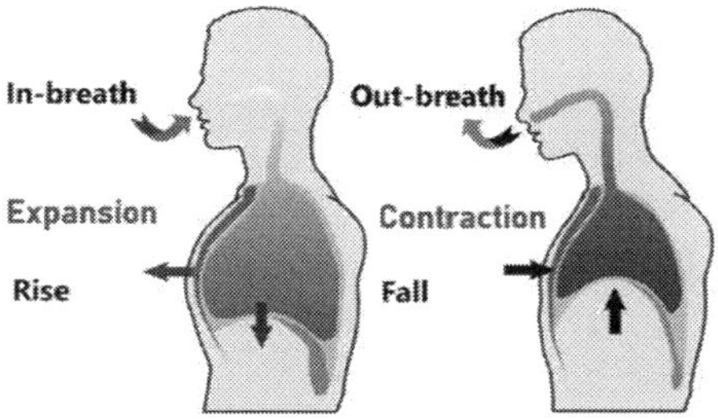

To do that, whenever you feel the in-breath, mentally note 'rise', and whenever you feel the out-breath, mentally note 'fall'. This mental noting is important to help you remember what to observe and thus to be mindful and aware.

In the first part of the observation, you become aware of the process simply as 'in-breath, out-breath... in-breath, out-breath... in-breath, out-breath...', and in the second part, you become aware of it as 'rise, fall … rise, fall …'.

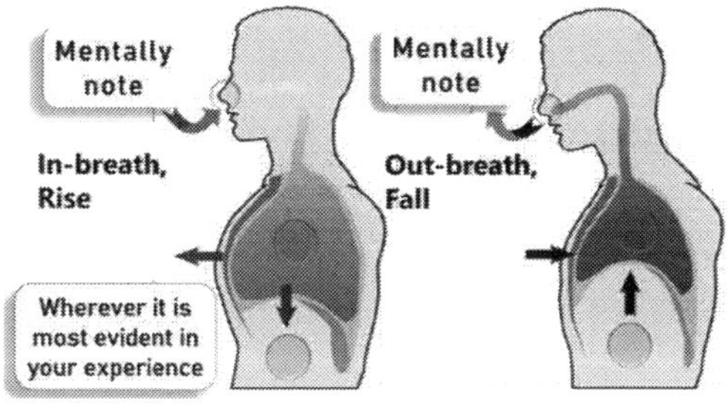

If you gradually deepen your observation, you can see more details and become aware of the in-breath itself as 'rise, fall' and of the out-breath itself as 'rise, fall'. For example, at the tip of the nose, the rise is when the air enters and begins touching the nostrils, and the fall is when it stops touching them. Therefore, whenever the in-breath begins, mentally note 'rise', and when it stops, mentally note 'fall'.

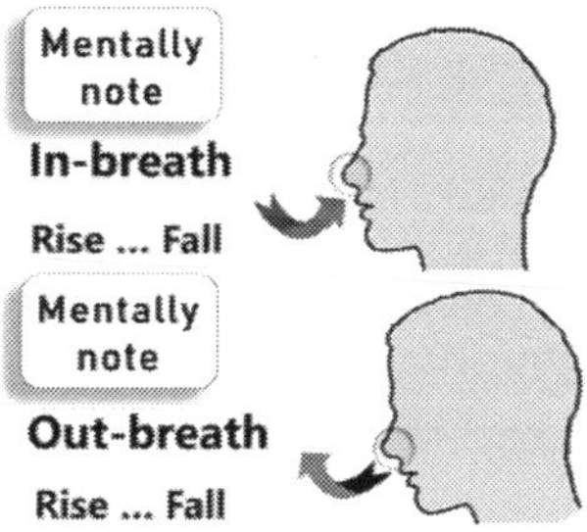

The same happens with the out-breath. The rise is when the air exits and begins touching the nostrils. The fall is when it stops touching them. Whenever it begins, mentally note 'rise', and whenever it stops, mentally note 'fall'.

This phenomenon can also be observed in other parts of the body, such as the chest and abdomen, where the beginning of the in-breath or out-breath is the rise, and its cessation is the fall.

Unlike serenity meditation, where emphasis is only on the in- and out-breath and the point where the air touches the nostrils, in insight meditation, emphasis is given on the impermanent nature of the breath as rise and fall, not on a specific point, but wherever it is most evident in the body.

Besides, the words you repeat mentally help you become aware of the whole process of the in- and out-breath. Later, when the mind becomes familiar with the process, you can omit repeating them, as the mind already knows what to focus on. Only repeat the words to refocus your mind when other thoughts arise and distract you. This also applies to the observations that follow, which have different objects but initially need to be mentally named with words in order to become aware of these objects.

The postures and movements of the body

Another way to mindfully make the observation is with the postures or movements of the body. That is, when walking, standing, sitting, or lying down, what is first observed is the posture (or movement) and then its impermanence, as it continuously changes through rise and fall. The Buddha says about the meditator:

> Again, when walking, he understands: 'I am walking.' When standing, he understands: 'I am standing.' When sitting, he understands: 'I am sitting.' When lying down, he understands: 'I am lying down.' Or in whatever way his body is positioned, he understands it accordingly.

Just like with the breath in the first part, you simply observe the movement occurring in your body when you walk, and mentally note 'I am walking' in order to understand the whole process. You can do the same with other movements or postures, as illustrated below:

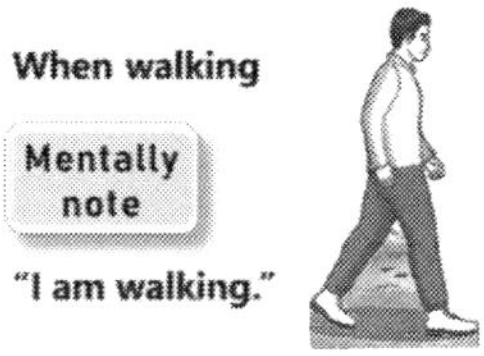

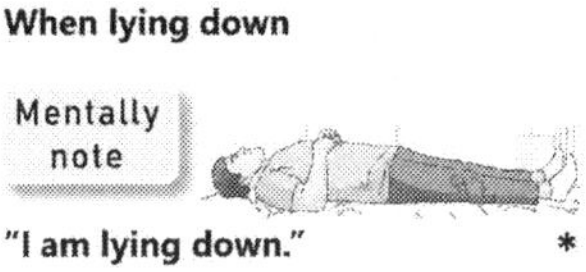

This is the first part of the observation.

Insight meditation

Now let's move on to the second part, where insight meditation begins. For this, the Buddha again says about the meditator:

> He abides observing in the body:
> its nature of rise,
> its nature of fall, or
> its nature of both rise and fall.

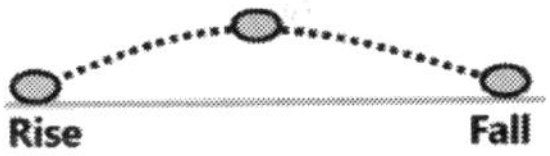

Therefore, this observation in the body, done with awareness and mindfulness, has the following two parts:

1st Part	2nd Part
Knowledge of the Object of Observation	*—Insight—* Observation of the Rise & Fall
BODY	✓

If we observe carefully, our body rises and falls with every movement we make. With every movement that falls, a new movement arises and falls as well, and so the whole process continues. If you gradually deepen your observation, you will be able to discern (in the case of walking, for example) the rise and fall in a very detailed manner, especially when walking slowly. At first, when walking, you can mentally note 'walking' and focus on the movement of your body. Try to see how you lift the foot, move it forward, and put it down, focusing on the details of the movement. For lifting, you can mentally note 'lifting'; for moving forward, 'moving'; and for putting down, 'placing'.

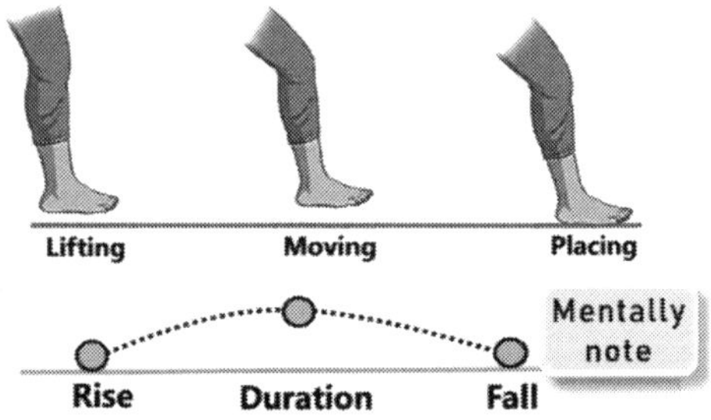

By observing this process, you will gradually discern the rise, the duration of the movement and the fall. To observe the impermanent nature of each single action, mentally note 'rise' when you lift your foot, 'duration' when moving it forward and 'fall' when placing it down.

If you deepen your observation further, you will notice that the rise, duration, and fall occur not only as lifting, moving, and placing, but also in between each phase of the process: in the actual lifting during the heel's raising, the actual movement during the lowering and touching of the foot to the ground, and also during the actual placing. Therefore, we can note small rises and falls in each of these phases. Try to discern them and mentally note 'rise, duration, fall' for each.

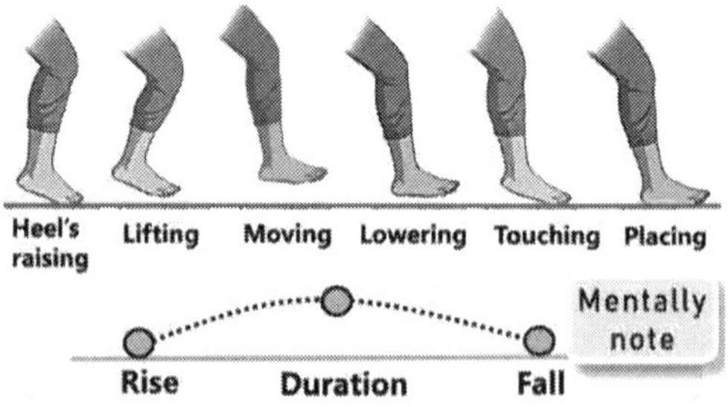

You can do the same when standing. First, you mentally note 'standing', and later, when you discern the rise, mentally note 'rise' at the moment you start standing, 'duration' as long as you continue standing, and 'fall' when you stop standing and begin to move. You can make the same observation when sitting or lying down, trying to distinguish rise, duration, and fall.

Conclusion

Through this meditation we can gain a clear understanding of the body, which is constantly in motion, or in a process of rising and falling, even though we consider it permanent, identify with it, and perceive it as *self*. Thus, the Buddha says regarding this:

> Mindfulness that 'there is a body' is established in [the meditator] just to the extent necessary for bare knowledge and continuous mindfulness.
>
> The meaning is that there is:
> only the body or the bodily process,
> not a being or a person,
> not a woman or a man,
> not a self or something that belongs to a self,
> not a 'me' or 'mine', and
> not someone or something that belongs to someone.

That is, when we observe bodily phenomena, we can see bodily or physical processes. Breathing, for example, is a bodily process. Although we are not aware at this moment that we are breathing in and out, the process of breathing continues automatically. If we observe many other movements we make with our bodies, we will see that we perform them because there is an external or internal stimulus that prompts us to execute them. These stimuli act as springs that push us to perform movements. Although we think we perform them of our own free will, they actually arise due to the existence of various needs, either internally or externally. Through observation, we will see that there are bodily processes that often we ourselves did not even think of performing, but are forced to do due to the circumstances of our lives.

With this meditation, then, we try to see the material body objectively and not to personify it, but simply view it as an impersonal bodily phenomenon. This is called *yathābhūta-ñāṇa*, knowledge of phenomena as they really are and not as we imagine them to be. The Buddha continues, saying:

> And he abides independent, not clinging to anything in the world.[4]

'Independent' means not dependent on craving (*taṇhā*) or on theories, speculations, and views (*diṭṭhi*) regarding the body. This is because the meditator understands that the body is simply a process of the rising and falling of physical phenomena that come into being and pass away at any moment.

'Not clinging to anything in the world' means not clinging to any body, thinking, 'This is mine, this is what I am, this is my self, or this belongs to myself', given that it changes at every moment. He instead only sees processes occurring according to causes and conditions, which themselves rise and fall.

The momentary 'rise and fall' of our bodies is also confirmed by scientific findings that show that in an adult, about 330 billion cells die daily and are replaced by other cells. In 80 to 100 days, 30 trillion cells will have died and been replaced, the equivalent of a new person. Indeed, the mass of cells we lose each year through normal cellular death almost corre-

---

[4] M I.56: '*Anissito ca viharati, na ca kiñci loke upādiyati.*'

sponds to our entire body weight. The Buddha also mentions that our mind changes much more rapidly compared to our body, meaning thoughts, feelings, and so on, are created and disappear at a faster pace. This can be confirmed by systematic self-observation, as we will explain below. Ultimately, the idea that there is a permanent, indestructible, immortal, eternal substance within us is just an illusion.

These are just some of the ways of observing the body. Additionally, the Buddha taught others as well. An example is the observation of small movements of the body, about which the Buddha says:

> And again,
> When looking ahead and looking around, one does so in full awareness.
> When flexing and extending the limbs, he does so in full awareness.
> When dressing, he does so in full awareness.
> When carrying things, he does so in full awareness.
> When eating, he does so in full awareness.
> When drinking, he does so in full awareness.
> When chewing, he does so in full awareness.
> When tasting, he does so in full awareness.
> When talking, he does so in full awareness.
> When keeping silent, he does so in full awareness.

In all these and any other movements, the purpose is to see their rise and fall.

Other ways of observing the body

Another example is the observation of the four primary elements that make up the body, namely the solid, liquid, heat, and air elements, as covered on p. 132. With insight meditation, one can observe their impermanent and transient nature as it is revealed at the moment of rise and fall. There is also the observation of the decomposition of a dead body and its comparison with our living body, which has the same mortal nature that it cannot escape, allowing us to perceive the impermanent nature of our body as rise and fall.

OBSERVATION OF FEELINGS

We will now explain the establishment of mindfulness on the observation of feelings. Feelings play a significant role in our lives. By observing them, we can discover the extent to which they influence our existence and the strong attachments they can create within us. Feelings can be pleasant, unpleasant, or neutral, and are associated with either material or spiritual pleasure or displeasure.

We observe feelings by locating them in our bodies or our minds. They can arise suddenly, at times being pleasant and at other times unpleasant. We typically don't anticipate unpleasant feelings, yet often experience them. Regarding the way such feelings appear, the Buddha gives an analogy referring to the winds, stating that:

Just as many various winds blow back and forth across the sky—easterly winds and westerly winds, northerly winds and southerly winds, dusty winds and dustless winds, sometimes cold, sometimes hot, those that are strong and others mild—similarly, various of feelings arise in this body: pleasant ones and unpleasant ones, and those neither-unpleasant-nor-pleasant (*neutral*).[5]

Our bodies, in other words, are surrounded and impacted by feelings, and we continuously try to respond to them, grasping at pleasant feelings and repelling the unpleasant ones, in a constant struggle between pleasure and displeasure.

If someone were to observe these feelings, however, it becomes quite easy to understand their transient nature and to overcome the influence they exert. We can make this observation gradually, first by identifying our feelings and then examining their nature. The Buddha says here about the meditator:

> And how does he in regard to feelings abide observing feelings?
>
> When feeling a pleasant feeling, he understands: 'I feel a pleasant feeling.'
>
> When feeling an unpleasant feeling, he understands: 'I feel an unpleasant feeling.'
>
> When feeling a neither-unpleasant-nor-pleasant (*neutral*) feeling, he understands: 'I feel a neither-unpleasant-nor-pleasant feeling.'

We are not trying to change anything, but remain aware and mindful by mentally noting what we feel, not what we 'should' feel. We do not try to welcome pleasant feelings or expel and suppress the unpleasant ones.

If a pleasant feeling is more evident, mentally note 'pleasant feeling'. If an unpleasant or neutral feeling is more evident, mentally note 'unpleasant feeling' or 'neutral feeling'. This is the first part of the observation.

---

[5] S IV.218, *Paṭhama-ākāsa-sutta.*

Insight meditation

Now we proceed to the second part, where insight meditation begins. The Buddha again says about the meditator:

> He abides observing in feelings:
> their nature of rise,
> their nature of fall, or
> their nature of both rise and fall.

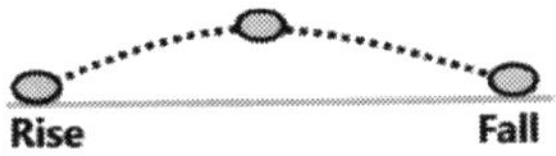

Therefore, this observation in feelings, conducted with awareness and mindfulness, also has the following two parts:

1st Part	2nd Part
Knowledge of the Object of Observation	—*Insight*— Observation of the Rise & Fall
FEELING	✓

In the case of feelings, however, one can also observe their duration phase. Often, when a feeling arises, it does not immediately fall, but lasts for a while. This can happen frequently. Therefore, the meditator needs to have the discernment to observe not only the rise and fall, but also the intermediate duration. Hence, the Buddha says about the meditator:

> Here, he knows feelings
> as they arise,
> as they last (endure), and
> as they pass away (fall).[6]

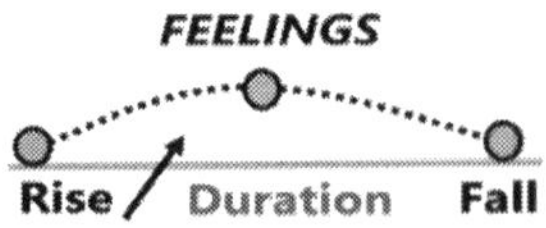

---

[6] A II.45, *Samādhibhāvanā-sutta*: '*Idha, viditā vedanā uppajjanti, viditā upaṭṭhahanti, viditā abbhatthaṃ gacchanti.*'

We see that there are three phases of which one can be aware: rise, duration, and fall. Some feelings rise and fall so quickly that we can only discern their rise or fall, or both. Others occur slowly, so we can also discern their duration.

If we cannot discern their rise, at least we try to discern their duration or fall. If we cannot discern their duration, then we try to discern their fall. Gradually, we will be able to discern all three phases.

Unpleasant feelings

Unpleasant feelings are usually felt more intensely by meditators than any other feeling. They can appear in the mind as grief or in various parts of the body, such as the knee, elbow, shoulder, or head, and can be felt in various ways, such as pain, numbness, itchiness, or stinging. Instead of using many words, we'll call all of these 'unpleasant feelings'. If these feelings are evident and preoccupy your mind, turn your attention to where you feel them and mentally note 'unpleasant feeling'.

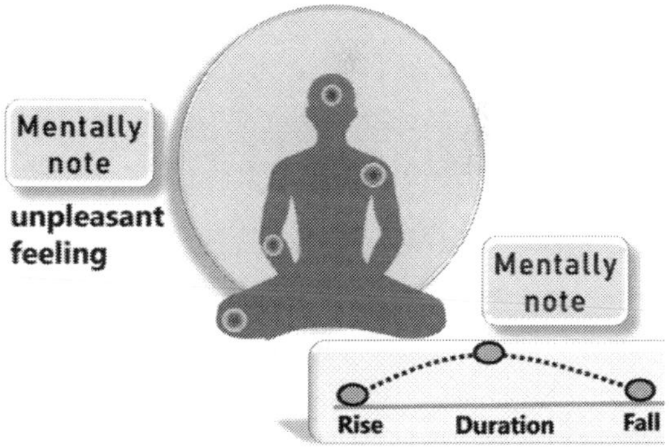

In this case, it is a feeling, not another process like breathing or thinking. Therefore, instead of simply naming it 'upleasant', it is good to name it 'unpleasant feeling' to differentiate it from other phenomena that are not feelings. Then, you can observe that the unpleasant feeling, like other phenomena, arises, lasts for a while, and then passes away. If you discern its rise, mentally note 'rise'. If you discern its duration, mentally note 'duration … duration', for as long as it lasts. If you see its fall, mentally note 'fall'.

Pleasant feelings

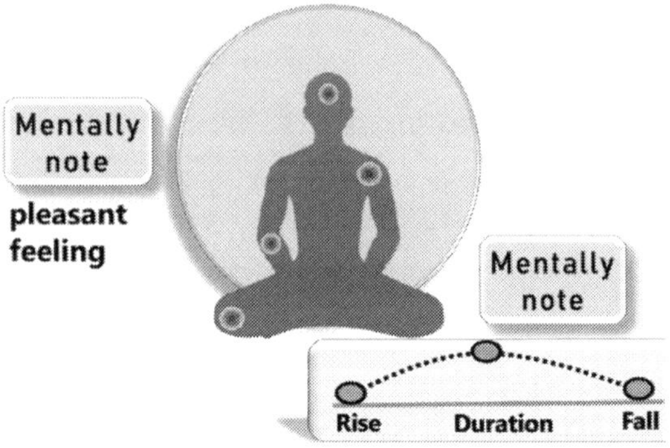

Pleasant feelings can appear in the mind as joy or in various parts of the body as pleasurable sensation. For instance, if the unpleasant feeling disappears, a pleasant feeling might appear in the same spot, which can be felt as pleasurable relief. If so, mentally note 'pleasant feeling' and then try to observe that it too arises, lasts, and falls. It is not everlasting. If you discern its rise, mentally note 'rise'. If you discern its duration, mentally note 'duration', for as long as it lasts. If you discern its fall, mentally note 'fall'.

Neutral feelings

Neutral feelings are those which are neither unpleasant nor pleasant. They can appear in the mind or in various parts of the body as 'indifference', a 'void', or a 'nothingness'. For example, when the pleasant feeling disappears, it leaves behind a void or a nothingness that cannot be identified as either pleasant or unpleasant. The same can happen with the unpleasant feeling when it disappears and creates a void that can sometimes be perceived as quietness or calmness.

If you identify a neutral feeling, you can mentally note 'neutral feeling' and then try to observe that it too arises, lasts, and falls. The neutral feeling is not everlasting. It has limits and can at any moment be replaced by an unpleasant or pleasant feeling. If you discern its rise, mentally note 'rise'; if you discern its duration, mentally note 'duration' for as long as it lasts. If you discern its fall, mentally note 'fall'.

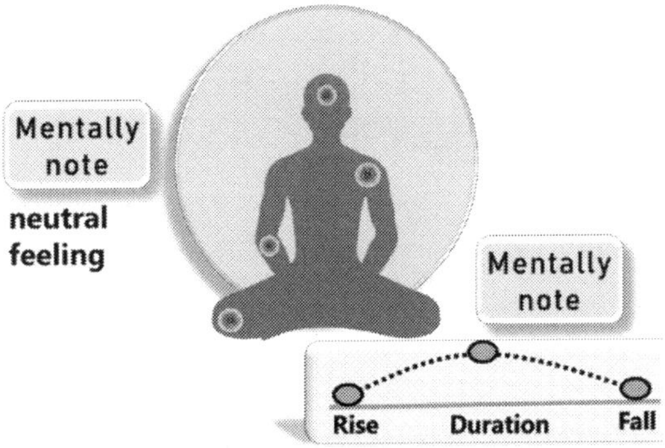

Conclusion

By observing feelings, we can eventually realize that they are not permanent or static but can pass away at any moment. Many meditators, however, tend to want to remove unpleasant feelings, like pain, because they feel uncomfortable and are in a hurry to get rid of them. This, of course, creates more tension and often results in anxiety, especially when the unpleasant feeling they want to remove does not go away. In such cases, we should observe the feelings objectively and without judgment. The more objectively we view them, the easier it becomes to understand their fleeting nature. This way, they leave much more easily than if we were trying to drive them away.

The opposite tendency is to want to hold onto pleasant feelings. When they go away, however, we become disappointed. In both cases, with unpleasant and pleasant feelings, the mind struggles to repel and to hold on. This is a common tendency of the mind.

What do we do in the case of insight meditation? We simply observe without interfering or participating, and without expecting a particular feeling to go away or stay. We just see its nature, which rises, lasts, and falls. In this way, we can see the transient nature of feelings much faster than when we were struggling to drive them away or hold on to them. With complete detachment of the mind, we observe them just as they occur, without intervening. When eventually there are no more feelings, we can return to observing the in- and out-breath in the manner mentioned before.

By practicing this meditation, we can gain clear knowledge about our feelings, which are in constant motion or flow—the process of rising and falling—even though we often consider them to be permanent, identify with them, and perceive them as *self*. The Buddha says the following about this:

> Mindfulness that 'there is feeling' is established in [the meditator] just to the extent necessary for bare knowledge and continuous mindfulness.

> The meaning is that there is:
> only the feeling or the sensory process,
> not a being or a person,
> not a woman or a man,
> not a self or something that belongs to a self,
> not a 'me' or 'mine', and
> not someone or something that belongs to someone.

That is, when observing feelings, we can notice processes that we often hadn't imagined could happen. Feelings frequently arise without us telling them to do so, and they fall without our command. Pleasant feelings that we want to keep usually disappear, while unpleasant ones that we wish to go away remain. Most of the time, they appear without being summoned. We have not asked them to come, to stay, or to leave. After all, do we want to experience unpleasant feelings? Yet, they come, they stay—causing distress—and when circumstances change, they leave.

Through this process, we observe that all these are a series of mental actions which appear and disappear depending on the circumstances. We try to see them objectively and not personify them. We simply view them as impersonal mental phenomena. This is called *yathābhūta-ñāṇa*, knowledge of phenomena as they really are and not as we imagine them to be. The Buddha continues, saying about the meditator:

> And he abides independent, not clinging to anything in the world.[7]

'Independent' means not dependent on craving (*taṇhā*) or on theories, speculations, and views (*diṭṭhi*) regarding feelings, because the meditator understands that feelings are simply a process of the rising and falling of phenomena that come into being and pass away at any moment.

'Not clinging to anything in the world' means not clinging to any feeling, thinking, 'This is mine, this is what I am, this is my self, or this belongs to myself', given that it changes at every moment. He only sees processes occurring according to causes and conditions, which themselves rise and fall.

Observation of Thoughts

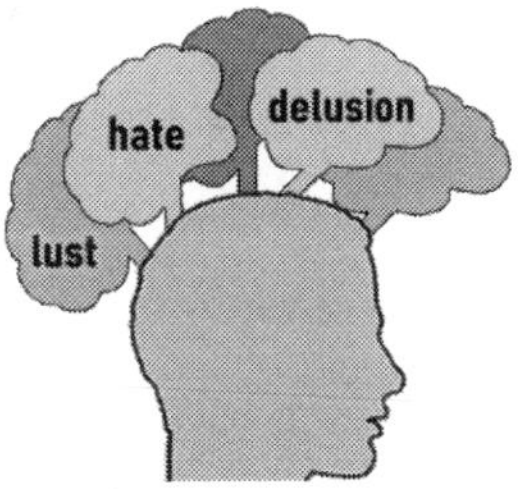

We will now explain the establishment of mindfulness on the observation of thoughts, which may include thoughts of lust, hate, delusion, and so on. Like feelings, thoughts are a common part of our existence and occur daily. They play a significant role in our lives, and by observing them, we will discover how much they influence our existence as well as the strength of the attachments they can create within us.

In observing thoughts, we discern them in our minds and see them objectively. As the Buddha says about the meditator,

---

[7] M I.59: '*Anissito ca viharati, na ca kiñci loke upādiyati.*'

'In regard to the thought, he abides observing the thought.'[8] This means that we observe a thought simply as thought and not as a *person*, *me*, *mine,* or my *self*, as we usually do when we personify thoughts.

Moreover, given that there are a myriad of thoughts that can occur every day, classifying them helps us distinguish them one from another and determine their qualitative, quantitative, or temporal nature. Otherwise, they will appear to be in a chaotic state and be difficult to observe. Therefore, the Buddha classifies our thoughts into various categories that have opposite properties, such as:

thought with lust	←→	thought without lust
thought with hate	←→	thought without hate
thought with delusion	←→	thought without delusion

Thought with lust

Regarding lust, the Buddha says about the meditator: 'He understands a thought with lust as a thought with lust.'

This means when lust arises within us, we try to understand that it is a thought with lust. Usually, lust arises within us when there is an attractive object that tempts, fascinates, or captivates us, something we crave and long for. Depending on its intensity, lust can take many forms. So there are many words to describe it, such as:

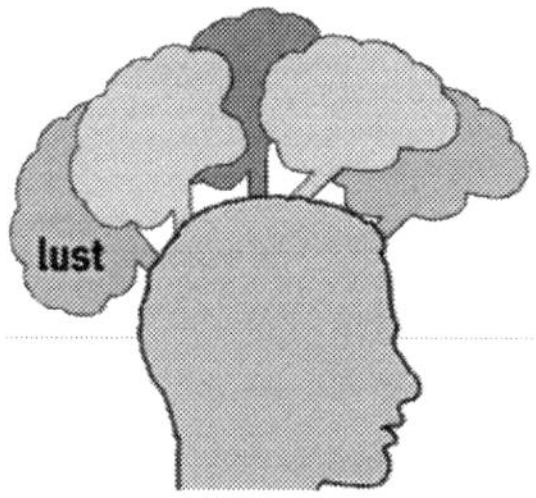

> Passion, desire, longing, yearning, craving, greed, covetousness, and more.

[8] M I.59: '*Citte cittānupassī viharati.*' *Citta*, derived from the verb *cinteti* (to think), can mean 'thought' or, more broadly, 'mind'. Please see PED.

However, to avoid confusion during meditation, we limit ourselves to using the word 'lust' or very close synonyms like 'desire' or 'passion', mindful of their broad meanings. Therefore, when lust arises within you, mentally note 'thought with lust'. Instead of just calling it 'lust', it is good to call it 'thought with lust' in order to differentiate it from other phenomena that are not thought.

Thought without lust

There are also moments when we have no lust within us, such as when we lose interest in something we once desired. In such cases, it is good to realize this, hence the Buddha says about the meditator: 'He understands a thought without lust as a thought without lust.'

Here we can observe the alternation between situations in which we experience lust and those in which we do not, specifically realizing how our minds often fluctuate between states of lust and non-lust. In both cases, we observe the changing nature of our mind, which is not constant or consistently aligned; instead, various thoughts and ideas can emerge in it at any moment. When this happens, we are not trying to modify the thought, but to observe it and understand its nature. Therefore, when non-lust appears within you, mentally note 'thought without lust'.

Thought with hate

The same observation can be made for hate. When hate arises within us, we try to understand it; so, the Buddha says about the meditator: 'He understands a thought with hate as a thought with hate.' Usually, hate arises within us when there is an unattractive object that causes us displeasure, dislike, dissatisfaction, annoyance, disgust, aversion, antipathy, disappointment, or frustration. Depending on its intensity, hate can take many forms, so there are many words to describe it, such as:

> Hatred, anger, ill-will, malice, malevolence, rage, wrath, grudge, repulsion, aggression, and so on.

Hate can begin from a minor displeasure and escalate into hatred or rage. Because such thoughts can be triggered within us, this meditation aims to make us aware of them. There are other forms of hate, like fear (which is also displeasure and aversion towards an object or person we perceive as a threat), jealousy (displeasure and aversion to others' success), sorrow, sadness, grief, depression, guilt, stress, and anxiety. All of these negative emotions stem from displeasure or antipathy towards the object of our experience.

Here too, to avoid confusion, we use only the word 'hate' or very close synonyms, such as 'anger', during meditation, keeping the broad spectrum of meanings in mind. Therefore, when hate arises within you, mentally note 'thought with hate'. Instead of simply naming it 'hate', it is good to call it 'thought with hate' to distinguish it from other phenomena that are not thoughts.

Thought without hate

However, there are moments when we do not feel hate, such as when the displeasure towards something or someone we once disliked fades away. In such cases, it is good to realize this. Hence the Buddha says about the meditator: 'He understands a thought without hate as a thought without hate.'

Here, we see the alternation between moments when we feel hate and those when we do not, specifically how our mind often fluctuates between states of hate and non-hate. In both cases, we observe the changing nature of our minds, which are not constant or consistently aligned; instead, various thoughts and ideas can emerge in it at any moment. Therefore, when non-hate appears within you, mentally note 'thought without hate'.

Thought with delusion

Delusion refers to a lack of knowledge, direction, or orientation of thought, or even the mistaken belief that something is real or achievable. Thoughts with delusion rapidly enter our mind, change direction quickly, cause confusion, and even bring us worries, uncertainty, or doubt, as if we are at a crossroad and do not know which direction to follow. Depending on its intensity, delusion can take many forms; hence, there are many words to describe it, such as:

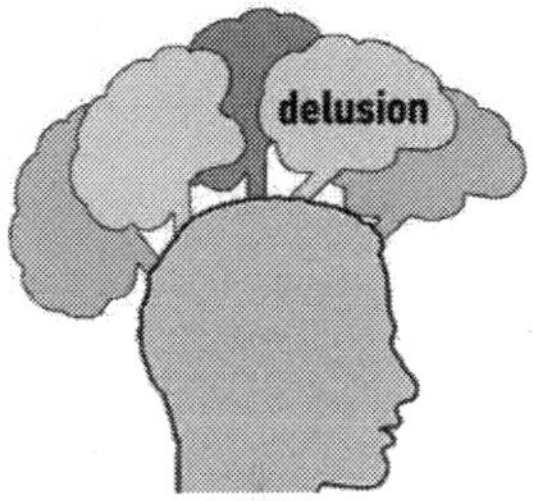

> Confusion, perplexity, uncertainty, doubt, ambiguity, vagueness, bewilderment, ignorance, illusion, fantasy, and daydreaming.

In such cases, the Buddha says about the meditator: 'He understands a thought with delusion as a thought with delusion.' Therefore, when delusion appears within you, mentally note 'thought with delusion'.

Thought without delusion

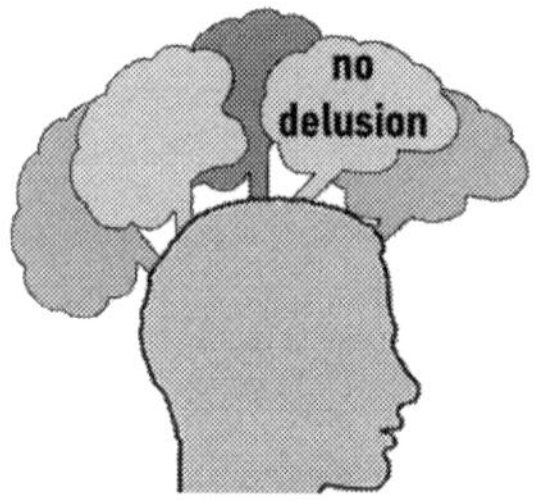

There are times when we have clarity and sobriety, and our thoughts are without delusion. In these cases, the Buddha says about the meditator: 'He understands a thought without delusion as a thought without delusion.' Therefore, whenever you experience a thought without delusion within you, mentally note 'thought without delusion'.

Here, we see the alternation of thoughts and the changing of our mind, how it often moves between states of delusion and non-delusion.

Categories of thoughts

The most common categories of thoughts one can identify within oneself are those with opposite properties that we have already mentioned, such as:

thought with lust	←→	thought without lust
thought with hate	←→	thought without hate
thought with delusion	←→	thought without delusion

Other categories of thoughts include:

contracted thought (due to drowsiness)	←→	distracted thought (due to worry)
concentrated thought	←→	unconcentrated thought
liberated thought	←→	unliberated thought

Insight meditation

Let us now move on to the part of insight meditation that examines the nature of these thoughts. Here, the Buddha says about the meditator:

He abides observing in thought:
its nature of rise,
its nature of fall, or
its nature of both rise and fall.

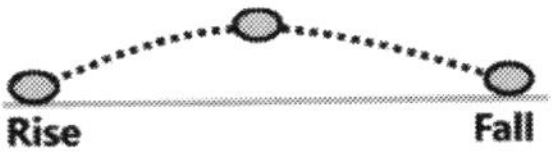

Therefore, this observation of thoughts, done with awareness and mindfulness, also has the following two parts:

1st Part	2nd Part
Knowledge of the Object of Observation	—*Insight*— Observation of the Rise & Fall
THOUGHT	✓

Just as with feelings, in the case of thoughts, one can also observe their duration phase because often, when a thought arises, it does not immediately fall but lasts for a whiles. This can happen frequently. So, the meditator needs to have the discernment to observe not only the rise and fall but also the intermediate duration. On this, the Buddha says the following:

Here, one knows thoughts
as they arise,
as they last (endure), and
as they pass away (fall).'[9]

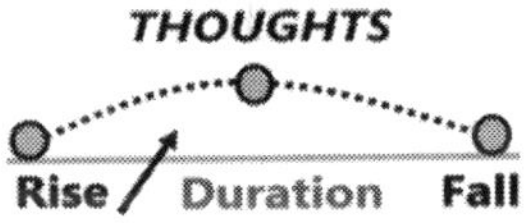

We can see from this that there are three phases of which one can be aware: rise, duration, and fall. Some thoughts rise and fall so quickly that we can only discern their rise or fall, or both. Others occur slowly, so we can also discern their duration.

[9] A II.45, *Samādhibhāvanā-sutta*: '*Idha, viditā vitakkā uppajjanti, viditā upaṭṭhahanti, viditā abbhatthaṃ gacchanti.*'

Many thoughts come to our minds against our will, without us ever asking them to. They come anyway, though, and trouble us. Likewise, many of the good thoughts, which we want to keep, leave without us telling them to go. Thus, we find ourselves in a struggle to keep the positive thoughts in our minds and expel those that trouble us. But if one observes thoughts, one can see the nature of their rise and fall without identifying with them, thereby remaining unaffected by them.

The mode of observation

If you cannot understand the category of a thought, simply name it 'thought' or 'thoughts'. Mentally note 'thought... thought... thought'. Then go to the second part and observe the thought's rise, duration, and fall. Mentally note 'rise... duration... fall'.

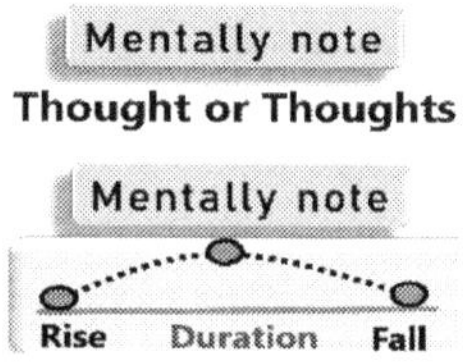

Whenever thoughts are persistent, however, try to analyse them according to the above categories. If you discern a thought with lust, mentally note 'thought with lust...'. Then go to the second part and observe its rise, duration, and fall. Mentally note 'rise... duration... fall'.

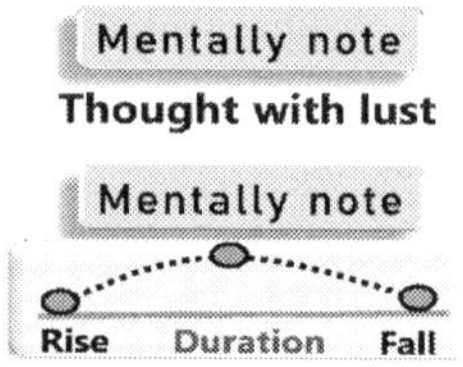

If the thought is without lust, mentally note 'thought without lust...', and observe its rise, duration, and fall by mentally noting 'rise... duration... fall'.

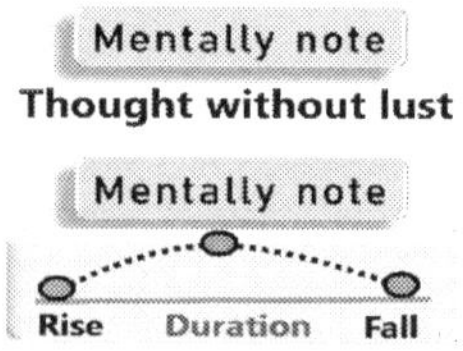

If you discern a thought with hate, mentally note 'thought with hate...', and observe its rise, duration, and fall by mentally noting 'rise... duration... fall'.

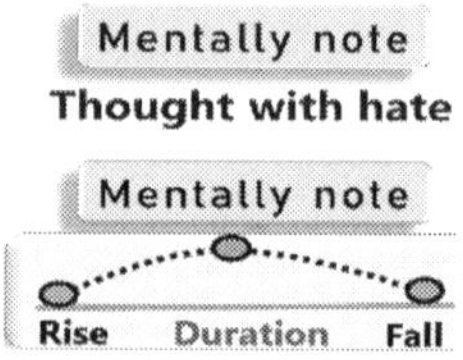

If the thought is without hate, mentally note 'thought without hate...', and observe its rise, duration, and fall by mentally noting 'rise... duration... fall'.

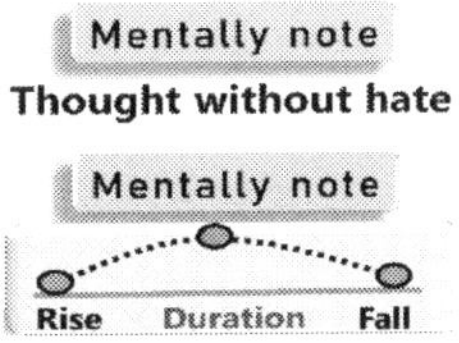

If you discern a thought with delusion, mentally note 'thought with delusion...', and observe its rise, duration, and fall by mentally noting 'rise... duration... fall'.

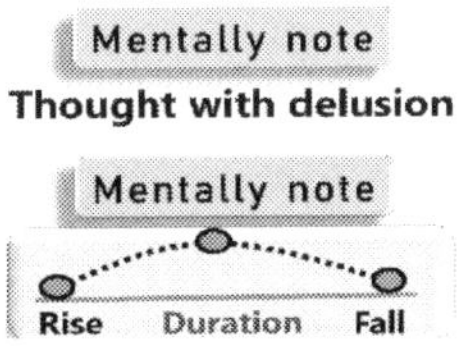

If the thought is without delusion, mentally note 'thought without delusion...', and observe its rise, duration, and fall by mentally noting 'rise... duration... fall'.

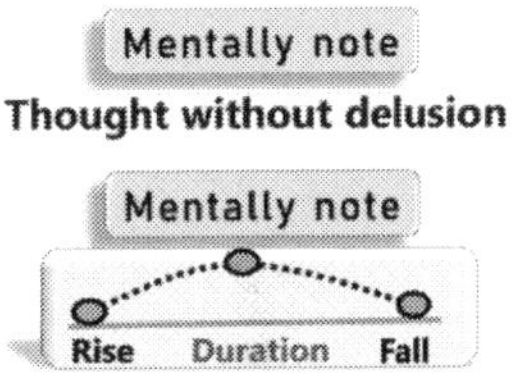

Conclusion

In this meditation, we are not trying to create thoughts of lust, hate, or delusion, and so on within ourselves. Instead, we objectively observe them as they appear, seeing how we get carried away and become involved in them without truly understanding the impermanence of their nature. Over time, we can gain clear knowledge about such thoughts and realize that they are not permanent or static but can pass away at any moment. They are constantly in motion, in a flux or in the process of rising and falling, even though we consider them fixed, identify with them, and perceive them as *self*. The Buddha says about this:

> Mindfulness that 'there is thought' is established in [the meditator] just to the extent necessary for bare knowledge and continuous mindfulness.
>
> The meaning is that there is:
>
> only the thought or the thought process,

> not a being or a person,
> not a woman or a man,
> not a self or something that belongs to a self,
> not a 'me' or 'mine', and
> not someone or something that belongs to someone.

That is, when we observe thoughts, we can see processes that often even we ourselves had not conceived could occur.

Thoughts arise frequently without us telling them to do so and pass away without our command. Positive thoughts that we want to keep often disappear, while negative thoughts that we want to disappear remain. These thoughts present themselves many times regardless of our will. We didn't invite them to come, stay, or leave. After all, who wants to experience distressing thoughts? Yet, they come and linger, causing distress, and leave as soon as circumstances change.

We observe that all of these are sequences of mental processes that appear and disappear depending on circumstances. We try to see them objectively. Instead of personifying them, we see them simply as impersonal mental phenomena. This is called *yathābhūta-ñāṇa*, knowledge of phenomena as they really are and not as we imagine them to be. The Buddha continues, saying about the meditator:

> And he abides independent, not clinging to anything in the world.[10]

'Independent' means not dependent on craving (*taṇhā*) or on theories, speculations, and views (*diṭṭhi*) regarding thoughts, because the meditator understands that thoughts are simply a process of the rising and falling of mental phenomena that come into being and pass away at any moment.

---

[10] M I.59: '*Anissito ca viharati, na ca kiñci loke upādiyati.*'

'Not clinging to anything in the world' means not clinging to any thought, thinking, 'This is mine, this is what I am, this is my self, or this belongs to myself', given that it changes at every moment. He only sees processes occurring according to causes and conditions, which themselves rise and fall.

Observation of Mind-Objects

We will now explain the establishment of mindfulness through the observation of mind-objects. This type of observation can be undertaken by more advanced meditators. The Buddha has mentioned various ways through which this observation is carried out. However, here we will provide a simple example of one of the easier ways to begin observing mind-objects.

The example concerns the sense organs, such as the eye and ear, and the sense objects, like visible forms, sounds, and so on. Both sense organs and sense objects are considered to be material phenomena.

When material phenomena, such as visible data (colours and shapes), impinge on our eyes, they impact our minds. From this impact, ideas and emotions can arise, becoming

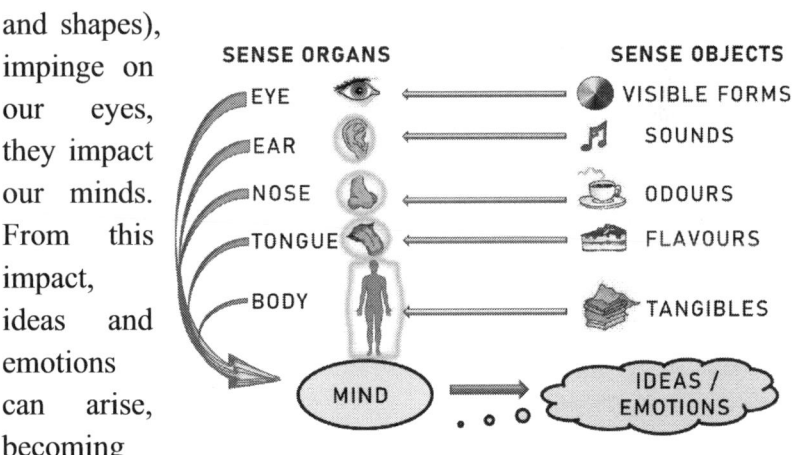

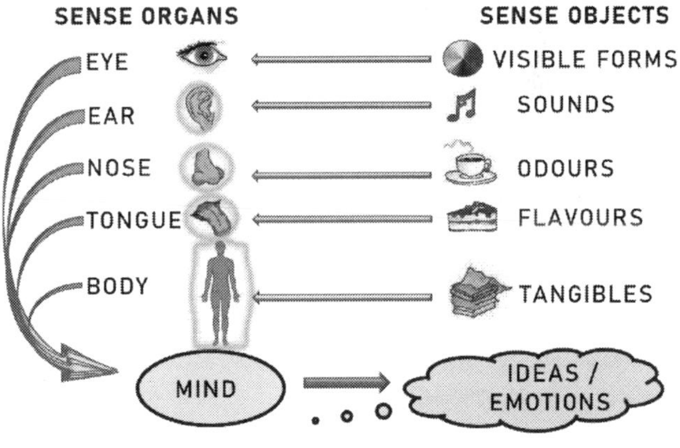

mind-objects. The same applies to the ear and sounds. When a sound impinges upon our ears, it impacts our minds and can evoke ideas and emotions within us. If the sounds are pleasant to us, they arouse pleasant ideas and emotions, which become mind-objects. Conversely, if they are unpleasant to us, unpleasant ideas and emotions arise. We observe, therefore, that many of these mental phenomena occur within us due to material phenomena, because of the stimuli we receive from our senses. In other words, material sense objects have an impact on our minds and affect the mind-objects.

The same happens with the nose and odours. When an odour impinges on our nose, it impacts our mind, and ideas and emotions related to odours are generated within us. Depending on whether the odours are pleasant or unpleasant, we have corresponding pleasant or unpleasant ideas and emotions.

A similar process occurs with our tongues and flavours. Flavours that impinge on our tongues can be pleasant or unpleasant and have a corresponding impact on our mind and ideas. One may have a desire for certain tastes and an aversion to others. Although we believe that we generate these ideas and emotions, they are actually result from the external stimuli received by our senses. There is a mechanism by which our minds are influenced by visible forms, sounds, flavours, and so on. They generate ideas and emotions within our minds that can change at any moment.

The same happens with our bodies. When they come into contact with tangible objects, these objects impinge upon them, impacting our minds and generating ideas and emotions.

In short, material objects, through the sense organs, are transformed into mind-objects that can change our moods and ideas at any moment. Moreover, mind-objects can create emotional ties or bonds, which the Buddha calls 'mental fetters' (*saṃyojana*). These are, for example, sensual lust (*kāma-rāga*), ill-will or anger (*vyāpāda*), conceit (*māna*), restlessness (*uddhacca*) and doubt (*vicikicchā*).[11]

---

[11] Please see the section on mental fetters (*saṃyojana*) on p. 188.

Therefore, if, upon seeing visible forms, hearing sounds, smelling odours, and so on, sense objects become evident, use them as objects of attention and mentally note 'visible form', 'sound', 'odour', 'flavour' and 'touch', as appropriate. Also, observe the 'mental fetter' that arises dependent on these objects and mentally note 'sensual lust', or 'ill-will/anger' and so on, as the case may be. This is the first part of the observation.

Insight meditation

Let's move on to the part of insight meditation that examines the nature of these objects. Here, the Buddha says about the meditator:

> He abides observing in mind-objects:
> their nature of rise,
> their nature of fall, or
> their nature of both rise and fall.

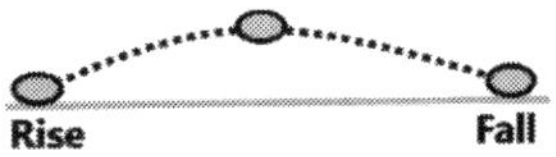

Therefore, this observation, which is made with awareness and mindfulness, also has the following two parts:

1st Part	2nd Part
Knowledge of the Object of Observation	—*Insight*— Observation of the Rise & Fall
MIND-OBJECTS	✓

The mode of observation

When there are stimuli from visible forms, sounds, and so on, observe how they arise, last and fall. For example, a pleasant sound causes pleasant emotions, which in turn create the mental fetter of sensual lust. But how long does the sound and the sense of lust last? Lust lasts for as long as the stimulus of the sound is present. When the stimulus ceases, sensual lust disappears. In short, mental fetters depend on the stimuli we receive from the environment and are equally impermanent and transient as anything else. We mistakenly identify with these mental fetters and, of course, suffer because of them, as we do not understand their transient nature.

So, when you hear a sound, try to observe that it arises, lasts, and falls. If you discern its rise, mentally note 'rise'; if you discern its duration, mentally note 'duration ... duration' for as long as it lasts; if you discern its fall, mentally note 'fall'. Also, discern the rise, duration, and fall of the mental fetter that arises dependent on sound and mentally note it accordingly.

You can apply the same observation to other sense objects whenever they are evident. For instance, while eating or drinking, observe the odour, taste, and touch, and discern their rise, duration, and fall. Also, discern the rise, duration, and fall of the *mental fetter* that arises dependent on these and mentally note it accordingly.[12]

Conclusion

Through this meditation, we can gain clear knowledge about the objects that affect our daily life. Although these objects are constantly in motion, in a flux, or in a process of rising and falling, attachment to them easily forms within us. We become captivated and identify with them mentally or emotionally, perceiving them as *self*. The Buddha says about this:

---

[12] For further details on the observation of mind-objects in terms of the sense organs and the sense objects, please see p. 286. For the other observations of mind-objects, please see p. 284ff.

> Mindfulness that 'there are mind-objects' is established in [the meditator] just to the extent necessary for bare knowledge and continuous mindfulness.

> The meaning is that there are:
> only mind-objects,
> not a being or a person,
> not a woman or a man,
> not a self or something that belongs to a self,
> not a 'me' or 'mine', and
> not someone or something that belongs to someone.

That is, when we observe such objects, we see a mechanism of how our emotions of sensual lust, anger, conceit, and so on are affected by the stimuli we receive when we come into contact with sense objects.

Although we might think that we generate our emotions and ideas, the reality is that the mind naturally reacts to colours, shapes, sounds, flavours, and similar stimuli, eliciting emotions and ideas within us that are often unexpected. These often arise without us asking them to and fall away in the same way. Those we wish to retain usually pass away, while those we want to go away tend to persist. We can observe that all of these are sequences of mental processes that appear and disappear depending on circumstances. We try to see them objectively and we do not personify them, but simply see them as impersonal mental phenomena. This is called *yathābhūta-ñāṇa*, knowledge of phenomena as they really are and not as we imagine them to be. And the Buddha continues, saying about the meditator:

> And he abides independent, not clinging to anything in the world.[13]

---

[13] M I.61: '*Anissito ca viharati, na ca kiñci loke upādiyati.*'

'Independent' means not dependent on craving (*taṇhā*) or on theories, speculations, and views (*diṭṭhi*) regarding mind-objects, because the meditator understands that mind-objects are simply a process of the rising and falling of mental phenomena that come into being and pass away at any moment.

'Not clinging to anything in the world' means not clinging to any mind-object, thinking, 'This is mine, this is what I am, this is my self, or this belongs to myself', given that it changes at every moment. He only sees processes occurring according to causes and conditions, which themselves rise and fall.

This is the general information required to comprehend the basic practice of insight meditation.

Dependent Origination

The more the meditator proceeds with the observation involved in insight meditation, the more they can reach deeper levels of knowledge and discern finer details of the way in which material and mental phenomena arise and fall. That is, they can discern that there is a mechanism contributing to their birth and their destruction, known as Dependent Origination (*Paṭiccasamuppāda*). This reveals the principle of the causal relationship of phenomena (*dhammaṭṭṭhitatā*), their natural order of occurrence (*dhamma-niyamatā*), and their specific conditionality (*idappaccayatā*). Regarding this, the Buddha says:

> Because of not understanding, not penetrating this teaching of Dependent Origination, this generation has become like a tangled skein, like a knotted ball of thread, like matted rushes and reeds, and does not pass beyond *saṃsāra* with its plane of misery, unfortunate destinations, and lower realms.[14]

[14] D II.54, *Mahānidāna-sutta*.

The teaching of Dependent Origination allows one to understand the specific conditions (*idapaccaya*) upon which the existence of a phenomenon depends. Therefore, we should mention here that there are two ways of observing the rise and fall:

1) the momentary rise (*khaṇika-samudaya*) and
the momentary fall (*khaṇika-vaya / atthaṅgama*), and
2) the conditional rise (*paccaya-samudaya*) and the
conditional fall (*paccaya-vaya /atthaṅgama/-nirodha*).[15]

We have already explained the first way. As for the second, we must understand that the rise and fall of a phenomenon do not occur by chance. Phenomena arise from causes and conditions and fall due to causes and conditions. In the ultimate reality (*paramattha-sacca*), there are only processes of physical and mental phenomena that continuously rise and fall depending on causes and conditions (*hetu-paccaya*), which themselves are also impermanent.

For example, how does desire rise and fall within us, and how do hate, delusion, and other emotions rise and fall? With continued practice, one can gradually ascertain that all of these phenomena do not happen by chance but depend on certain causes and conditions. They are produced by a chain reaction of causes and conditions. Without it, such phenomena cannot occur.

When, for example, we walk on the street and see an attractive object with a beautiful colour and shape, our eye is immediately drawn to it, and a desire is born within us to go closer, see it more clearly, and admire it. So, what happened? If this object did not exist, we would not have approached it. We only approached it because it appeared before us. In this example,

[15] Ps I.54, *Udayabbayañāṇaniddeso;* SA II.74, *Dukkha-sutta-vaṇṇanā*. Cf. S II.42, *Paccaya-sutta.*

the attractive object is the cause, and the result is the desire that arose within us. The object, functioning as the cause, gives rise to the result—the desire that draws us towards the object.

Additionally, there are conditions. For instance, if the attractive object is a beautiful flower, there must be light for us to see it and for desire to arise within us. Light is a suitable condition that allows us to see the flower; otherwise, it would be impossible to perceive it visually.

Colour also plays a role. If the flower is red and it is in front of a wall that is also red, then we cannot distinguish it from the wall. There must be a contrast of colours; for example, the wall must be white, or the flower yellow.

These are some of the external conditions. There are also internal ones, such as:

1) our eyes, which must function,
2) visual consciousness, to cognize that the flower exists,
3) feeling, to directly experience whether the flower is pleasant or unpleasant,
4) perception, to have a good or bad impression given by the feeling,
5) the thought process, to think about the flower, and
6) desire, for the beautiful flower.

We see that there is a procedure, that desire did not arise out of the blue. We can state that it is causal and conditioned, as it is produced by a series of causes and conditions, depending on them. This is called 'Dependent Origination' of phenomena.

A similar process occurs with the desire for sounds, odours, flavours, and ideas, and emotions such as hate, fear, or sorrow around them. Eventually, a domino effect emerges, not by chance but due to a sequence of events. We can comprehend this only through methodical observation and analysis. Assuming that it is a random occurrence obscures a clear understanding of how so many material and mental phenomena appear within us and the mechanism that lies behind them.

When a meditator observes all of these phenomena, they realize that phenomena are causal and conditioned, but also that the specific causes and conditions are not everlasting. The flower we mentioned, that is, the object or the cause, changes at any moment. The external conditions (for example, the light) as well as the internal ones—consciousness, feelings, perceptions, and thought processes—also change. The causes change, the conditions change, and the results of the causes and conditions also change, as all are in continuous alternation of rise and fall.

Furthermore, the meditator will be able to ascertain that the causes and conditions depend on other causes and conditions for their appearance and duration. Thus, they can gain an overall knowledge and understanding of Dependent Origination' of phenomena.

This contributes to the purification (*visuddhi*) of the mind from passions and anything else that causes suffering and distress due to attachment to impermanent, unstable, and conditioned phenomena. In this way, the meditator can overcome sorrow and lamentation, eliminate pain and sorrow, and achieve the true method and realization of Nibbāna, the supreme bliss—an ideal state of equilibrium that transcends the cycle of rebirth and death.

SUMMARY

Let us summarize what we have covered so far. We will also make further reference to the four stages of Enlightenment achieved through insight meditation.

Insight meditation is practised through ardentness, mindfulness, awareness, and observation of the body, feelings, thoughts, and mind-objects.

The insight that one needs to develop is based on the observation of the rise and fall of material and mental phenomena. Wherever we observe, we shall see that phenomena possess different characteristics (*paccatta-lakkhaṇa*)—for example, the body with its breathing has characteristics different from feelings; thoughts have their own characteristics as well, as do mental and material objects. However, all share a universal characteristic (*sādharaṇa-lakkhaṇa*): they rise and fall. Whether we observe the body, feelings, thoughts, or anything else, in essence, we observe the same thing: their rise and fall.

With this meditation, we can change the object of observation according to what is most evident in our experience, while still discerning the same universal characteristic. For example, if, while observing the body, or the breath specifically, a feeling arises that is prominent and occupies our mind, we can shift our observation from the breath to the feeling. We will see that the same thing happens there—the feeling rises and falls, like our breath. When the feeling fades away, we can return to observing the breath. If, while we are observing a feeling, a thought appears that is intense and occupies our mind, we can interrupt the observation of the feeling and observe the thought. We will see that the same phenomenon occurs there, too—the thought rises and falls just like our feelings and breath. When the thought fades away, we either return to the observation of the feeling, if it is still persisting, or, if it too has disappeared, we return to the breath, which is always present.

This particular meditation has as its object of observation that which is most evident, distinct, clear, obvious, and apparent in our experience. This allows us to change the object of observation without losing the thread of observation, because the purpose of insight is to discern the universal characteristic of rise and fall. Therefore, we discern rise and fall whether we observe the body, feelings, thoughts, the mind-objects.

'Rise and fall' forms a continuum. We can discern it wherever we direct our attention, and that is when our concentration increases. The mind does not become lost in the multitude of objects since it discerns their fundamental principle, which is the continuous cycle of rise and fall. This concentration is called 'concentration through insight meditation' (*vipassanā-samādhi*).[16]

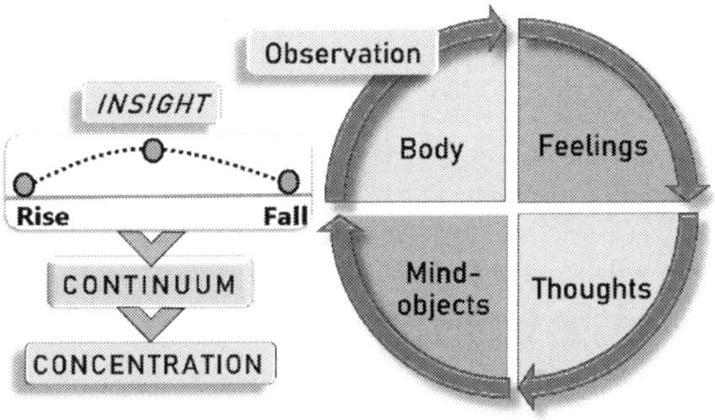

Concentration through insight meditation

The concentration through insight meditation is a process referred to by the Buddha as the 'development of concentration' (*samādhi-bhāvanā*) leading to mindfulness and full awareness (*sati-sampajaññā*). Regarding this, the Buddha states:

> And what is the development of concentration that leads to mindfulness and full awareness? Here one knows feelings ... thoughts ... perceptions as they:

[16] This type of concentration is also referred to in the Buddha's discourses as 'signless concentration of mind' (*animitto cetosamādhi*), for instance, in S IV.268. It involves the mind concentrating on impermanence (rise and fall) and abandoning the sign of permanence, etc. (SA III.90). Impermance (*anicca*) is characterized in the discourses as: 'Impermanent, alas, are formations; their nature is to arise and fall (*uppāda-vaya-dhammino*).' See, for example, S II.103, *Vepullapabbata-sutta*.

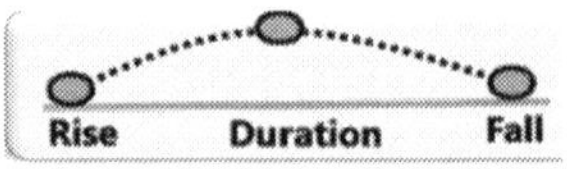

arise (*uppajjanti*),
last/endure (*upaṭṭhahanti*), and
pass away (*abbhatthaṃ gacchanti*).[17]

This concentration is attainable because there is a continuous pattern upon which the mind can focus amidst the multiplicity and variability of phenomena. This continuous pattern is phenomena's incessant rise, duration, and fall.

When starting this meditation, avoid thinking, 'Oh, there are so many things to meditate upon!' Instead, be more aware of observing rise, duration, and fall. Gradually, your mind will become concentrated on this pattern and be able to observe these phenomena in greater detail.

Even when walking, eating, speaking, drinking, or making any movement, you can observe rise, duration, and fall.

The Buddha referred to the rise and fall in the Discourse on the Establishment of Mindfulness, as well as in numerous others. His following statement, as noted in the introduction of this book, illustrates the importance he gave to understanding rise and fall:

Better to live one day
seeing the rise and fall of phenomena
than to live a hundred years
without ever seeing their rise and fall (*udaya-vaya*).[18]

And the last words of the Buddha were:

All conditioned phenomena have the nature to fall (*vaya-dhamma*). Strive to understand this diligently.[19]

---

[17] A II.45, *Samādhibhāvanā-sutta.*
[18] Dhp, 113.
[19] D II.120, *Mahāparinibbāna-sutta.*

The Four Stages of Enlightenment

Those who delve deeper into insight meditation can gradually attain the four stages of enlightenment, which are:

1) attainment of the stream-enterer (*sotāpanna*),
2) attainment of the once-returner (*sakadāgāmī*),
3) attainment of the non-returner (*anāgāmī*),
4) attainment of the Worthy One (*Arahant*).

1. *Attainment of the stream-enterer*

A stream-enterer is a noble person (*ariya-puggala*) who has fully entered the stream of the Noble Eightfold Path,[20] which irrevocably carries him towards entrance into Nibbāna. They have fully understood the following fundamental principle:

> All that has the nature of arising also has the nature of cessation/fall.[21]

This understanding is called the 'dhamma eye' (*dhamma-cakkhu*), meaning 'the eye of the true nature of all phenomena'. Here, *dhamma* means 'nature', and the eye is the comprehension of the aforementioned fundamental principle.

Having seen this truth through observation of the rise and fall of all mental and material phenomena, the stream-enterer has severed the first three of the ten mental fetters (*saṃyojana*) that keep the mind in bondage to continuous wandering in the dreadful cycle of rebirth (*saṃsāra*). For the first time, they enter the 'stream' that inevitably moves towards Nibbāna, which is the complete cessation of rise, duration, and fall. They have

[20] The Noble Eighth Path (*ariya-aṭṭhaṅgika-magga*) consists of: 1) right view, 2) right thought, 3) right speech, 4) right action, 5) right livelihood, 6) right effort, 7) right mindfulness, and 8) right concentration.

[21] '*Yaṃ kiñci samudayadhammaṃ, sabbaṃ taṃ nirodhadhamman'ti.*' E.g. D I.148, *Kūṭadanta-sutta*; M I.379, *Upāli-sutta*; M I.500, *Dīghanakha-sutta*; Ud 48, *Suppabuddhakuṭṭha-sutta.*

attained the first supramundane path and its fruition and now possesses excellent and liberating wisdom, ensuring that they will be reborn at most seven more times and only in human or divine realms of existence. They are no longer subject to rebirth in lower worlds, such as those of animals, spirits, demons, titans, and hell beings, and are firmly established on the path, destined for enlightenment (*sambodhi*) and complete cessation of existential suffering.

2. *Attainment of the once-returner*

If the stream-enterer continues with insight meditation, they can attain the state of once-returner while still in the human world. A once-returner is a noble person who has attained the second supramundane path and its fruition, has severed the first three of the ten mental fetters, has weakened the fetters of sensual desire and hate, and is destined after death to be reborn in this world only one more time, thereby putting an end to existential suffering.

3. *Attainment of the non-returner*

If a once-returner continues with insight meditation, they can attain the state of non-return. A non-returner is a noble person who will not return to the sensual world of existence because they have attained the third supramundane path and its fruition, having severed the first five of the ten mental fetters. If they fail to attain the state of the Worthy One in this life, they reappear in the higher divine world of the 'Pure Abodes' (*Suddhāvāsa*) and, without returning from that world to the human or any other sensual world, attain the state of the Worthy One and final Nibbāna, thus putting an end to the existential suffering.

4. *Attainment of the Worthy One*

A Worthy One (*Arahant*) is a noble person who, through insight meditation, has attained the fourth supramundane path and its fruition, having severed all ten mental fetters. Their mind is free from all mental defilements (*kilesa*) such as lust, hate, delusion, ignorance, and conceit, and all mental corruptions (*āsava*). They are not destined for further rebirth, thereby putting an end to existential suffering.

The term *Arahant* is used for the Buddha and his noble disciples who attained the highest level of knowledge (*aññā*) of the Four Noble Truths. This knowledge brings about final liberation and the attainment of the highest enlightenment (*sambodhim'uttama*).[22] As the Buddha describes it:

> There is no future round (*vaṭṭa*) of rebirth in the case of those who are *Arahants* because 1) they have eliminated the mental corruptions (*āsava*), 2) lived the holy life (*brahmacariya*), 3) finished what had to be finished (*katakaraṇīya*), 4) laid down the burden (of the five aggregates of existence, or *khandha*), 5) reached their own final goal, 6) destroyed the fetters of becoming (*saṃyojana*), and 7) are completely liberated through the final knowledge (*sammadaññā vimuttā*).[23]

It should be noted here that what is meant in Buddhism by the word 'enlightenment' is not some enigmatic flash of a mysterious light—individual, divine, cosmic, and so on—or a divine power or divine grace, but the supreme understanding (*bodhi*) that leads to the complete realization of the Four Noble Truths. In English, it is metaphorically translated as 'enlightenment' or 'awakening', and the derived word *Buddha* as 'Enlightened One' or 'Awakened One'.

---

[22] Cf. A II, 14, *Cara-sutta.*

[23] M I.141, *Alagaddūpama-sutta.*

The Buddha gives the following definition: 'It is because He has fully understood the Four Noble Truths as they really are that the Buddha is called the Worthy One (*Arahant*), the Perfectly Enlightened One (*Sammā Sambuddho*).'[24]

The Four Noble Truths (*cattāro ariyasaccāni*) comprise 1) the noble truth of existential suffering (*dukkha*), 2) the noble truth of the origin of suffering, which is craving (*taṇhā*), 3) the noble truth of the cessation of suffering, which is Nibbāna, and 4) the noble truth of the liberating Eightfold Path that leads to the cessation of suffering.

Liberation from mental fetters

The ten mental fetters (*saṃyojana*) mentioned above are those that bind beings to the stream of existence (*bhava-sota*) and continuous wandering in the dreadful cycle of rebirth (*saṃsāra*). They are:

1) the identity view (*sakkāya-diṭṭhi*) within or outside the five aggregates of mind and matter,
2) doubt (*vicikicchā*),
3) distorted grasp of rules, rituals, or ascetic practices (*sīlabbata-parāmāsa*) in the belief that only through them purification and redemption are attained,
4) sensual lust (*kāma-rāga*),
5) ill-will or anger (*vyāpāda*),
6) lust for fine-material existence (*rūpa-rāga*),
7) lust for immaterial existence (*arūpa-rāga*),
8) conceit (*māna*),
9) restlessness (*uddhacca*), and
10) ignorance (*avijjā*).

---

[24] S V.433, *Sammāsambuddha-sutta*: '*Imesaṃ ... catunnaṃ ariyasaccānaṃ yathābhūtaṃ abhisambuddhattā tathāgato 'arahaṃ sammāsambuddho'ti vuccati.*'

The first five of these are called 'lower fetters' (*orambhāgiya-saṃyojana*) because they are connected with the sensuous world of existence. The last five are called 'higher fetters' (*uddhambhāgiya-saṃyojana*) because they are connected with the higher worlds, namely, the fine-material and immaterial ones. In order to cut off and abandon these fetters, one must develop the five spiritual faculties of faith, energy, mindfulness, concentration, and wisdom (insight knowledge).

There are four stages of liberation from the mental fetters leading to the end of existential suffering (see also the table below):

a) One freed from the mental fetters 1-3 is a stream-enterer.
b) One who, besides these three mental fetters, has overcome 4 and 5 in their grosser form by weakening them is called once-returner to this sensuous world.
c) One who is completely freed from the mental fetters 1-5 is a non-returner to the sensuous world.
d) One who is freed from all then mental fetters is called a Worthy One (*Arahant*) and is not reborn into the cycle of existence.

The table here summarises the key data for the four stages.

<table>
<tr><th>4 Stages of Liberation</th><th colspan="2">Elimination of Fetters</th><th>Rebirth</th></tr>
<tr><td>Stream-enterer</td><td>1. identity view
2. sceptical doubt
3. distorted grasp of rules, rituals</td><td rowspan="3">lower mental fetters</td><td>up to seven rebirths in the human world or in divine worlds</td></tr>
<tr><td>Once-returner</td><td>weakening of 4 and 5</td><td>once again in the human world</td></tr>
<tr><td>Non-returner</td><td>4. sensual lust
5. ill-will, anger</td><td>in the divine world of the Pure Abodes</td></tr>
</table>

Worthy One	6. lust for fine-material existence 7. lust for immaterial existence 8. conceit 9. restlessness 10. ignorance	**higher mental fetters**	no rebirth

The Buddha concludes the *Discourse on the Establishment of Mindfulness* with a statement of assurance, vouching for the effectiveness of the method. He states that the fruits of continuous practice are either the achievement of Arahantship or Non-returning within a minimum of seven days or a maximum of seven years.

In the next chapter, we will extensively analyse the concept of Nibbāna for a better understanding of this wonderful state which, according to Buddhism, is the highest bliss possible, and which is achieved through the practice of insight meditation.

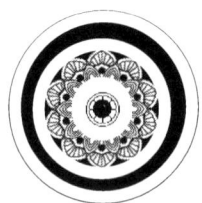

PART III

NIBBĀNA OR NIRVĀNA

INTRODUCTION

Nibbāna in Pāli or *Nirvāna* in Sanskrit, is, according to Buddhism, the supreme bliss and well-being that arises as a result of concentration and penetrative insight knowledge. It is a perfect state of equilibrium that transcends the dreadful cycle of rebirth, signifying the liberation from *saṃsāra*, the continuous wandering in the round of birth and death. It represents the highest and ultimate goal of all Buddhist endeavours, which is the complete cessation of lust, hate, and delusion. Consequently, it signifies the final and complete liberation from all future rebirths that entail ageing, sickness, death, and all forms of suffering, misery, distress, and pain across all realms of existence—human, non-human, and divine. As stated in the discourses of the Buddha:

> The elimination of lust (*rāga-*), the elimination of hate (*dosa-*), the elimination of delusion (*moha-khayo*): this is called Nibbāna....[1]

> This is peaceful, this is sublime; that is, the stilling of all activities (*saṅkhāra*), the relinquishing of all attachments (*upadhi*), the elimination of craving (*taṇhākkhayo*), dispassion (*virāgo*), cessation [of suffering] (*nirodha*), Nibbāna.[2]

In response to the question of how Nibbāna is directly knowable, the Buddha's answer is:

> One whose mind is possessed by lust, hate, or delusion thinks for his own affliction, for the affliction of others, or

[1] S IV.251, *Nibbānapañhā-sutta*; It.38, *Nibbānadhātu-sutta.*
[2] A I.132, *Ānanda-sutta.*

for the affliction of both, and experiences mental suffering and dejection. But when lust, hate, or delusion are abandoned, he does not think for his own affliction, the affliction of others, or the affliction of both, and does not experience mental suffering and dejection. It is in this way that Nibbāna is directly knowable.[3]

Suffering and the cessation of suffering are two crucial themes in the Buddha's teachings. As he states, 'What I teach is suffering (*dukkha*) and the cessation of suffering (*dukkhassa ca nirodhaṃ*).'[4] Therefore, his teachings focuses on the following two key issues of human existence:

1) Physical and mental suffering, including dejection, sorrow, lamentation, grief, stress, depression, and despair.
2) Complete liberation and deliverance from these conditions.

The central problem of suffering is explained by the Buddha in the First Noble Truth he taught. However, the truth of suffering is not the final word in his teachings—it is only the starting point. The Buddha begins with an explanation of suffering because his teaching is designed for a specific purpose: to lead to liberation from suffering and the realization of Nibbāna, which he describes as 'the supreme bliss' (*Nibbānaṃ paramaṃ sukhaṃ*).[5] In order to achieve this, he must give us a reason to seek liberation.

If a person is unaware that their house is on fire, they will continue to dwell within it, indulging in enjoyment, play, and laughter. To prompt their exit, they must first be made aware of the danger surrounding their home.

---

[3] A I.159, *Nibbuta-sutta.*
[4] M I.140, *Alagaddūpama-sutta.*
[5] Dhp, 204.

Similarly, the Buddha proclaims that our existence is consumed by the flames of ageing, sickness, and death, and our minds are burning with greed, hate, and delusion. It is only upon recognizing this imminent threat that we become prepared to pursue the path of liberation.

Two kinds of search

According to the Buddha, there are two kinds of search: the ignoble search and the noble search.

What is the ignoble search? It is when someone, being themselves subject to birth, ageing, sickness, death, sorrow, and mental defilements, seeks that which is also subject to birth, ageing, sickness, death, sorrow, and mental defilements. This is the ignoble search that leads to existential suffering.

And what is the noble search? It is when someone, being themselves subject to birth, ageing, sickness, death, sorrow, and mental defilements, understands the danger inherent in these conditions and seeks the unageing, unailing, deathless, sorrowless, and undefiled supreme security from bondage, Nibbāna. This is the noble search that leads to liberation from existential suffering.[6]

In the Second Noble Truth, the Buddha points out that the primary cause of existential suffering is the triple craving, namely:

1) craving for sensual pleasures through the five senses of sight, sound, smell, taste, and touch,
2) craving for existence or becoming, and
3) craving for non-existence or annihilation.

The key to achieving the cessation of existential suffering is the elimination of craving, to which the Buddha refers in the Third Noble Truth as follows:

---

[6] M I.161, *Ariyapariyesanā-sutta* or *Pāsarāsi-sutta.*

> And what is the noble truth of the cessation of suffering? It is the complete fading away and cessation of that very craving (*taṇhā*), the giving up and relinquishing of it, freedom from it, and non-reliance on it.[7]

This complete cessation of craving is related to Nibbāna. As the Buddha says, 'The total elimination of craving, its complete fading away and cessation, is Nibbāna.'[8]

The practice to attain liberation and the cessation of suffering is expressed by the Buddha in the Fourth Noble Truth, which is the practice of the Noble Eightfold Path, the highest good of which is Nibbāna. As he himself says:

> It is this Noble Eightfold Path ... that is the middle way, which gives rise to vision and to knowledge, which leads to peace, to direct knowledge, to enlightenment, to Nibbāna.[9]

The Noble Eightfold Path, as mentioned before, consists of:

> 1) right view, 2) right thought, 3) right speech, 4) right action, 5) right livelihood, 6) right effort, 7) right mindfulness, and 8) right concentration.

Etymology of Nibbāna

Etymologically, the word 'Nibbāna' is derived from the verb *nibbāti*, which literally means 'to extinguish'. It signifies the extinguishment of the 'fires' of lust (*rāgaggi*), hate (*dosaggi*), and delusion (*mohaggi*). When these fires are extinguished and there is no longer fuel to sustain them, Nibbāna is achieved, marking the liberation from *saṃsāra*.[10]

---

[7] D II.304, *Mahāsatipaṭṭhāna-sutta.*
[8] Ud.33, *Loka-sutta.*
[9] S V.421, *Dhammacakkappavattana-sutta.*
[10] It.92, *Aggi-sutta.*

Another etymology of Nibbāna, proposed by Pāli commentators, is 'exit (*nikkhantatta*) from the entanglement of craving (*vāna*)'. The word *vāna* is synonymous with *taṇhā* (desire).[11] In this case, the word *Nibbāna* is derived from *ni* + *vāna* (non + desire), which becomes *ni+bbāna*, with the transformation of the consonant 'v' (*-āna*) to 'b' (*-āna*).[12] This means that as long as one is entangled with desire, one remains bound to *saṃsāra*; however, when all desire has disappeared, one attains Nibbāna, or liberation from *saṃsāra*. As the Buddha says:

> This is peaceful, this is sublime; that is, ... the elimination of craving (*taṇhākkhayo*), ... Nibbāna....[13]
> The elimination of craving (*taṇhākkhayo*) is Nibbāna.[14]

Conceptual definition of Nibbāna

No concept in the Buddha's teachings has proven as difficult to comprehend as the state achieved when craving is fully extinguished, known as Nibbāna.

In a sense, such difficulty is to be expected, given that the Buddha describes Nibbāna precisely as 'peaceful and sublime, unattainable by mere reasoning, subtle, difficult to see and understand by those who delight in attachment, live in lust and hate, and are shrouded in darkness.'[15]

However, in the same passage, the Buddha also says that Nibbāna can be experienced by the wise, and in his discourses, he provides ample details about the nature of Nibbāna in order to illustrate its benefits.

---

[11] SnA I.300, *Maṅgalasuttavaṇṇṇanā*: '*vāna-saññitāya taṇhāya nikkhantattā "nibbānan"ti vuccati.*'

[12] Such transformation of the consonant 'v' to 'b' occurs in other words, such as *ni+vida* = *nibbidā* (revulsion).

[13] A I.133, *Ānanda-sutta.*

[14] S III.190, *Satta-sutta.*

[15] M I.167, *Ariyapariyesanā-sutta* or *Pāsarāsi-sutta.*

He also offers numerous descriptions and praises of Nibbāna. It is worth mentioning at this point the words of Rh. Davids:

> One might fill columns with the praises [of Nirvāna], many of them among the most beautiful passages in Pali poetry and prose, lavished on this condition of mind, the state of the man made perfect according to the Buddhist faith. Many are the pet names, the poetic epithets, bestowed upon it, each of them—for they are not synonyms—emphasizing one or other phase of this many-sided conception.[16]

Some of these names and epithets are:

> the other shore (*pāraṃ*), freedom (*mutti*), shelter (*tāṇaṃ*), supreme security from bondage (*anuttaraṃ yogakkhemaṃ*), the refuge (*saraṇaṃ*), the final end [of suffering] (*parāyanaṃ*), the sublime (*paṇītaṃ*), the auspicious (*sivaṃ*), the wonderful (*acchariyaṃ*), the serene (*santaṃ*), the pure (*suddhiṃ*), the undefiled (*asaṃkiliṭṭhaṃ*), the truthful (*saccaṃ*), the unageing (*ajaraṃ*), the ageless (*ajajjaraṃ*), the unailing (*anītikaṃ*), the unafflicted (*abyāpajjhaṃ*), the sorrowless (*asoka*), the stable (*dhuva*), the non-disintegrating (*apalokita*), the deathless (*amata*), cessation of the cycle of rebirth (*vaṭṭūpaccheda*), the free from mental corruptions (*anāsava*), the unconditioned (*asaṅkhata*).[17]

The Buddha affirms the outstanding reality of Nibbāna by referring to it as the 'supreme foundation of wisdom and truth' (*parama paññā/sacca adhiṭṭhāna*), whose nature is real and which ranks as the supreme noble truth (*paramaṃ ariyasaccaṃ*), encompassing the knowledge of the eradication of all existential suffering.[18]

---

[16] Davids, T. W. Rhys (1908), *Early Buddhism*, p. 72.
[17] E.g. S IV.361-373.
[18] M III.245, *Dhātuvibhaṅga-sutta.*

His discourses provide sufficient evidence to refute the view of some interpreters that Nibbāna itself is complete annihilation. Even a more sophisticated view, which holds that Nibbāna itself is simply the elimination of mental defilements and passions, cannot withstand close examination.

A particularly strong testimony countering that view is probably the Buddha's renowned statement about Nibbāna, in which he says:

> Verily, there is an unborn (*ajāta*), unbecome (*abhūta*), uncreated (*akata*), and unconditioned (*asaṅkhata*), the existence of which makes it possible to escape from the born, become, created, and conditioned.[19]

At this point, it is necessary to distinguish between Nibbāna itself and the attainment of Nibbāna. Through the practice of the Noble Eightfold Path, particularly through insight meditation (*vipassanā*)—an integral component of the Path—one achieves the eradication of mental defilements and the purification of one's mind. However, this process does not cause Nibbāna to come into existence or to be annihilated. Rather, it uncovers something that already exists: the cessation of mental defilements, which are not born, do not become, and are not created. For only a purified mind, one without attachments, can perceive this cessation, Nibbāna. Therefore, as mentioned earlier, the Buddha says, 'Verily, there is an unborn, unbecome, uncreated, and unconditioned.'[20] He also describes this as a state (*āyatana*) completely different from anything else, saying:

---

[19] Ud.80, *Tatiya-nibbāna-paṭisaṃyutta-sutta.*
[20] Ud.80, *Tatiya-nibbāna-paṭisaṃyutta-sutta.*

> There is this state (*āyatana*)[21] where there is no solid element (*pathavi*), no liquid element (*āpo*), no heat element (*tejo*), no air element (*vāyo*), no base of infinite space, no base of infinite consciousness, no base of nothingness, no base of neither-perception-nor-non-perception, not this world, not other world, no moon and sun. There, too, I say, there is no coming, no going, no standing, no passing away, no rebirth. It is without support, without occurrence, without an object. Just this is the end of (existential) suffering.[22]

While Nibbāna itself has no object (*anārammaṇa*), it appears as an object to a purified mind and cannot be perceived by someone who indulges in attachment and lives with lust, hate, and delusion. However, Nibbāna can be perceived through insight meditation (*vipassanā*) if one understands that 'anything existing within material and mental phenomena—such as the material body, feeling, perception, mental formations, and consciousness—is impermanent, suffering, and not-self'[23] and abandons attachment or clinging (*upādāna*) to these.

Then one can understand that, as the Buddha says:

> Indeed, I have long been tricked, cheated, and defrauded by this mind. For when I have been clinging, it was just to material form … to feeling, to perception, to mental formations, to consciousness. With my clinging as the condition, becoming (of karmic actions) comes to be; with becoming as the condition, birth; with birth as the condition, ageing and death, sorrow, lamentation, pain, grief, and despair come to be. Such is the origin of this whole mass of suffering.[24]

---

[21] In this context, 'state' or 'sphere' (*āyatana*) means 'object' (*ārammaṇa*), according to the commentary SA.389.

[22] Ud.79, *Paṭhama-nibbāna-paṭisaṃyutta-sutta.*

[23] M II.435, *Mahāmālukya-sutta.*

[24] M II.511, *Māgaṇḍiya-sutta.*

With insight meditation, when practiced correctly, one will know and see that:

> With the cessation of clinging to material and mental phenomena comes the cessation of becoming (of karmic actions). With the cessation of becoming comes the cessation of birth. With the cessation of birth, ageing and death, sorrow, lamentation, pain, grief, and despair cease. Such is the cessation of this whole mass of suffering.[25]

Then one turns their mind away from material and mental phenomena and directs it towards the deathless element (*amatadhātu*) of Nibbāna thus:

> This is the peaceful, this is the sublime; that is, the stilling of all activities, the relinquishing of all attachments, the elimination of craving, dispassion, the cessation [of suffering], Nibbāna.
>
> In this way, one can see Nibbāna, and if they remain in it as an object (*tattha ṭhito*), they attain the elimination of mental corruptions (*āsava*).[26]

Here, it is essential to provide an interpretation of the description 'elimination of the mental corruptions' or 'elimination of lust, hate and delusion' attributed to Nibbāna. Nibbāna itself is, as mentioned above, the unborn, the uncreated, and the unconditioned.[27] However, it is due to Nibbāna (*taṃ āgamma*) serving as an object (*ārammaṇa*) that, upon its realization, there arise: a) the complete elimination of mental corruptions, and b) liberation from conditioned existence. But

---

[25] Ibid.
[26] M II.435, *Mahāmālukya-sutta.*
[27] Ud.80, *Tatiya-nibbāna-paṭisaṃyutta-sutta.*

Nibbāna itself cannot be reduced to these two events, which are, in reality, conditioned and occur in time.

Nibbāna as an unconditioned phenomenon

A conditioned phenomenon is one that depends on causes and conditions for its existence. The Buddha has clearly explained the main difference between conditioned phenomena, which include all material and mental or spiritual phenomena, and one unconditioned phenomenon, which is Nibbāna, by describing their fundamental characteristics. He says the following in one of his discourses:

> There are these three characteristics that define a conditioned phenomenon (*saṅkhata-lakkhaṇa*):
>
> 1) a rise can be seen (*uppādo paññāyati*),
> 2) a fall can be seen (*vayo paññāyati*), and
> 3) a change in its duration can be seen (*ṭhitassa aññathattaṃ paññāyati*).[28]

So, the nature of a conditioned phenomenon is that it is composed of conditions, depends on conditions, and is produced by a combination of causes and conditions that are impermanent and mutable; that is, they rise and fall.

'Rise and fall' is the characteristic of a phenomenon that is transient, temporary, short-lived, impermanent, momentary, fleeting, unstable, and not lasting. This characteristic is dominant and omnipresent in all material and mental phenomena.

The rise and fall of a phenomenon does not happen randomly. It arises due to causes and conditions and falls due to causes

[28] A I.152, *Saṅkhatalakkhaṇa-sutta.*

and conditions. Rise and fall is the essential characteristic of conditioned phenomena. In the ultimate reality (*paramattha-sacca*), there are only processes of physical and mental or spiritual phenomena that continuously rise and fall according to causes and conditions (*hetu-paccaya*) which themselves are transient.

All phenomena in the material, physical, mental, or spiritual world, and generally throughout the entire universe, are composed, formed, shaped, moulded, produced, and created from a combination of causes and conditions. They are not absolute, self-existing, unchangeable, unaltered, independent, or unrelated to other things. They depend on conditions and are interdependent with them. These conditions, in turn, continuously rise and fall according to other causes and conditions. Therefore, rise and fall reveals the nature of conditions: transient, temporary, momentary, fleeting, and not permanent. This is why they are called 'conditioned phenomena'.

These phenomena are classified in Buddhism as the five aggregates of existence—the aggregate of the material body, feeling, perception, mental formations, and consciousness.

In contrast, the unconditioned phenomenon, Nibbāna, has different characteristics. The Buddha says the following about it in his next discourse:

> There are these three characteristics that define the unconditioned phenomenon (*asaṅkhata-lakkhaṇa*):
>
> 1) no rise can be seen (*na uppādo pañññāyati*),
> 2) no fall can be seen (*na vayo paññāyati*), and
> 3) no change in its duration can be seen
> (*na ṭhitassa aññathattaṃ paññāyati*).[29]

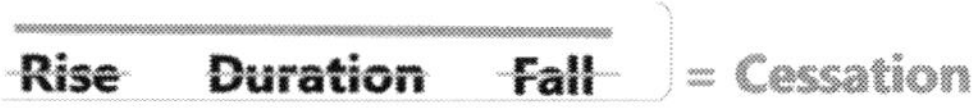

---

[29] A I.152, *Asaṅkhatalakkhaṇa-sutta.*

Regarding its nature, an unconditioned phenomenon is not composed of conditions, does not depend on conditions, and is not produced by a combination of causes and conditions. It is the cessation of all processes and activities, which the Buddha describes:

> … the peaceful, the sublime, the stilling of all activities (*saṅkhāra*), the relinquishing of all attachments (*upadhi*), the elimination of craving, dispassion, cessation (*nirodha*), Nibbāna.[30]

As an unconditioned phenomenon, Nibbāna can be perceived by a consciousness or a mind, which, through practice in insight meditation, abandons conditioned elements and takes as its object the unconditioned element of Nibbāna. Someone who practices correctly can see Nibbāna with a mind that is purified, refined, and unobstructed by worldly desires. As the Buddha stated after his enlightenment:

> The mind has attained the unconditioned.
> The elimination of craving has been achieved.[31]

He has also said in another discourse:

> If one has abandoned lust [for the conditioned five aggregates of existence], the basis is cut off and there is no support for the establishment of consciousness. When that consciousness is unestablished, not coming to growth, nongenerative, it is liberated. By being liberated, it is steady; by being steady, it is content; by being content, he is not agitated. Being unagitated, he personally attains Nibbāna.[32]

---

[30] A I.132, *Ānanda-sutta.*
[31] Dhp, 154.
[32] S III.53, *Upaya-sutta.*

The direct path to Nibbāna

The direct path (*ekāyano maggo*) to Nibbāna is insight meditation (*vipassanā*), which is part of the Noble Eightfold Path as 'right mindfulness' and 'right view'. This is pointed out in the discourse called *The Establishment of Mindfulness* (*Satipaṭṭhānasutta*), where the Buddha explicitly and unequivocally states that:

> This is the direct path ... for the realization of Nibbāna, namely, the four establishments of mindfulness (*cattāro satipaṭṭhāna*).

The four establishments of mindfulness are the methodical observation through mindfulness and awareness of 1) the material body, 2) feelings, 3) thoughts, and 4) mind-objects, through insight meditation. The fundamental principle of insight meditation is the observation of the rise (*samudaya*) and the fall (*vaya*) of every material and mental or spiritual phenomenon. This principle is constantly and repeatedly referred to in the *Satipaṭṭhāna Sutta* as 'observing the nature of rise and fall' (*samudaya-dhamma/vaya-dhamma-anupassana*) for every material and mental object.

With continuous observation, the meditator establishes mindfulness as well as the knowledge that there are only processes of material and mental phenomena that constantly arise and fall according to causes and conditions. There is not a being, not an individual, not a woman, not a man, not a self, not something that belongs to a self, not an 'I', and not mine, not someone or anything that belongs to someone. This observation leads to understanding of the three central characteristics of existence, which are:

1) Impermanence (*anicca*) of all conditioned phenomena, which have the nature of rise and fall.

2) Suffering, pain, or distress (*dukkha*) due to the unstable nature of all conditioned phenomena that are constantly subjected to the rise and fall, and thus become the basis of suffering in a changing world.

3) Non-self, non-soul, non-ego (*anattā*), which means that, ultimately, there is nothing eternal or immutable in human nature that one can call a 'self', 'soul', or 'I' to anchor a stable sense of 'me'. The whole concept of 'I' is actually a mistaken notion that tries to establish itself in an unstable and temporary aggregate of material and mental elements. It is simply the tendency of humans to personify conditioned phenomena and identify with them, rather than analyse them objectively by their components and understand them.

The suitable practice for attaining Nibbāna

Understanding the three characteristics of existence is what the Buddha calls 'the suitable practice for attaining Nibbāna', which he describes as follows:

> Here, one sees the eye as impermanent, suffering, non-self. He sees visible forms as impermanent, suffering, non-self. He sees eye-consciousness and eye-contact as impermanent, suffering, non-self. He also sees as impermanent, suffering, non-self whatever feeling arises with eye-contact as condition, whether pleasant or unpleasant or neutral.
>
> He sees the ear ... the sounds ... the nose ... the odours ... the tongue ... the flavours ... the body ... the tangible objects ... as impermanent, suffering, non-self.
>
> He sees the mind as impermanent, suffering, non-self. He sees the mind-objects as impermanent, suffering, non-

> self. He sees mind-consciousness and mind-contact as impermanent, suffering, non-self. He also sees as impermanent, suffering, non-self whatever feeling arises with mind-contact as a condition, whether pleasant or unpleasant or neutral.[33]

By thoroughly understanding the three characteristics of existence, this practice helps one to eliminate craving for all material and mental phenomena, to remain independent (*anissito*), and not to cling to anything in the world (*na ca kiñci loke upādiyati*), considering it as 'myself' or as belonging to 'myself'. One becomes detached and does not identify with anything.

Then, the mind turns away from conditioned phenomena and directs itself towards the unconditioned and deathless element of Nibbāna, of which the Buddha says:

> This is the peaceful, this is the sublime, that is, the stilling of all activities, the relinquishing of all attachments, the elimination of craving, dispassion, cessation [of suffering], Nibbāna. In this way one can see Nibbāna and, if one remains in it as an object, attains the eradication of mental corruptions (*āsava*).[34]

The four stages of enlightenment

Those who see Nibbāna for the first time have attained the first stage of enlightenment and are called 'stream-enterers' (*sotāpanna*). They have understood the following fundamental principle that:

> Whatever has the nature (*dhamma*) of arising, all that also

[33] S IV.133, *Anicca-, Dukkha-, Anatta-nibbānasappāya-sutta.*

[34] M I.435, *Mahāmālukya-sutta.*

has the nature (*dhamma*) of ceasing (fall).[35]

This understanding is called 'the eye or vision of the true nature of all phenomena' (*dhamma-cakkhu*) which arises when one understands the impermanent nature of all conditioned phenomena and has as its object the cessation of these, the unconditioned Nibbāna.

The understanding or knowledge that arises from seeing Nibbāna, when the darkness obscuring the three characteristics of existence is dissolved, is like the clear moon appearing behind the clouds and dispelling the darkness of the sky.

If a stream-enterer continues with insight meditation, they can reach the other three stages of enlightenment, which are more profound degrees of absorption in Nibbāna. These stages are:

- Once-return (*sakadāgāmi*). If a once-returner does achieve the next stage, they will be reborn only once more in the human or heavenly world.

- Non-return (*anāgāmi*). If a non-returner does not achieve the next stage, they will not return to rebirth in the human or heavenly worlds, but will be reborn in the 'Pure Abodes', located in the fine-material plane of existence.

- Arahantship (*arahatta*). If this final stage is achieve, there will be no more rebirths. In this case, they are called 'a Worthy One' (*arahant*). An *arahant* has fully abandoned craving and passion, cutting them off at their root, so that they no longer arise in the future. They have lived the holy life, finished what had to be finished, laid down the burden (of the five aggregates of existence, or *khandha*), reached

---

[35] '*Yaṃ kiñci samudayadhammaṃ, sabbaṃ taṃ nirodhadhamman'ti.*' E.g. D I.148, *Kūṭadanta-sutta*; M I.379, *Upāli-sutta*; Ud.48, *Suppabuddhakuṭṭha-sutta*.

their own final goal, destroyed the fetters of becoming, and is completely liberated through the final knowledge.[36]

Is Nibbāna conditioned by its path?

A common question regarding Nibbāna concerns its attainment, with many pointing out that, if it is attained through the practice of the Noble Eightfold Path, does this not imply that it is a conditioned phenomenon, a product of the path? Does this not mean that Nibbāna is a consequence of its cause, the path?

In this context, it is essential to differentiate between Nibbāna itself and the realization of Nibbāna. The practice of the path does not bring Nibbāna into existence; it leads to the discovery of something that already exists, in the sense of the absence of the mental defilements that cause existential suffering, and the absence of conditioned mental and material phenomena that rise and fall. As the Buddha says:

> Verily, there is an unborn, unbecome, uncreated and unconditioned. If there were not that unborn, unbecome, uncreated and unconditioned, there would be no escape from the born, become, created and conditioned. But because there is an unborn, unbecome, uncreated and unconditioned, therefore there is an escape from the born, become, created and conditioned.[37]... Just this is the end of existential suffering.[38]

Therefore, while the path leading to Nibbāna is conditioned, Nibbāna itself is referred to as the unborn, uncreated, and un-

---

[36] M I.489, *Mahāvaccha-sutta.*
[37] Ud.80, *Tatiya-nibbāna-paṭisaṃyutta-sutta.*
[38] Ud.79, *Paṭhama-nibbāna-paṭisaṃyutta-sutta.*

conditioned. In the Buddhist text *Milinda Pañha* it is compared to a mountain that does not depend on the path leading to it.[39]

Nibbāna and non-self (*anattā*)

Fully grasping the reality of non-self or non-soul (*anattā*)—the egolessness and insubstantiality of all forms of existence—is essential not only for the actual realization of the goal of Nibbāna but also for its theoretical understanding.

Without such an understanding, one will inevitably misinterpret Nibbāna, according to one's materialistic or metaphysical inclinations, either as annihilation and extinction of an ego/self, or as an eternal state of existence into which an ego or a self enters or merges with.

Nibbāna is the cessation of existential suffering, and the Buddha was clear when he said:

> One with the right view does not cling to the idea of 'my self' (*attā me*)'. He has no doubt that what arises is only suffering arising, what ceases is only suffering ceasing.[40]

Something similar has been said by his disciples:

> There is not a being here. This is just a heap of (material and mental) processes. Just as, with an assemblage of parts, the word 'chariot' is used, so when the (material and mental) aggregates exist, there is the convention 'a being'. In fact, it's only suffering that arises, and suffering that endures and falls away. Nothing but suffering arises, nothing but suffering ceases.[41]

---

[39] Miln.269, *Akammajādipañho.*
[40] S II.17, *Kaccānagotta-sutta.*
[41] S I.135, *Vajirā-sutta.*

Hence, it is said in the Pāli commentaries:

> For there is just suffering,
> but not a sufferer.
> Action exists, but not an actor.
> Nibbāna as the extinguishment (of suffering) exists,
> but no extinguished person.
> The path exists, but not a wayfarer.[42]

Misconceptions and fantasies about *Nibbāna*

There are groundless views by eternalists (those who believe in an eternal self, soul, or ego-entity), who have misunderstood the Buddha's teaching about Nibbāna thinking that it presupposes the annihilation (*uccheda*) of an existing being considered as 'self'. The Buddha states that, in the ultimate sense, a living being is not a 'self' but simply an aggregation of factors—material and mental events—linked in a process which is inherently suffering (*dukkha*). He also explains that Nibbāna, the cessation of suffering, is not the annihilation or extermination of a being, but the termination of the inherently unsatisfactory process of existential suffering. That's why he says that 'Both in the past and now what I teach is suffering and the cessation of suffering.'[43] In fact, he compares Nibbāna to health (*ārogya*) and suffering (*dukkha*) to the presence of a fundamental illness and affliction in beings.[44]

Therefore, there is no one entity to be eliminated or annihilated. What should be eliminated is the subjective illusion of a self. In other words, as the Buddha says, what needs to be eliminated are the mental defilements (*kilesa*) of lust, hate, and

---

[42] Vism.513, Ch. XVI; VbhA.89; PsA I.198.
[43] M I.140, *Alagaddūpama-sutta.*
[44] M I.510, *Māgaṇḍiya-sutta.*

delusion.[45] As he says in his discourses, 'The elimination of lust (*rāga-*), the elimination of hate (*dosa-*), the elimination of delusion (*moha-khayo*): this is called Nibbāna.'[46]

Another misconception is that the term 'Nibbāna' (or Nirvāna) is Hindu. However, the most ancient texts of Hinduism, such as the *Vedas* and the early *Upanishads*, do not mention the word 'Nirvāna'.[47] This word is found in texts such as the *Bhāgavad Gītā*[48] and the *Nirvāna Upanishad*, which were likely composed after the time of the Buddha[49] and misrepresented the meaning of *Nirvāna*.

According to Zaehner, Johnson and other scholars, 'Nirvāna' in the *Bhāgavad Gītā* is a Buddhist term adopted by Hindus. Zaehner states that it was first used in Hindu texts in the *Bhāgavad Gītā*. Johnson contends that Hindus took the term *Nirvāna* from Buddhists in order to confuse the Buddhists themselves, linking the Buddhist state of Nirvāna with the pre-Buddhist Vedic tradition of the metaphysical absolute, known as 'Brahman'.[50] Hence, the concept of Nirvāna is misrepresented in Hindu literature, where it is described as the union or identification of the self or individual soul (*ātman*) with *Brahman*, the Supreme or Universal Soul (*Paramātman*).[51]

Nevertheless, according to Buddhist texts, the concept of Nibbāna existed in India before the appearance of the historical Buddha Gotama and was used by ascetics. As Buddha Gotama himself states, Nibbāna and the Noble Eightfold Path leading

---

[45] A IV.174, *Verañja-sutta.*

[46] S IV.251, *Nibbāna-pañhā-sutta*; It.38, *Nibbāna-dhātu-sutta.*

[47] Fowler, Jeaneane D. (2012), *The Bhagavad Gita: A Text and Commentary for Students*, Sussex Academic Press.

[48] Ibid.

[49] Olivelle, Patrick (1992), *The Samnyasa Upanisads: Hindu Scriptures on Asceticism and Renunciation*. Oxford University Press.

[50] For Zaehner and Johnson, see. Fowler, Jeaneane D. (2012), *The Bhagavad Gita: A Text and Commentary for Students*, Sussex Academic.

[51] Brian Morris (2006), *Religion and Anthropology: A Critical Introduction*. Cambridge University Press, p. 51.

to it were taught by previous Buddhas (including Buddha Kassapa and Koṇāgamana) but, over time, the concept of Nibbāna was misunderstood and misrepresented by naive commoners.[52]

Particularly because Nibbāna is described as the supreme bliss and happiness, ordinary people who have not experienced this state have often attempted to imagine it and equate it with mundane experiences.

In a comprehensive discourse, the Buddha explains five distorted notions of Nibbāna that existed in his time and included the concept of the self or soul (*atta*/*ātman*). These obviously prevail even in our time, and the first one is:

> 1) When the self (*atta*) is equipped with sensual pleasures (*kāma*) and enjoys them with the sense organs, then it attains 'the supreme Nibbāna in this very life' (*parama-diṭṭhadhamma-nibbānaṃ*).[53]

This is a hedonistic conception of Nibbāna, which some identify with the full enjoyment of sensual pleasures (*kāma*) experienced by the self (*attā*). There were even ascetics and teachers who preached that the body is Nibbāna because, whenever they were healthy in body, had no discomfort, and felt happy (*sukhī*),[54] they considered Nibbāna to be the sensual or physical feeling of happiness.

Others, however, identified Nibbāna with the spiritual bliss achieved in the mundane meditative absorptions (*jhāna*). Thus, they propagated the distorted notions 2), 3), 4) and 5), claiming that:

---

[52] M I.509, *Māgaṇḍiya-sutta.*
[53] D I.36, *Brahmajāla-sutta.*
[54] M I.508, *Māgaṇḍiya-sutta.*

> When the self (*atta*) attains the first ... second ... third ... or fourth *jhāna*, it attains the supreme Nibbāna in this very life.[55]

This is the meditative or spiritually pleasant conception of Nibbāna, as the *jhānas* produce such intense feelings of rapture, bliss, and equanimity that if the idea of self still lingers in the meditator's mind, they are likely to consider these feelings as a manifestation or expression of the True, Higher, or Divine Self, which appears when the clouds of their dialectical thought have been dispersed through the practice of concentration.[56] In this particular case, it is possible for the meditator to identify themselves with the fictional projection of a Divine Self. This identification is represented by the non-dualistic spiritual traditions, such as Advaita Vedanta.[57]

Advaita Vedanta teaches a radical non-dualistic view, the one and indivisible ultimate reality, in which there is no distinction between the *ātman*, the innermost self or the individual soul that constitutes relative reality, and the *Paramātman*, the Supreme or Universal Soul which constitutes the Absolute, the Divine Reality (*Brahman*), which is the fundamental substratum of the world. There is only one Reality—which is simultaneously the *ātman* and the *Brahman*—and the purpose of the spiritual search is to recognize that one's true self, the *ātman*, is Existence (*Sat*), Awareness (*Cit*), and Bliss (*Ānanda*).

---

[55] D I.36, *Brahmajāla-sutta*.

[56] B. Bodhi (2007), *The All-Embracing Net of Views*, Buddhist Publication Society, Kandy, Sri Lanka.

[57] Advaita Vedanta is perhaps the most well-known among all the schools of Vedantic philosophy in Hinduism. It teaches the radical non-dualistic view, the one and indivisible ultimate reality where there is absolutely no distinction between the Absolute (*Brahman* or Supreme Soul) and the relative reality (or individual soul). The term 'Advaita' is sometimes translated as 'non-dualism' or 'non-dualistic philosophy', which is essentially a form of monism. Among the greatest teachers of Advaita in the 20th century were Swami Vivekananda, Ramana Maharshi, and Nisargadatta Maharaj.

Similar searches characterise other traditions where one visualises various things or entities and tries to connect with a higher self or God.

From a Buddhist perspective, every search for the discovery of selfhood, either as a permanent individual self or as an absolute universal self (spirit, God, etc.), is a delusion and a fallacy, a mental construct arising from a misunderstanding of the true nature of experience, especially of the desires and cravings that produce such fantasies and its feelings of bliss. As mentioned above, the Buddha explained the deception of feelings, namely how 'feelings condition craving; craving conditions clinging; clinging conditions becoming (of karmic actions); becoming conditions birth; birth conditions ageing and death, sorrow, lamentation, pain, suffering and distress.'[58] He also explained how he 'has understood the rising (*samudaya*) and the passing away (*atthaṅgama*) of feelings as they really occur, their pleasure, their danger, and the escape from them, and how he was liberated through non-attachment or non-clinging (*anupādāvimutto*).'[59]

Therefore, those who identify Nibbāna with physical or spiritual bliss and enjoy, desire, or crave this state are imagining Nibbāna with desire and craving. Boasting that 'I have attained Nibbāna', they imagine Nibbāna with conceit. Thinking that this imaginary Nibbāna is permanent and their 'self', they imagine it with wrong view. Regarding such misconceptions the Buddha said:

> An untaught ordinary person perceives Nibbāna as Nibbāna.[60] Having perceived Nibbāna as Nibbāna, he imagines (*maññati*) [himself as] Nibbāna; he imagines [himself] in

---

[58] D I.45, *Brahmajāla-sutta.*

[59] Ibid. I.39.

[60] He perceives it with the distorted and misconceived notions of Nibbāna that were mentioned above on p. 213 ff.

> Nibbāna; he imagines [himself apart] from Nibbāna; he imagines Nibbāna to be 'mine'; he delights in Nibbāna. Why is that? Because he has not fully understood Nibbāna, I say.[61]

In this case, the object of perception, imagination and delight is Nibbāna, that is, the feeling of a sensual or spiritual bliss at the mundane level of experience. The ordinary person imagines it with three types of imagination: imagination due to craving (*taṇhā-maññanā*), imagination due to conceit (*māna-maññanā*), and imagination due to wrong view (*diṭṭhi-maññanā*). However, a person who has eradicated ignorance and is completely liberated through final knowledge is said not merely to perceive (*sañjānāti*), but to directly know (*abhijānāti*) Nibbāna, as well as the imagination that arises because of it. Therefore, the Buddha says about such a person:

> He directly knows Nibbāna as Nibbāna. Having directly known Nibbāna as Nibbāna, he does not imagine [himself as] Nibbāna; he does not imagine [himself] in Nibbāna; he does not imagine [himself apart] from Nibbāna; he does not imagine Nibbāna to be 'mine'; he does delight in Nibbāna. Why is that? Because he has fully understood it, I say.[62]

The Buddha made it also clear that the foremost achievement in attaining the supreme Nibbāna in this very life (*etadaggaṃ paramadiṭṭhadhamma-nibbānaṃ*) is liberation through non-clinging (*anupādā vimokkha*), which comes after fully understanding, as they truly are, the arising (*samudaya*) and passing away/fall (*atthaṅgama*) of the six sense organs of

---

[61] M I.4, *Mūlapariyāya-sutta.*
[62] Ibid.

contact[63] and the resultant feelings, their gratification, danger, and escape from them.[64]

Another misinterpretation of Nibbāna is that it is the 'One', indivisible fundamental substratum of the world from which everything emanates. This interpretation is essentially a form of monism or non-dualism, resembling the Vedic conception of the metaphysical absolute *Brahman*. However, as mentioned above, Nibbāna is the extinguishing of the 'fires' of lust, hate, and delusion, and the cessation of existential suffering. Something that is extinguished ceases to exist. So, it cannot become a substratum for something else. If it did, it would, according to Buddhism, be a source for the emergence of existential suffering, which is not the case with Nibbāna.

Nibbāna is beyond the concept of non-dualism found in mystical, metaphysical, idealistic, or ontological notions of monism and monotheism, whether speaking of the One, the Absolute, the All, the Anonymous, or the Tao, or God, Creator, Supreme Mind, Father, Universal Mother, Goddess, Godhead, Deity, or Brahman as the foundation or substratum of the world. It is also not what is termed in Mahāyāna Buddhism as 'non-differentiation' between:

- *saṃsāra* and Nirvāna (Nibbāna),
- mental defilements (*kilesa*) and purification (*visuddhi*),
- ignorance (*avijja*) and enlightenment (*bodhi*).[65]

---

[63] '*Channaṃ phassāyatanānaṃ samudayañca atthaṅgamañca assādañca ādīnavañca nissaraṇañca yathābhūtaṃ viditvā anupādā vimokkho.*' A V.64, *Paṭhamakosala-sutta.*

[64] D I.39, *Brahmajāla-sutta.*

[65] E.g. Nāgārjuna, *Mūlamadhyamakakārikā, Nirvāṇa parīkṣā*, f. 19, 20, and Bodhi, Bhikkhu (1994): *Dhamma and Non-duality*, Buddhist Publication Society.

The twofold Nibbāna

Nibbāna is itself a single, undifferentiated ultimate reality. It is exclusively supramundane and has one intrinsic nature (*sabhāva*), which is that of being the unconditioned deathless element totally transcendent from the conditioned world.

Nevertheless, Nibbāna is said to be twofold by reference to a basis for distinction. This basis is the presence or absence of the five aggregates of existence. The element of Nibbāna as experienced by Arahants or Buddhas is called 'with the residue remaining' (*saupādisesa*), because, though the mental defilements of lust, hate, delusion, and so on have all been extinguished, the 'residue' of the aggregates acquired from past clinging in previous lives remains during their present life.

However, the element of Nibbāna attained with an Arahant's or a Buddha's demise is called that 'without the residue remaining' (*anupādisesa*), because the five aggregates are discarded and never acquired again.[66]

In the Pāli commentaries, the first element of Nibbāna is also called 'the extinguishment of the mental defilements' (*kilesa-parinibbāna*), and the second, 'the extinguishment of the aggregates' (*khandha-parinibbāna*).[67]

Nibbāna after the death of a Buddha or an Arahant

The question is sometimes asked: What happens after the death of a Buddha or a Worthy One (*Arahant*) whose mind is liberated (*vimuttacitto*) from mental defilements (*kilesa*) and the aggregates (*khandha*), and who has attained the final Nibbāna

---

[66] The distinction of the twofold Nibbāna is found in It.38, *Nibbānadhātusutta*, and the above explanation in Bodhi, Bhikkhu (1993, 1999): *A Comprehensive Manual of Abhidhamma – The Philosophical Psychology of Buddhism,* p. 259.
[67] E.g. DA III.899.

(*parinibbāna*)? Do they reappear (*upapajjati*) after death? Do they not reappear (*na upapajjati*)? Do they both reappear and not reappear? Do they neither reappear nor not reappear?

To these questions, the Buddha responded that the terms 'reappear', 'not reappear', and so on do not apply (*na upeti*). Only the final extinguishment (*parinibbāna*), which can be likened to an extinguished fire, applies. Therefore, when an Indian ascetic named Vaccha posed such questions, the Buddha answered with a simile of an extinguished fire, as follows:

'What do you think, Vaccha? Suppose a fire was burning in front of you. Would you know: "This fire is burning in front of me"?'

'I would know, Master Gotama.'

'If someone were to ask you, Vaccha: "Depending on what does this fire burn in front of you?"—what would you answer?'

'I would answer: "This fire burns dependent on fuel of grass and sticks."'

'If that fire in front of you were to be extinguished (*nibbāyeyya*), would you know: "This fire in front of me has been extinguished (*nibbuto*)"?'

'I would know, Master Gotama.'

'If someone were to ask you, Vaccha: "When that fire in front of you was extinguished, to which direction did it go: to the east, the west, the north, or the south?"—what would you answer?'

'That does not apply, Master Gotama. The fire burned depending on fuel of grass and sticks. When that is used up, if it does not get any more fuel; being without fuel, it is reckoned as extinguished (*nibbuto*).'

'So too, Vaccha, the Buddha (Tathāgata) has abandoned that material form ... feeling ... perception ... mental formations ..., and consciousness by which one describing the Buddha might describe him; he has cut them off at the root, made them like a palm stump, done away with them so that these are no longer subject to future arising.

The Buddha is liberated from reckoning in terms of material form ...feeling ... and consciousness; he is profound, immeasurable, hard to fathom like the ocean. 'He reappears' does not apply; 'he does not reappear' does not apply; 'he both reappears and does not reappear' does not apply; 'he neither reappears nor does not reappear' does not apply.'[68]

Here, the view that a Buddha appears or exists after death is a form of eternalism (*sassata-diṭṭhi*). It regards the Buddha or an Arahant as possessing a self that attains eternal deliverance after the death of the body. The opposite view, that a Buddha does not appear or exist after death also identifies the Buddha as a self but holds that this self is annihilated upon the death of the body. This view is known as annihilationism (*ucchedadiṭṭhi*). The third view attempts to combine these two, which the Buddha rejects because both components involve wrong view. The fourth view seems to be a sceptical attempt to turn down both alternatives or to avoid taking a definite stand. The Buddha rejects this as well.

Just as an extinguished fire cannot be described as moving in any direction, so a Buddha who has attained the final Nibbāna cannot be described in terms of these four alternative views. The simile of the fire concerns solely the legitimacy of conceptual and linguistic usage. It is not intended to suggest, as some scholars have held, that the Buddha attains some mystical absorption in the Absolute. The words 'profound, immeasurable, hard to fathom' point to the transcendental dimension of the liberation attained by the Buddha, its inaccessibility to discursive thought.

---

[68] M I.486 ff, *Aggivaccha-sutta.*

The threefold Nibbāna

Nibbāna is also threefold, according to its different aspects:

1) It is called the void (*suñña*) because it is devoid of a) mental defilements (*kilesa*), such as lust, greed, hate, and delusion; b) a self (*atta*); and c) all that is conditioned (*saṅkhata*).

2) It is called signless (*animitta*) because it is free from a) the signs of mental defilements like lust and b) the signs of all conditioned phenomena.

3) It is called desireless (*appaṇihita*) because it is free from the desire for mental defilements, and because it is not desired by craving.

Above all, Nibbāna is called the cessation of existential suffering (*dukkha-nirodha*). This understanding is sufficient to motivate those who seek the end of suffering in *saṃsāra* to engage in the practice of the Noble Eightfold Path, leading to Nibbāna.

PART IV

QUESTIONS AND ANSWERS ON MEDITATION

The questions have been asked by students of meditation seminars conducted by the author. They have been answered by him in order to clarify frequent questions regarding the aforementioned meditations.

1. Questions and answers on the meditation on breathing

Question 1: Should we pull our abdomen inwards during the out-breath?

Answer: No, this is not necessary. We simply focus all of our attention on the tip of the nose where the air comes into contact with the nostrils and observe the natural rhythm of in- and out-breath. If you cannot perceive the out-breath, pay more attention to when the air exits as out-breath or take a deep in-breath and wait until the out-breath exits through the nose. If you feel bloating in the abdomen, you may pull the abdomen inwards if it brings relief. Usually, however, we try to focus our mind on the nostrils.

Question 2: Is it okay if the in- and out-breath are done through the mouth?

Answer: When breathing is done through the mouth for an extended period, saliva, the mouth, and the throat become dry, causing coughing. The rhythm of breathing is more natural through the nose, so we focus our attention there, where the observation of the in- and out-breath can be done for hours without any discomfort.

Question 3: After practicing meditation on friendliness, can we return to focusing on the breath?

Answer: Yes, when the mind has calmed down from negative emotions through meditation on friendliness, we can return to the breath. By then, distracting thoughts will have subsided, making it easier to observe the breath.

Question 4: What do you mean when you say ‘unification of the mind’? Does it mean having no thoughts during the concentration on the breath? And what do we gain when we achieve calmness, serenity, and unity of the mind?

Answer: If we observe the mind, we will see that it is like an unruly horse, constantly running from place to place. We can also say that it is lost and scattered, fragmented by a deluge of information, which causes psychological problems for most people and creates a sense of stress and dissatisfaction within them. They are annoyed by everything and feel anxiety or other kinds of negative emotions.

With unification, we take this scattered mind that has flung itself in various directions and focus it on a single point, bringing all of its mental energy closer and closer, over and over again. This is where one feels the energy of the mind pulling together, achieving deep concentration and a stillness and bliss that emanate from deep within.

Unity of mind means that our mind remains on one single point. That is, we unite it with an object, which in this case is the breath. Our breath can be observed because it is repetitive, with a continuous rhythm. While other objects change and we constantly have to make various mental manoeuvres to follow them, with the breath, we don't need to do that because it is a very simple, rhythmic object that lends itself to observation and concentration. The mind easily unites with the breath.

In ancient Indian language, the word *yoga* (in our times, the word has taken other dimensions) meant exactly this: joining, connecting or unifying the mind with an object so that the mind is not swayed, disturbed, or encouraged to jump from object to object—not scattered everywhere, but channelling all its energy into a single object. Then one feels within oneself all the mind's dynamism to such an extent that even the perception of the body is lost. Feeling very light, receiving the energy of the mind within—this is what causes the bliss, calmness, serenity, and stillness that many people long to find in the external environment but cannot, because their mind is fragmented and scattered.

With the mind's unification, its entire potential comes closer to us, and as a result, we feel well-being. The first signs are that one feels lighter and more blissful, while tranquillity and mental peace arise within.

When we talk about tranquillity and calmness, we say that at certain times we must remain undisturbed by external situations, but these are only words. As long as the mind is unfocused and scattered, it is impossible to remain undisturbed. However, unifying the mind by focusing on an object can bring about tranquillity and serenity.

Question 5: Can this energy of the mind help us to gain abundance, whether spiritual or material, in our lives?

Answer: Spiritual, yes. Some people might also gain material abundance. As already discussed, a person with a chaotic and scattered mind cannot concentrate. When given advice, for example, on how to set up a business, they are unable to follow it because their mind is scattered, leading them to forget some details, to not pay attention well, and generally being unable to focus their mind or have direction in life. The energy of their mind is fragmented and dispersed. But if someone acquires concentration and unification of the mind, then they can focus and achieve a goal much more easily than a confused person.

Meditation prevents confusion and brings clarity of mind, enabling someone to achieve their goals in life more effectively. Focusing on the breath is a goal on which we must repeatedly concentrate, an exercise that prevents us from forgetting what is in front of us. This helps both in memory and awareness, as well as in concentration, focus, and unity of the mind. It's something many people cannot achieve normally because they let their minds are distracted by all kinds of information.

As you may have heard, many businesses collaborate with meditation teachers for this reason. Employees work long hours, become tired, lose their concentration, cannot focus, and make mistakes. Many errors in businesses occur this way because employees become distracted. How does distraction arise? It arises because these people work hours on the computer processing a multitude of information, resulting in their minds becoming overwhelmed.

Through meditation, they try to concentrate their minds on one object for an extended period, on something experiential, something close to them; they try to bring all the energy of the mind closer and not let it turn outward. The closer they bring it, the more they gain mental unity, stabilise their minds, and calm down. Then they feel all of this energy of the mind, and they feel energised and recharged, ready to work more efficiently than before.

Many companies, such as Google, try to ensure their employees have time set aside for meditation, sometimes at least 20 minutes a day. Just as they set a daily fitness schedule, they also set a meditation schedule. The mind, just like the body, needs exercise, so we should not only exercise the muscles of the body but also our mental muscles. This way, material abundance can also be achieved if someone wants to use this exercise for such purposes.

Question 6: When I focus on my breath, it stops being spontaneous, and it feels like I am controlling it. How can I make it more natural?

Answer: It requires a bit of patience and practice. Before you start meditating, bring your attention to your entire body and say to yourself a few times, "relax, relax". This will remind the mind that there is no need to hurry. The mind will relax, concentrate on its own, and naturally follow the normal pace of breathing. Try it, and you'll see that gradually you will be able to follow the breath's natural rhythm.

Question 7: My breathing was so fast that I could barely note "beginning, middle, end". Is that normal?

Answer: When our breathing is already fast, it is normal to have difficulty noticing the details and distinguishing the beginning, middle, and end. When this happens, return to the first step and mentally repeat "in-breath, out-breath... in-breath, out-breath...." This way, you observe the in- and out-breath more broadly. Once your breathing calms down, gradually start to observe its beginning, middle, and end.

Question 8: If, during meditation, we notice our heartbeat or feel the breath in our stomach, should we ignore that or focus our attention there?

Answer: We should ignore it and focus our attention on the nostrils. When we change the object of attention, concentration is disrupted, the mind becomes scattered, and we start speculating: *Why does my heartbeat like this? How does the stomach move up and down with the breath?* So, we ignore any kind of thinking or other function of the body and focus our attention on the tip of the nose where the air comes into contact with the nostrils, mentally noting "in-breath, out-breath... in-breath, out-breath...." The more we focus, the more the perception of the body fades, and eventually, we remain only with the awareness of the breath.

Question 9: Is it better for breathing to be thoracic or abdominal?

Answer: There are people who, due to their physiology, breathe with their abdomen and feel the breath more prominently in this area. Others experience the same with their chest. Therefore, there is no specific appropriate area—what is good for one person is not necessarily good for everyone. With the meditation on breathing, we observe the in- and out-breath at the tip of the nose or nostrils, because this is the point where one can concentrate and achieve unity of the mind. If the mind tries to focus on the chest or abdomen, which are large areas, it will eventually scatter and not achieve proper concentration. And since the nose is the gateway through which air enters our body, it is more natural to observe our breath there.

Question 10: Is there a pause between breaths?

Answer: Sometimes there is, as it depends on our current mood. Occasionally, when we remember emotional things, there is a momentary pause in our breathing. Other times, there isn't, but we think that there is. We think about something and believe our breathing has stopped. In reality, it hasn't stopped. Of course, when someone develops very deep concentration, there are moments when the breathing stops even for half a minute. This happens because the calmness is so profound that the body does not need much oxygen. This affects the heart and the nervous system, making one feel like the breathing has stopped. If it has, it will resume naturally on its own.

In those who achieve the fourth meditative absorption (*jhāna*), breathing completely ceases for an extended period of time.[1] Due to the deep calmness in this state, a meditator's body requires only a minimal amount of oxygen to survive, while they experience great bliss. For beginners, though, it is very rare for breathing to stop.

---

[1] S IV.216, *Rahogata-sutta*: "*Catutthaṃ jhānaṃ samāpannassa assāsa-passāsā niruddhā honti.*"

2. Questions and answers on the meditation on friendliness

Question 1: According to my beliefs, it is not easy for me to say: "May I be happy, may I be happy...", because it is like feeding my ego, which we do not want to nurture; on the contrary, we want to eliminate it. I prefer to say: "health, health..., love, love..., light, light..., to help the world, to help...." Overall, I felt so overwhelmed with emotion that I cried.

Answer: Although the wish "May I be happy" seems selfish, it is meant to stimulate positive feelings within us. Because if we ourselves are unhappy, if we suffer, we cannot give happiness to others. We should realise this!

We need to have the source of joy and happiness within us so that we can give to others the good we think we can offer. For example, when we want to do good deeds for both ourselves and others, we should consider what kind of goodwill we can offer when we ourselves are depressed. All people want happiness. When we say, "May I be happy", it also implies, "If I am not happy, how can I offer happiness to others? If I am overwhelmed by negative emotions and feel unhappy, what kind of happiness can I offer others? What sort of kind words can I say to them? Only words of sadness and grief will come out of my mouth. But if I am happy, I can say good and pleasant words, be in a good mood, and do good deeds."

So, don't consider the wish "May I be happy" to be something selfish. The purpose of this meditation is not only to feel good ourselves but also to share the happiness we feel with others. Thus, you take the people you call to mind, the people you live your life with, as an object of attention and wish them to be happy, too. We start with ourselves in order to develop altruism. First, though, we should be ready and have all the necessary strength within us to be altruistic.

Sometimes people think that all forms of egoism are negative, but that is not the case. Without egoism, we can't do anything! We wouldn't be able to do many things in life, not even eat to survive. Of course, there is negative egoism, the one that annoys others and causes them trouble.

But there is also positive egoism, when we are not a trouble to others. For instance, sitting and reading a book instead of going out and doing social work to help our fellow humans may seem egoistic and selfish to some. But from this book, we may learn a lot, like how to live our lives or be healthy. We first need to learn how to be healthy ourselves, so that we can then help others to be healthy as well.

Therefore, we should not always consider egoism as something negative. We need to work on our ego, to cleanse it, so that we can later offer goodness to others. For if we have dirt inside us, how can we offer cleanliness to others? We first need to remove the dirt from within us (grief, fear, anger, hate, and hostility). When we clean ourselves and feel that we have happiness within us, wishing "May I be happy, happy, happy...", then we can offer others cleanliness, genuine happiness, and health.

But if we say "health, health..., love, love..., light, light..., to help the world, to help..." and then start crying, we have not experienced genuine happiness and, therefore, cannot offer it to others.

Question 2: What is Buddhism's stance on forgiveness? What does someone do when they are deeply hurt and unable to forgive, choosing to distance themselves instead?

Answer: Certainly, if there is resentment of others, it is very difficult to forgive. The mind cannot find the logic to do so and resists, and that is absolutely normal. We need to identify what prevents us from forgiving. We remember the bad things they have done to us, the injustices we have suffered, and we become hurt. The essential cause of this hurt is the anger, hatred, hostility, and annoyance we have experienced because of them. Continuous annoyance or the continuous memory of the annoyance results in hostility towards other people. When an-ger has reached the level of hostility, as soon as we see the person who caused it, we feel that we want to take revenge. Forgiving them is nearly unthinkable! We think that forgiving them would be the greatest injustice we could do in the world!

In such cases, according to Buddhism and what I teach here, we need to identify the emotion that prevents us from forgiving others. Buddhism does talk about forgiveness, but it also teaches how to first get rid of negative emotions, such as held grudges, resentment, hostility, or hatred, which prevent us from achieving forgiveness. When we identify these emotions, then, of course, we try to eliminate them, because they primarily hurt us.

When people commit an injustice, it is a sign that they were also a victim of negativity, just as we often are. We are both victims.

When practicing meditation on friendliness, we first try to eliminate this negativity. Only then will we see that others are also victims of the very same negativity, and thus realise that we can forgive them. Without eliminating negative emotions, it is difficult to forgive others. No matter how much advice we receive, no matter how many books we read with tips like "Forgiveness is a good thing, we must forgive others", these are just words. After a while, negative feelings return and dictate the opposite!

So, we need to identify the problem and eliminate it. Only then will we have the clarity and a sober enough mind to see what primarily is hurting us, whether it's hatred, enmity, anger, rage, or so on. The Buddha has said that a person who is angry is like someone holding a hot iron to throw at others, but the first one who gets hurt is oneself. Anger is like a hot iron, and we must be careful not to grasp it, not to be swept away by anger and rage, because it's us who will get hurt first. Only by eliminating negative emotions can we have clarity and see that others suffer from similar emotions and are also victims. Only then can we sincerely and effectively forgive them.

Question 3: Since emotions are part of human nature, what can be done when one gets very angry? Can we do this exercise to calm down?

Answer: Definitely. Try this exercise. The mind, and human nature in general, is not static, and we can change it at any moment. It is up to us what we choose to focus on. For example, when you go to a forest, everything is natural, including the poisonous plants there. But if we eat them, we will die. There are also plants and fruits that, if we eat them, will make us feel good and fill us with energy and freshness. So everything is natural. It is up to us what we choose to benefit from.

Something similar happens within our mind. All emotions are natural, but we need to choose which ones to use, which emotions we want to nourish. Many use anger as a weapon. If they don't get angry, they cannot impose themselves on others. Eventually, day by day, this anger becomes incredibly strong, bringing great difficulties into their lives. Their good relationships start to fall apart, their good friends begin to distance themselves, and when they face problems, no one goes to help them. *Why would I help them?* they think. *That neurotic person, who said all those bad words to me... I'm supposed to help them?* Anger can turn against us, poisoning both ourselves and others. All because we think that anger is 'human nature' and should guide us.

If we realise that vicious emotions like anger are profoundly negative, we should try to eliminate them and with the meditation on friendliness wish: "May I be without this or that negative emotion." We withdraw our minds from that emotion and do not give it the fuel it needs to exist, which is our own interest in it. When it is not fuelled, the specific emotion ceases to have substance and leaves. Until then, however, we have been the ones fuelling it with our own interest in it.

Anger, for example, may exist because we want to take revenge on the person or persons who hurt us. Even when we sit and talk, complaining about one person or another, we try to highlight their faults. Eventually, this anger redounds to us and hurts us.

Through friendliness meditation, one can gradually realise the problem, namely what the specific negative emotion is. We are not talking about something abstract here, and we should not put veils in front of us and camouflage the negative emotion as if it didn't exist. If it exists, we must admit it and recognise it, as we cannot eliminate it without recognising it first. We must recognise it and then wish to be without that specific emotion. Indeed, such emotions are part of human nature. We should not feel guilty when we feel angry. Everyone gets angry. However, we can eliminate such emotions at any time, provided there is the will to do so.

Question 4: I don't think there is hatred towards others, but bitterness. We feel bitterness due to the injustices of others towards us.

Answer: This bitterness is sorrow. Initially, we are saddened by an injustice that occurred. However, if this injustice happens repeatedly, sorrow can evolve into hatred. That's why I said that with the meditation on friendliness, one can investigate all of the negative emotions in such a way as to understand them, whether it is sadness, sorrow, or bitterness, and say "May I be without sorrow...", or "May I be without bitterness...", and so forth. Then one becomes aware of what is going on within oneself, with this awareness acting almost like a flashlight, illuminating the murky depths of our minds in order to investigate exactly what is happening. This is a state of self-awareness or self-knowledge. We do not try to camouflage negative emotions and pretend they do not exist; instead, we aim to recognise them. Then we try to eliminate them, but not aggressively. Peacefully, we try to withdraw our minds from this bitterness, wishing "May I be without bitterness...". You will then see that, when our minds withdraw from this emotion, they cease to fuel it, and gradually this bitterness, having no substance, leaves us and does not evolve into hatred.

Of course, if this bitterness has existed for months or years, do not expect it to go away with five or ten minutes of meditation. You have to work on it. You will feel, at least, some initial relief from the negative emotion, though. This is the first sign that you can really shake off the bitterness.

Question 5: If the other person does not show remorse, do we continue to work on freeing ourselves from whatever negative emotion we have and forgive them?

Answer: Usually, we expect others to show forgiveness or remorse. However, with meditation on friendliness, we try to make the first step ourselves, since with it we at least have a technique to eliminate toxic emotions. Others do not. Where would they learn it from? Who would teach them? Did anyone ever tell them at school how to work on eliminating feelings of anger or hostility? Is there a school to learn these things? They do not have a technique, whereas you, through the lessons you take, can at least learn that there is such a technique, that there is a way to eliminate negative emotions, provided that you make the effort. Do we expect those who do not have the technique to show remorse or forgiveness? Impossible.

We, however, have the technique and should make use of it. We start with ourselves, and then we can influence others. As I said, when we eliminate negative emotions and awaken positive ones within us, we share these positive emotions with others, wishing them to be happy, or without anger, or without hatred as we do for ourselves, because others suffer from the exact same negative emotions. You will find that in this way you can change the behaviour of other people as well, almost like telepathy!

If we visualise a person whom we hate or with whom we have a grudge and wish them to be without anger, without hatred, without any grudges, and to be happy, after three or four days of meditation, we will find that this person behaves in a completely different way than in the past because we have influenced them mentally.

It's like sunlight, for example, which is diffused everywhere. When we focus the sun's rays onto paper using a lens, we see the paper begin to smoke and eventually burn. Something similar happens with our mind. If we focus our mind on one point for a long period of time, it gains so much power that we can not only eliminate negative emotions but also free others from them by focusing our positive thought on them. That is, we can influence their mood. Because of all this, we start this practice ourselves, without expecting others to show forgiveness and remorse.

Question 6: I find it difficult to meditate, because I have been trapped for a long time in bad and negative thoughts that flood my mind; I cannot avoid them. They hinder the joy and peace of my everyday life. At some point, I had very bad thoughts about a loved one, and now I have guilt and panic attacks. Psychologists say that we all have such thoughts at some point, but since we don't act on them, we should calm down and let them go. How can meditation help me get rid of all these bad thoughts and negative emotions?

Answer: I don't know if you've tried the serenity meditation on friendliness. As I already mentioned, it is very effective, because we are not trying to attack these emotions or fight them, but simply withdraw our mind from them and not get involved. The key is to identify the negative emotion and wish to be without it.

Usually, it is aversion or anger; guilt in particular is anger against oneself. It's like taking a knife and stabbing ourselves because we feel guilty and remorseful that something was our fault. Sometimes we feel this aggression towards ourselves and, if given the opportunity to lash out elsewhere, will do so—we see ourselves and others as enemies and look for an opportunity to vent. So, guilt is a form of anger. You, of course, can label your emotions and thoughts as you wish, depending on how you perceive them. What you need to understand, however, is that they belong to a specific category.

Take jealousy, for example. We are jealous of a person who has certain qualities that we do not have. Because we don't have them for one reason or another, we don't want others to have them, either, because we consider it unfair and feel annoyed that they have them and we do not. All of these feelings are forms of anger. Anger comes from the annoyance we feel because of ourselves or others.

Identify the emotion you feel, naming it in your own words—I have simply given some examples. Focus all your attention on your body, specifically on the place where you strongly feel this emotion (for example, in the chest, stomach, back, or head) and wish: "May I be without anger..." or "without fear..." or "without guilt..." and so on.

So, we make a wish. We do not command, but we wish, withdrawing our mind from the specific emotion. Without access to fuel, it weakens and disappears. To achieve this, however, continual practice is necessary. And since, as I understand, these feelings have been inside you for a long time, don't expect them to disappear in two or three minutes. You need to have some patience and practice in a relaxed rather than an aggressive or hostile manner. With repeated practice these emotions become less intense, and then you will feel calmer and more at peace.

Anger, guilt, and remorse are like poisons within us. When we see the danger, we withdraw our mind so as not to provide fuel to these emotions, which, no longer having any substance, disappear. However, when we don't know how to escape from them and become involved in them, they multiply.

It is worth spending more time on this meditation. Even when you are walking, sitting, or lying down, keep meditating, wherever you are. We don't meditate only while seated, and emotions don't only appear then, either. On the contrary, they can appear at any moment: when we are walking, when we are washing the dishes, when we are cleaning the table, and at any other time. We should be aware of them, identify them, and wish to be without them.

Question 7: Events and stimuli from the external environment can be very distressing and affect more sensitive individuals. In your opinion, how can these people maintain positive emotions and thoughts as well as hope for the future?

Answer: I have spoken about positive emotions and how they can be awakened within oneself. However, when people have negative emotions, they feel like they are missing something, thinking, *I used to have positive emotions, and now I don't!* They begin to feel depressed at some point in their lives, feeling sadness and sorrow due to the lack of positive emotion and the presence of negative emotion. They feel that they previously had something positive that they have now lost.

This is due to the desire people have to obtain something and the sorrow they feel when they don't get it. There is a saying in ancient Greek: 'It is not lack of something that causes sorrow, but the desire.' We desire something, and when we don't have it, we grieve. Many people believe that desire is a very positive thing, that we should have desires. However, when they don't have or acquire what they desire, they become sad and dejected. People often think about what they had before and now do not have, and this causes them grief.

But there is a way to overcome this sadness. One must first identify the emotion that is tormenting oneself and causing trouble, which is robbing one's peace and tranquility, and name it. Is it sadness? Is it sorrow? Sadness is also a kind of annoyance, when grieving *Formerly I had..., now I don't...* Then, one wishes to be without this sadness or sorrow.

As a result, this emotion of sadness or sorrow is no longer a burden, and the person can better adapt to their situation, not considering it as something very sad. In this way, we can more clearly understand the reality of life and accept our situation, not as victims of fate, but with the awareness that there are negative emotions which cause us more distress than the actual distress of the situation itself.

By dispelling this sadness from within, we gain greater clarity, which helps us decide what to do and how to adapt by utilising the little things we have in life, without feeling stress.

When this sadness or sorrow is appeased, we can wish for ourselves "May I be happy..., may I be happy..., may I be happy...." Positive emotion can arise within us when we have created these positive thoughts. For example, we can recall other happy moments we spent with friends or loved ones and, remembering ourselves as we were then, say, "May I be happy..., may I be happy...."

We will find that when we do not let our minds generate negative thoughts and generate positive thoughts instead, our attitudes begin to shift. This is due to our own effort. We don't let the mind follow its own trajectory, its own mindset, which brings us negative emotions. Once we let it loose, our chatty mind starts to tell its own stories! But when we guide it by saying, "May I be happy... may I be happy...", those few negative emotions that have been left behind will disappear, and we will start to feel joy within us and accept situations as they are, without anxiety.

Then, if other people come to mind, we can also wish for them to be "happy, happy, happy" and thus create a very harmonious atmosphere around us. We understand that our happiness depends not only on the material goods we have but also on how we see and perceive the world.

If we believe that only material goods bring happiness, and we do not have them, then of course we become anxious and depressed. However, if we are satisfied with even just a few possessions, then the mind adapts to having fewer things. In this way, it becomes very easy for someone to give up things, meaning that they do not feel stressed if they do not possess them or lack the comforts they had before.

Apply this meditation, and you will see that when you dispel sadness or sorrow by wishing to be happy, you will gain deep spiritual happiness that comes from within and will bring you fulfilment and hope for the future.

Question 8: Are you saying that even in situations where nothing changes in the external environment, there is a way to be well within ourselves by eliminating the desire to change reality?

Answer: Certainly. Experiments related to this question have been done, but we can also draw from relevant human experiences in order to answer. I will give you some examples of people who have ended up in prison. Being in prison is the worst thing that can happen to a person—that is the prevailing opinion, at least. However, when meditation teachers go and teach meditation to prison inmates, after a period of practice, the inmates exhibit different personalities and change their mindsets. They become calmer, their irritation gradually fades, and they no longer feel the weight and anxiety that oppresses them knowing that they will remain in prison for many years, if not for life. Despite their very bleak situation, they overcome their sadness through meditation. It pleases them to sit and meditate, accepting their situation as it is.

We are not in prison, although many of us may have felt like prisoners during the coronavirus crisis when we were forced to stay in our homes, unable to go out whenever we wanted for shopping or other activities due to the strict measures that were imposed. The psychoses created by such situations of confinement and prohibition are normal, but we can overcome them through meditation and see reality from a different perspective.

There are meditators who need very few things in their lives, such as water, food, or other simple living conditions, to do their meditation calmly. They do not expect many goods and are satisfied with a few necessities.

I'm not telling you that you should become ascetics, but I am showing you how the human mind functions. The mind can become very flexible, adapting to how we tune it. Depending on how we adjust it, the mind reacts. If we tune it with positive perceptions, the mind reacts accordingly, and we feel fulfilment. If, on the contrary, we leave it untuned, free to have its own wild passions, we feel disturbed.

It depends on how we regulate or tame our mind. Meditation is actually the taming of the mind. The mind is like a wild horse that needs to be tamed. Once we do, the mind attains peace and calmness, and we can see reality as it is.

Question 9: What happens when it is not a matter of the absence of material goods but a matter of non-existent values? That is, values that we perceive to exist even though they really don't.

Answer: This is something that can be easily overcome with medita-tion, especially if we understand that these values are nonexistent and that our perception creates them, and if we realise the delusion and illusions we have about them.

Regarding material goods, it is true that many people get anxious if they cannot go to stores to buy what they want. Some material goods are essential for our life, and our body needs them to survive. On the other hand, non-existent values created by our minds are easily overcome by meditation. Of course, this requires patience and effort, because these tendencies were not created in us yesterday, or the day before yesterday, or last week; they have been there for many years, resulting in us expecting things to happen as we have planned. When this does not happen, we become disappointed.

However, with meditation, we at least gain some self-awareness so that we understand what is happening inside us—which negative emotions destroy our peace and calm, and how we can recover from them by bringing positive thoughts into our minds.

Question 10: Are you talking about accepting reality as it is?

Answer: Everyone perceives reality differently. I'm talking about reality as it happens within us. That's why meditation has to do with introspection, so we can understand what things disturb us. This is our reality. What disturbs others is their reality.

We need to understand what makes us suffer, identify it, and categorise it (as anger, sorrow, fear, etc.). Then we are in reality and accept reality—that is, that this emotion exists within us—without putting up screens and pretending it doesn't exist. Instead, we recognise it and try to overcome it. If we do not recognise this reality, in other words the existence of a particular emotion within us, we won't be able to over-come it.

Accepting reality as it is, then, is recognition of the emotions that we have within us. But we don't stop there. We try to overcome these negative emotions. We don't just accept; we transcend.

Question 11: When an event occurs that causes anger, should we meditate at that moment or recall the issue later and meditate then?

Answer: Both work. But usually the event consumes people so much that they forget they need to be aware of the anger that is arising within them. Only those who have already practiced this meditation are able to immediately identify the anger within them and have the awareness to wish "to be without anger... without anger...".

It may not be possible for someone to identify anger the moment it arises. Later, when sitting quietly and starting to recall events and the anger that was sparked in them, they may wish to be without anger.

When we recall events, and see what we have done and how we have behaved, we gain self-awareness, understanding how we behave and react to different situations. It's like we have filmed ourselves on video and are watching ourselves back. This meditation helps us to become more self-aware. We can observe ourselves and see what emotions appear in each situation, how they affect us, and how they cause us to act and react. In short, we are able to see a fuller picture of ourselves.

Meditation on friendliness is not limited in space or time but can be practised even when one is walking down the street, washing dishes, clearing the table, eating, sitting, and drinking, and generally any moment one perceives that anger or another negative emotion is arising, as these emotions are also not limited in space and time but arise at any moment. We identify them in ourselves and wish to be without them. Then, since they don't have any real substance, they fade away.

Question 12: I continue to struggle to concentrate fully. Whether counting the breaths or wishing to be without a specific emotion, thoughts constantly flood my mind. My mind doesn't calm down at all. What else can I do?

Answer: Thoughts exist; don't try to combat them. Even when you practise meditation on friendliness and wish to be without this or that emotion, thoughts will continue to come; for example, thoughts about the episode that caused the emotion from which you wish to be freed. There will some be parallel thoughts. Do not pay attention to the thoughts, but keep wishing: "May I be without this emotion..." With this meditation, we don't try to fight thoughts and stop the mind by putting a curtain in front of us or cutting the thoughts with a knife. This is impossible! No one can achieve it in this way!

Don't be afraid of these thoughts. Let them come and go, and focus more on the emotion, because it is the emotion that causes the thoughts. It can be anxiety about something, sadness, sorrow, even hate. So, it is good to start identifying these emotions within you, naming them, and realising their intensity and how big a role they play in your daily life, to the point where you cannot concentrate.

Again, when you wish to be happy but the mind doesn't calm down, it means that there's a strong emotion of guilt, anger, or remorse inside you, agitating your mind. Whenever you have free time, sit in a quiet place without noise and try to identify this emotion, wishing to be without it. Do it calmly, without pressure. If there are parallel thoughts, accept them and continue to focus on the emotion that generates them, in the way I have suggested.

Question 13: Is it possible for your thoughts to merge with someone else's thoughts? Or, to put it differently, is it possible for the thought of one mind to stimulate the thought of another mind?

Answer: Yes, there is such a possibility. Not in the sense of merging, but in the sense of influence. We can influence others' thoughts, somewhat akin to the phenomenon of telepathy.

This is particularly true with meditation on friendliness. For example, if we remember people who have harmed us and want to change their bad behaviour, we can focus on them as the object of our attention and wish them to be happy, to be without hate, without anger, and so on. We can focus on their foreheads especially and wish them to be without hate and hostility and to be happy. We repeat this over and over for two or three days. We will find that if we meet these people again, they will treat us in a completely different, much more pleasant way.

This has been confirmed by many testimonies and does not only apply to humans but also to animals. For example, if you are walking down the street and a dog attacks you, all you need to do is focus on the dog's forehead and wish it to be "without hate..., without hate..., without hate..." and "to be happy..., happy..., happy...". You will see that the dog will stop barking and start wagging its tail. It may even want to play with you!

This is a frequently confirmed fact, and the Buddha had suggested this approach especially for monks living in forests so that they could live in harmony with the wild animals that dwell there. Those who practice meditation on friendliness can ward off many dangers that appear around them, not only from humans but also animals.

Therefore, if you have toxic people around you, people whom you greatly dislike, with whom you have a bad relationship, who harass you and put you into difficult situations, you can use this meditation and change their behaviour.

Of course, patience and a period of a few days are required to achieve this. Don't expect that with just five or ten minutes of meditation you can miraculously change everything as if you took some magic pill. You need to practice. In this way, the thought of one person can influence the thought of another.

3. Questions and answers on four elements meditation

Question 1: When I focus on a particular organ, what exactly should I do? Should I make it function well?

Answer: No, because our goal is to understand the material aspect of our nature, not to modify something. For example, we see that the heart cannot exist or function without the solid, liquid, heat, and air elements, because without even the air element there would be no movement, and the heart would stop. Essentially, we try to understand that our physical nature and substance are composed of these four elements and that our bodies, which we so adore, are not made of indestructible diamonds and rubies but are a composition of these perishable elements, which are constantly changing and transforming.

People are obsessed with their bodies! They nourish them, beautify them, adore them! With this meditation, we eliminate and deconstruct this adoration, narcissism, and vanity. We develop a detachment towards the body and see it simply as a process of material elements, without becoming its adorers. By ceasing to feel attracted to our body, we achieve equanimity.

Our body is like a puppet, and our mind is the puppeteer who pulls its strings. It is not our 'self' or something of our own; it just has its own functions and processes for its existence. What we do in this case is not to heal the body, but our mind from attachment and vanity. We care for it daily, trying to satisfy its needs, but do not realise that we are its slaves.

Doing this meditation, you will gradually experience a relief that brings peace. At the same time, you will realise that, although we 'carry' this body with us constantly, we have not understood it, just as we have not understood to what elements it owes its existence and, ultimately, who we are. Do we have self-knowledge? And what does self-knowledge mean? Is it simply an attempt to know what ideas, thoughts, and emotions we have? And what are these based on? How are they produced—randomly? No, many of them are produced in dependence on the material body!

According to Buddhism, in the realm of our material existence there is mentality and materiality (*nāma-rūpa*), which are interdependent and mutually supported. They are like two upright sheaves of reeds leaning one against the other so as not to fall. Our mentality (consciousness, thoughts, ideas, moods, and emotions) is greatly influenced by the material body and influences it in turn.

Have we truly understood this material body, however? Where do you think most of our life's problems come from? If we didn't have this body, would we run to find food? Certainly not! Would we run to find water, clothing, and other necessities? No! Would we run to find work and money? We basically work for this body!

Why does someone go to work? To protect and maintain the body, to dress it, to feed it, to give it drink, to give it medicine in order to heal it, to give it a house in order to protect it from weather conditions, vermin, even wild animals. How much money is spent overall on this body? Have we understood it, though? No! We just serve it. We are servants of this body.

Practicing this meditation, one can understand some shocking truths, like what it means to carry these material elements within us. We speak pompously about high ideas and lofty philosophies without realising that we are rooted in matter, immersed in matter, stuffed with matter. Yet have we understood our material nature? No.

To understand it, then, we need to realise how we are grounded in the material body, which affects our lives, emotions, ideas, and moods.

It is good, therefore, not only from a psychological but also rational point of view to understand what this body is and how it affects us, what it consists of, how it functions, and how to analyse it. So, we undertake an analytical examination to finally understand a reality we usually avoid seeing.

Question 2: What is the purpose of this type of meditation?

Answer: One reason is to eliminate the vanity we have about the body, to overcome attachment, passion, narcissism and the tendency to identify with it. Another reason is to see clearly what this body is and what it consists of, in order to deconstruct the illusions and fanciful image we have of it and our existence.

We feed it with food and fluids, try to protect it from the heat and cold with clothing and much else, and generally struggle with it from the moment we are born. Most of our effort and toil is spent on the body.

But if we understand what our bodies are and what they are made of, we will have a clearer understanding of them and can eliminate our attachment to them. This does not mean that we will neglect and stop caring for our body, but it is essential to understand what something we use, serve, and carry with us every day consists of. Everyone can examine and study what this body is and how it functions, which ultimately is not ours but simply a composition of elements that we have borrowed and can lose at any moment. Borrowed from whom? From our parents. For example, our genetic material, or DNA, which produces every cell in our body, comes from our parents. Without it, it is pointless to talk about a body. And our parents, in turn, got it from their parents, and they from theirs, and so on, stretching back millions of years. Thus, our bodies are not ours or 'ourselves' but merely material borrowed from generations of ancestors, who may belong to different ethnicities. For if we analyse our DNA, we will find that it is multiethnic, even that of our parents.

When we stand in front of the mirror and admire our physical body, what we are really admiring is a temporary composition of the four primary elements in our DNA, which has given the body a specific shape that can change at any moment. But we don't realise this, and that is why we struggle and toil to maintain it in the form and shape we desire. And when the body doesn't respond the way we want it to, we become frustrated. When we are attracted to the bodies of other atoms, we are actually attracted to an assembly of the solid, liquid, heat, and air element in others. If this assembly is ugly, we see them as ugly people and not as a solid, liquid, heat, and air element. If they are beautiful, we consider them attractive as individuals and not as an assembly of elements.

Because we do not understand these elements, our psychological world is repelled or attracted by their temporary composition, perceiving them as beautiful or ugly. Beauty and ugliness, however, are nothing but temporary appearances of the four elements. What is beautiful today can become ugly tomorrow and vice versa. And as these material elements change, so too do our perceptions of beauty and ugliness.

Our psychological world is greatly influenced by the material world. If we do not understand the material world, we cannot comprehend what is happening inside us and how much we are influenced by material elements, which take various forms and prompt us to form ideas and opinions about them.

In conclusion, if one analyses the body, one can gain profound knowledge about the material aspect of our existence. Whether someone is ugly or beautiful, we see them as a composition of elements, and the matter ends there. Through continual meditation on the elements and the material body, one can memorise them, 'scan' them, gain great concentration, dissolve all fantasies and wrong views about the body and its elements, and be freed from attachment. The mind is liberated, no longer feeling attraction or repulsion, but only equanimity accompanied by penetrative knowledge of the true nature of the material body.

Question 3: When I visualise a single organ or body part, like teeth, I have good concentration. But when I visualise something that is expansive or moving, like blood, which is fluid, I lose my concentration. How can I correct this?

Answer: Certain body parts and organs appear very clearly in a meditator's mind, while others do not. In such cases, we try to focus more on the clear and distinct ones. Teeth, for example, are often seen in the mirror, making them easier to bring to mind. The same is true of any other part or organ of the body, like the heart, liver, and stomach, with which we are familiar through pictures in anatomy books or through our experience (for example, if we have been to a butcher for meat).

Each meditator differs from another due to different experiences and knowledge. When someone pays more attention to specific organs, it is natural that these organs appear clearer in their mind.

In this case, with a fluid like blood, we try to concentrate on an organ that is more clear, like the heart, where our concentration can be significantly increased. Continuing the observation, eventually, the blood in the heart becomes evident to us. Later, we can also see the arteries and veins as solid elements through which the liquid blood flows.

Question 4: If, while examining an organ or a body part, emotions such as fear, aversion, or attraction arise, what should we do?

Answer: In this case, you should continue repeating the same pattern ("solid element..., solid element..., solid element..." or "liquid element..., liquid element..."), because these words are crucial for focusing and maintaining our attention on the part or organ we want to observe objectively, without being swayed by emotions of fear, aversion, attraction, and so on. Otherwise, our mind will focus on whatever it wants to.

4. Questions and answers on insight meditation

Question 1: When a feeling is neutral, how can we recognise when it rises and when it falls? Isn't it difficult to identify it?

Answer: It is true that beginners find it difficult to identify a neutral feeling. The indication that it exists is when we feel a sense of emptiness within us, when nothing seems to be happening, when there is inertia, when our thoughts have calmed down, when we think of nothing, and generally when we are in a state that is neither pleasant nor unpleasant. When such a feeling appears, we identify it and name it as "neutral feeling, neutral feeling...". Then, we mentally note "duration, duration, duration...", until it falls after a while. We start observing the duration because, as with many feelings, we cannot always detect exactly when they arise, but we can identify that there is a pleasant, unpleasant, or neutral feeling and observe its duration. Then we can see its fall.

Generally, most people misinterpret neutral feelings and try to give them a mystical meaning, thinking that they have come into contact with the emptiness of all things or something similar. However, by observing more carefully, we realise that they are like small waves that come and go, rise and fall, without any element of permanence.

Question 2: Listening to various sounds, like those of birds, I tried to think what that sound was. Then, a thought of guilt from the past appeared, and I tried to examine it. Next, feelings of anxiety and fear appeared, and I tried to think about where they came from. For every kind of thought that appeared, I tried to see where it came from and why it was there. Is this the right way to meditate?

Answer: In insight meditation, we do not try to find the cause of a phenomenon by speculation and assumption. Instead, we initially try to understand its impermanent nature and how much we identify with it and suffer as a result. If a thought of guilt appears and we focus on it, the mind can become involved in trying to speculate about its original cause, which may lead to a labyrinth of thoughts.

Thoughts themselves do not have their own specific essence, unless we choose to assign one. Of course, when we do, the mentally constructed essence disappears due to its impermanence, and we have to try to regain it. This is our struggle to identify with the thoughts that the mind manifests, and naturally, we also become emotionally involved.

Therefore, when we detect any thought, we do not focus on its cause but on the way it behaves. We observe it and see that it has a duration and that, after a certain period, it fades and falls. It may reappear, and we can see its rise and then observe its duration and fall again. In short, initially we try to see the impermanent nature of the thought, not its cause. Whether it's thoughts of anger, guilt, or any emotion, we see that they repetitively rise, last, and fall in an endless cycle, without having a stable essence.

At this point, a meditator begins to become detached. They see thoughts objectively, without being swept away by them. They notice that thoughts don't appear because they call them and don't leave because they told them to, but that they appear of their own accord, last for a while, and then leave on their own. A meditator just lets that process happen, being a mere observer witnessing the fleeting nature of their thoughts.

That's how we start insight meditation. Of course, later, we can see that there is a causality behind the rise, duration, and fall of thoughts, but this knowledge comes afterwards. We will find that there is always one phenomenon causing another phenomenon, feeling, or thought, and that this cause is also not permanent but arises, lasts for a time, and falls. In this way, we discern impermanence either in the cause of the phenomenon or in the phenomenon itself.

Start to observe impermanence by mentally noting "rise, duration, fall" for all categories of thoughts, whether of desire, anger, or delusion, until your mind becomes used to seeing these phenomena as they actually occur, without identifying with them.

Thoughts of guilt, anxiety, and fear belong to the category of anger, because when we remember something negative that we did, we feel anger towards ourselves, and we become anxious and fear that something bad might happen to us. When such thoughts appear, we observe their rise, duration, and fall, and do not get involved in the drama that accompanies identification with it.

We see thoughts as bubbles that superficially reflect different colours but which burst and disappear in the next moment. We are fascinated by the spectacle and go close to see what is inside the bubbles. But as soon as we observe them for a while, they dissolve, and we realise their hollow nature. In the same way, we see thoughts completely objectively and try to understand their fleeting nature.

Question 3: So, whatever kind of thoughts we have, do we not analyse them, but focus on their impermanence?

Answer: We do analyse them, but in the way I described. When thoughts are intense and repetitive, we try to see what kind they are, what their nature is, what category they belong to, rather than what their hypothetical cause is. We observe whether they are thoughts of lust, hate, or delusion.

The Buddha, in his discourses, classified thoughts and emotions into sixteen categories.[2] However, for beginners, we teach the three most apparent categories we mentioned: lust, hate, and delusion. These categories are the most difficult for a meditator to overcome, due to identification with them. We carry them around all day, every day, for weeks, months, even years. They become our personality, our identity—this is who I am!

We carry this burden of thoughts and label it 'I' and 'me'. However, if we saw their content, we would be surprised by these thoughts' transient and fleeting nature. *What am I doing? What are these things that I carry? How is it possible to have clung to such transient things that constantly change?* we wonder. Realising the delusion we are in by identifying with such unstable and transient things, our mind becomes detached, now possessing the ability to make judgements unaffected by impermanent phenomena. Liberation from attachment and

---

[2] See p. 283, "Observation of Thoughts".

identification can be achieved, but it requires continual effort, not just a little meditation of five to ten minutes a day.

Question 4: So, we don't sit down to visualise or imagine various things and try to connect with a higher self or god, as some believe. On the contrary, by observing phenomena, we see their impermanent nature, stop being attached to them, and consequently, the mind calms down. Is that correct?

Answer: Correct. In other traditions, emphasis is placed on visualisation, but then people are trying to create and construct something inside of them rather than observing the desires and passions that produce such fantasies. They do not observe the transience and impermanence of mental phenomena as they really are but see things as they want them to be. It's just a mental construct and a fabrication of theirs.

Question 5: During insight meditation, I focus on rising, duration, and falling, without having trouble perceiving phenomena's impermanence and 'death'. In fact, many times, recognising the absence of a self, I feel happy, as if I have been relieved of a burden. However, when I do my workout and observe rising, duration, and falling, I wonder, *Why am I doing a workout? To have good health. Why do I want to have good health? To live well and have longevity. Why do I want to have longevity?* Logically, the answer to the question of longevity would be, in the best case, to have time to become an Arahant or, in the worst case, simply a better person, or to study the Dhamma, or something similar. But instinctively, I think, *I want to have longevity because I don't want to die! I want to live forever! To be immortal!* That is, there is a huge gap between logic and emotion. What should I do to eliminate this gap?

Answer: This is called *bhava-taṇha*, (desire or craving for continued existence), and it exists in the subconscious mind as a latent tendency. We want to promote our existence beyond this life. In insight meditation, we do not try to combat this impulse. Instead, we try to detect it, become aware of it, and see its nature. When this desire for immortality arises in us, we name it "desire..., desire..., desire..., desire..." and observe how long it lasts. Then we see that it falls. Then it appears again, lasts, lasts, lasts, lasts, and falls again. We observe this phenomenon objectively, without being swept away by this impulse, this desire without identifying with it, because it is nothing but a tendency of the mind.

Question 6: This desire has been in me since I was a child. I have always wanted to be immortal, to never die. But now that I am practicing insight meditation, the contrast between emotion and logic has become more pronounced. Before, I didn't realise the extent of this attachment to immortality. The perception of impermanence makes me see the enormous extent of my desire for existence. So, is it a matter of time and practice to overcome it?

Answer: It definitely takes time. Many meditators discover things within themselves that they had not previously detected. Not because these things didn't exist—they were always there, but such tendencies are present within us and manifest spontaneously, without our realisation. With insight meditation, however, we gradually become aware of them.

Something similar is happening in your case. You discovered that this impulse for immortality and longevity has always been within you, but you did not realise that it was so intense. With insight meditation, you are realising it now, because through this practice the mind gains greater clarity and becomes aware of this impulse and its rise within. This impulse or desire can be directed towards various objects like the body. Many people want their body to remain young and immortal, and to that end, they seek various elixirs and techniques like those used by Chinese Taoists when they try with drugs, herbs, and other ways to keep their body alive for many years, even two or three hundred.

With insight meditation, we detect not only the impermanence of the impulse by observing its rise, duration and fall, but also the object on which this impulse, this desire, is established. We come to realise that all desire has specific objects and things on which it becomes established. 'Established' here means that it takes root like a tree, which, no matter how much we pull it, is very difficult to uproot.

Comment: For me, it is not so much rooted in the enjoyment of material goods as in the desire for youthfulness of body and form, and for acquiring more knowledge.

Answer: You are not alone in this! Many share this desire. With insight meditation, we detect these emotions of desire and understand how much they mislead us.

At the same time, we eliminate ignorance, that is, the lack of knowledge about the mechanism of desire, simply by observing it. Since we don't see anything permanent in it, only transience, we don't get carried away by it. We see the pathways desire wanders along and we find that these too have an end. Desire itself has an end, because the energy of desire is not eternal; it eventually fades and disappears. It flares up again, and again it fades away, dependent on various causes and conditions. It appears when the right causes and conditions are present, and disappears when they are gone.

One simply becomes aware of what is happening within themselves, notices the transient nature of desire, and realises how they are being carried away by a phenomenon that is impermanent. Then the mind becomes detached and liberated from the enslavement of desire.

Question 7: Bhava-tanhā is the desire for existence and *kāma-taṇhā* is sensual desire, such as the desire I have for my favourite food or music, or for sex. When I want to go out for coffee, what kind of desire is it?

Answer: It is *kāma-taṇhā,* the desire for material or sensual pleasure. We want to enjoy the taste, smell, and the pleasant experience of coffee. We crave the coffee, and there it is. We jump up from our chair like a spring to go out and drink coffee.

Question 8: I would also like to ask about feelings, because, during meditation, I felt intense neck and stomach pain, and then after a while I felt warmth. Are there pleasant feelings that we should welcome when they appear?

Answer: Certainly, pleasant feelings arise as well. For example, when we have an unpleasant feeling that later goes away, we feel relieved—*Oh, how good it is that it's gone now!* It is something pleasant, but in this case, too, we must not forget that what is pleasant is also changeable and has a transient nature. We must continue our observation, that is, observation of the pleasant feeling's rise and fall. Thereby, we feel neither aversion to unpleasant feelings nor attraction to pleasant ones. When we expect something pleasant to happen and it does not, an unpleasant feeling arises. However, by seeing the rise and fall of both, we neither anticipate the pleasant feeling nor have aversion to the unpleasant one.

This cannot be achieved immediately. Gradually, with observation, one can achieve tranquillity and equanimity, so as to treat these feelings objectively, impartially, without taking a position towards them (*I like this and I want* this or *I don't like that*). Essentially, this is what we do every day in life: we welcome the pleasant and repel the unpleasant. This is a tendency of the mind to be attracted to objects or to resist them. In meditation we see them objectively. Simply put, the fundamental nature of all feelings, whether unpleasant or pleasant, is change and impermanence. When we feel aversion to something unpleasant, we are disappointed if it does not go away. When we feel a pleasant feeling and it goes away, we are disappointed again. We suffer because we identify with things we expect to behave in ways that we want, and eventually, when they don't, not only are we disappointed but also anxious! *Why don't things go the way I want*? we wonder.

In meditation, we observe what is unpleasant, and when it goes away and we feel relief and pleasure, we do not welcome the pleasant, but again observe it in a completely objective way, mentally noting "pleasant feeling, pleasant feeling, pleasant feeling". Then we move on to the next step, which is to observe the rise, duration, and fall of this feeling.

Question 9: If a buzzing in my ears occurs during meditation, how can we ignore it and continue? Maybe by putting on suitable music?

Answer: Isn't music also some kind of hum? In such cases, we can use insight meditation to make the buzzing itself the object of our attention, observing its transient nature—that it arises, lasts, and falls—without identifying with it or being troubled by it.

The more we identify with it, the more we nourish it, whereas when our mind becomes detached from it, it ceases and goes away.

5. General questions and answers on meditation

Question 1: What kind of meditation can we do in the evening?
Answer: It depends on our state of mind. When the mind is not disturbed, we can do meditation on breathing or insight meditation. However, if the mind is agitated by negative emotions such as fear, anger, sadness, or anxiety, and cannot concentrate on the breath, we simply do meditation on friendliness.

Question 2: What is the best duration of meditation? From 40 minutes onwards?

Answer: Beginners can start with short periods and then increase from 20 to 30 minutes, then to 35 and 40 minutes, until they reach one, two, or three hours at a stretch. This is very beneficial for concentration, as it achieves unification of the mind. Some people enjoy meditation so much that they can sit for a long time, losing their sense of time. A lady recently told me that, although she meditated for two and a half hours, it seemed to her that only ten minutes had passed. When meditation is pleasant, the meditator forgets about time, and it no longer plays a major role. However, the more time one can spend, the better.

Question 3: I have a chronic problem with sleep. I sleep intermittently and only get deep sleep in the morning hours. How can meditation help me?

Answer: In such a case, meditation on breathing is very helpful. Before going to sleep, try to be aware of your breathing as much as possible. Should you have any distracting thoughts, you can use the method of counting from one to five in order to avoid them. Count the in- and out-breaths: "one... two...

three... four... five...." Continue in this way, and in the end, you will see that as the mind gets closer to the breath, it calms down more, and it's easier to fall asleep. You will notice that the mind has relaxed so much that it eventually lets itself sink into sleep.

Even if you wake up at night, immediately bring your attention back to your breath, without thinking about anything else. If intense negative emotions arise like the ones I mentioned, and they disturb your mind and prevent you from sleeping, you need to identify them to see if they are fear, anger, or sadness. Name them as you perceive them and start wishing to be free from them, practising meditation on friendliness. If you wake up at night and realise you are feeling an intense emotion, tell yourself, "May I be free from this emotion."

Question 4: What do we do about sleep and drowsiness during meditation?

Answer: There are times when the tendency to sleep is natural, especially after fatigue, after eating, after sunset, etc. We feel sleep coming sweetly as a friend, but eventually, we realize that it stole our time and left like a little thief.

Generally, the morning hours are the best for meditation because the mind and body have rested after so many hours of sleep. Especially the mind is more flexible and clear, and we can concentrate it easily. Drowsiness at those times does not come or, if it does, it is weak and lasts only a short time. However, in case we feel drowsy, we can drink a cool juice, some tea, or coffee. Of course, it is best to meditate on an empty stomach or after a light breakfast. Especially after a full meal, we should avoid meditating immediately, because most of the blood goes to the stomach for digestion, thus reducing the amount of blood in the brain, which brings some drowsiness. It is good to walk for about half an hour, so that digestion is done well, and then sit for meditation.

However, if you feel drowsy and tend to sleep, stop meditating, get up and walk a few steps up and down in the fresh air. Alternatively, turn your attention to a bright spot, the sun, a lamp. Light has a good effect on the mind. You can even wash your face with cold water.

If you meditate regularly, you can catch your mind when it has escaped and is ready to sink into sleep, and bring it back to concentration. Especially in insight meditation, you can name the drowsiness you feel and observe its rise, duration, and fall.

In general, try to find times when you are energetic, i.e., you are not tired or sleepy, so that you are alert.

PART V

The Great Discourse on the Establishment of Mindfulness (*Mahā Satipaṭṭhāna Sutta*)

INTRODUCTION

The Great Discourse on the Establishment of Mindfulness (*Mahā Satipaṭṭhāna Sutta*) is one of the Buddha's most significant and comprehensive discourses on meditation, with particular emphasis on the development of insight meditation (*vipassanā*). It is the most widely studied and practically applied discourse of the Buddha, rightly called 'the heart of Buddhist meditation'. It presents the most direct and straightforward path for achieving the Buddhist goal of Nibbāna or Nirvāna. It is, as the Buddha calls it, 'the direct path for the realisation of Nibbāna'.

This discourse lays out a complete system of insight meditation, with the aim of training the mind to observe, with minute precision, the impermanent nature of the body, feelings, thoughts, and mind-objects, thereby overcoming attachment to them.

Insight meditation is unique in its kind and was first taught by the historical Buddha Gotama. As previously discussed, it was through insight meditation that he attained enlightenment and became the Buddha.

The purpose of *Satipaṭṭhāna*

The purpose of the *Satipaṭṭhāna* is outlined at the beginning of the discourse with the statement:

> This is the direct path (*ekāyano maggo*)
> for the purification (*visuddhi*) of beings,
> for the overcoming of sorrow and lamentation,
> for the disappearance of pain and grief,
> for the attainment of the true method, and
> for the realisation of Nibbāna—

> namely, the four establishments of mindfulness (*cattāro satipaṭṭhānā*).[1]

It is called the 'direct path' because it goes in one direction, that is, towards the purification of beings, and because it differs from other categories of meditations. These may lead, to a certain extent, to concentration and serenity, but not to Nibbāna. They may even lead to deviations from it. Conversely, insight meditation in *Satipaṭṭhāna* leads directly to the ultimate goal of Nibbāna.

The 'purification' (*visuddhi*) referred to here means the cleansing of the mind from mental defilements caused by lust, hate, and delusion. As the Buddha himself explains:

> For a long time, this mind has been defiled by lust, hate, and delusion. Through the defilements of the mind, beings are defiled; with the cleansing of the mind (*citta-vodānā*), they are purified (*visujjhanti*).[2]

Right mindfulness

While one may be mindful of many events and occurrences in one's everyday life, mindfulness concerning *Satipaṭṭhāna* is called 'right mindfulness' (*sammā sati*). This is what contributes to resolving central and urgent issues of human existence, leading to liberation from suffering, pain, stress, depression, sorrow, and grief through the purification (*visuddhi*) and cleansing (*vodāna*) of the mind, and to the realisation of Nibbāna.

The establishment of right mindfulness

Right mindfulness has the following four establishments through observation:

---

[1] D II.290, *Mahāsatipaṭṭhāna-sutta.*
[2] S III.151, *Dutiyagaddulabaddha-sutta.*

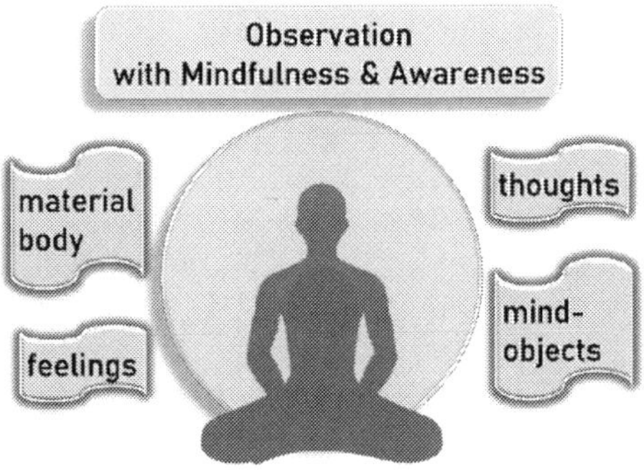

1) observation of the body (*kāyānupassana*),
2) observation of feelings (*vedanānupassana*),
3) observation of the mind or thought (*cittānupassana*), and
4) observation of mind-objects (*dhammānupassana*).

For successful observation, a meditator needs to be:

- ardent (*ātāpī*),
- fully aware (*sampajāno*), and
- mindful (*satimā*).

The observation fails when they are:

- sluggish, passive, lacking in energy (*anātāpī*),
- unaware (*asampajāno*), and
- unmindful, mindless, forgetful (*asatimā, muṭṭhassati*).

Therefore, the Buddha explains in the *Satipaṭṭhāna Sutta*:

> One abides observing the body ... the feelings ... the thoughts ... the mind-objects **ardent** (*ātāpī*), **fully aware** (*sampajāno*) and **mindful** (*satimā*).

In another discourse, the Buddha also mentions that one must be concentrated (*samāhita*) with a 'one-pointed' or unified mind (*ekaggacitta*) for effective observation in *satipaṭṭhāna*, in order to know the body, feelings, thoughts, and mind-objects as they really are (*yathābhūtaṃ*).[3] This makes it clear that concentration

[3] "*Kāya- ... vedana- ... citta- ... dhammānupassino viharatha ... samāhitā ekaggacittā.*" S V. 144, *Sāla-sutta.*

(*samādhi*) is essential for successful observation in mindfulness or insight meditation.

Types of observation

Satipaṭṭhāna does not employ the usual methods of meditation. Instead, it uses systematic and methodical observation of material and mental phenomena in order to penetrate their true nature. It includes training in insight meditation with mindfulness, awareness, and concentration, which are used for observing and understanding the unstable, impermanent, and transient nature of all mental and material phenomena, attachment to which creates unhappiness and suffering. It deals with a total of twenty-one types of observations:

1) Observation of the body includes fourteen types of observation.
2) Observation of feelings is considered one type of observation, although it includes nine ways.
3) Observation of thoughts or mind is also considered one type of observation, although it includes sixteen ways.
4) Observation of mind-objects includes five types of observation.

Each observation has two aspects:

1) basic observation through serenity meditation (*samatha*) and
2) advanced observation through insight meditation (*vipassanā*).

The fundamental principle of observation in serenity meditation (*samatha*) is concentration on a single object for an extended period of time. This type of meditation includes practices such as 'mindfulness of breathing' (*ānāpānasati*), 'attention to the foulness of the body' (*paṭikūlamanasikāra*), 'attention to the material elements of the body' (*dhātumanasikāra*), and the 'nine charnel ground contemplations' (*navasivathika*).

The fundamental principle of observation in insight meditation (*vipassanā*) is the observation of the rise (*samudaya*) and fall (*vaya*) of every mental and material phenomenon. This type of meditation can include any object of observation, even those from serenity meditation. Essentially, it is the observation of the rise and fall of any observed phenomenon, in order to deepen one's understanding of all phenomena's transient, impermanent, temporary, momentary, fleeting, and unstable nature.

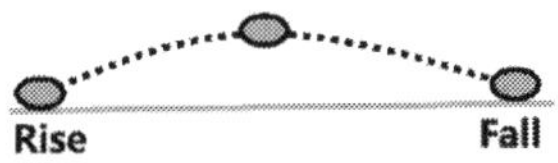

Particular and universal characteristics

'Rise and fall' is a dominant characteristic that is universally present in all material and mental phenomena. The Buddha urges meditators to repeatedly observe this characteristic. Although there are 21 types of observations in the *Satipaṭṭhāna Sutta*, each focusing on different and varied objects with separate characteristics, they all share a universal and general characteristic, that is, of rise and fall. This characteristic is repeatedly mentioned for all 21 types of observation, from the beginning to the end of the *Satipaṭṭhāna Sutta*, and forms the basis of insight knowledge.

Therefore, we have different objects of observation, each with its particular and individual characteristics (*paccatta-lakkhaṇa*), but which all have the universal characteristic (*sādhāraṇa-lakkhaṇa*) of rise and fall.

Two ways of observing the rise and fall

There are two ways of observing the rise and fall. The first is the initial way and the second is the advanced, namely:

1) momentary rise (*khaṇika-samudaya*) and momentary fall (*khaṇika-vaya*), and
2) conditioned rise (*paccaya-samudaya*) and conditioned fall (*paccaya-vaya*).

A meditator may begin by observing how each phenomenon rises and falls at any given moment. Then, as their understanding matures, they will be able to see that this rise and fall does not happen by chance, but is due to causes and conditions, and vanishes due to causes and conditions. They see that, in the ultimate reality (*paramattha-sacca*), there are only processes of material, mental or spiritual phenomena that continuously rise and fall according to causes and conditions (*hetu-paccaya*).

'Rise and fall' is a fundamental characteristic of all conditioned phenomena and the entire universe. Both conditionality and causality are integral parts of existence. All phenomena in the physical and spiritual world are produced by a combination of causes and conditions. They are not absolute, self-existent, immutable, or independent, but are related to other things. They are formed, shaped, moulded, and created by conditions. They depend and interdepend on conditions. Because of this, they are called conditioned. The conditions themselves also continuously rise and fall according to other causes and conditions. Rise and fall reveals that the nature of conditions is transient and unstable.

The method of liberation

Satipaṭṭhāna is the method of self-observation, self-knowledge, personal independence, self-reliance, self-support, self-help, and, above all, self-liberation. It does not require any complicated techniques or external gimmicks. Everyday life—the body, feelings, thoughts, and mind-objects—is the fabric of this practice. *Satipaṭṭhāna* neither involves exotic rituals or ceremonies nor requires 'initiation' or 'occult knowledge'. Its specific aim is self-enlightenment, that is, a deep understanding of the three characteristics of existence—impermanence, existential suffering, and non-self—and the Four Noble Truths (*ariya-sacca*).

Based on the law of karma (volitional actions), which implies responsibility and personal accountability for one's actions, *Satipaṭṭhāna* is incompatible with belief in a representative system of salvation, such as divine grace, priesthood, or 'meditation gurus'. It is free from dogma and dependence on 'divine revelations' or any external authority in spiritual matters. It relies solely on firsthand knowledge, knowledge from direct perception of one's immediate experience. It teaches how one can purify and enhance the essential quality of true knowledge: direct experience.

The Buddha's words in *Satipaṭṭhāna* are accepted and valued by meditators as detailed travel instructions from an experienced traveller who has traversed a road and reached its end, and thus deserves trust. The Buddha has travelled this path, applied everything in practice, and having reached the journey's end, can show the way. Effort must be made by the meditator, however, to gain empirical knowledge. This knowledge becomes their intellectual property only when verified through their own experience. Only by traveling the path of practical application can one verify, through one's own experience, what the Buddha said. *Satipaṭṭhāna* comes as a message of personal independence and self-help, as evidenced by the Buddha himself, when he states:

> Dwell with yourselves as your own island, with yourselves as your own refuge, with no other refuge; with the Teaching (*Dhamma*) as your island, with the Teaching as your refuge, with no other refuge. And how does one dwell with themselves as a ... refuge, ... with no other refuge? One dwells observing the body ... feelings ... thoughts ... mind-objects, ardent, fully aware, and mindful, having put aside covetousness and grief for the world....[4] Thus he abides independent, not clinging to anything in the world.[5]

Personal independence and liberation should be developed progressively, and *Satipaṭṭhāna's* path towards self-liberation begins with gradual steps that even the most hesitant can follow.

[4] D II.100, *Mahāparinibbāna-sutta.*
[5] "*Anissito ca viharati, na ca kiñci loke upādiyati.*" D II.292, *Mahāsatipaṭṭhāna-sutta.*

THE LONG COLLECTION, DISCOURSE 22

DĪGHA NIKĀYA, SUTTA 22

THE GREAT DISCOURSE ON THE ESTABLISHMENT OF MINDFULNESS

MAHĀ SATIPAṬṬHĀNA SUTTA

(Preamble)

Thus have I heard. On one occasion the Blessed One was staying in the Kuru country where there was a town of the Kurus named Kammāsadhamma.[6] There the Blessed One addressed the monks thus: 'Monks!'[7] — 'Venerable sir,' they replied. The Blessed One said this:

'This is the direct path for the purification of beings, for the overcoming of sorrow and lamentation, for the disappearance of pain and grief, for the attainment of the true method, and for the realisation of Nibbāna—namely, the four establishments of mindfulness.

'What are these four? Here, in regard to the body, a monk abides observing the body, ardent, fully aware, and mindful, having put aside covetousness and grief for the world. In regard to feelings, he abides observing feelings, ardent, fully aware, and mindful, having put aside covetousness and grief for the world. In regard to thoughts, he abides observing thoughts, ardent, fully aware, and mindful, having put aside covetousness and grief for the world. In regard to mind-objects, he abides observing mind-objects, ardent, fully aware, and mindful, having put aside covetousness and grief for the world.'

---

[6] According to some scholars, the town of Kammāsadhamma was located near modern New Delhi, India. (Malalasekara, G.P., *Dictionary of Pali Proper Names*).

[7] It should be understood that 'monks' can refer here to any meditator.

(Observation of the Body)

(*1. Mindfulness of Breathing*)

'And how does he, in regard to the body, abide observing the body?

Here, he goes to the forest or to the root of a tree or to an empty house, sits down, folds his legs crosswise, sets his body erect, establishes mindfulness in front of his face,[8] and ever mindful he breathes in, ever mindful he breathes out.

Breathing in a long breath, he understands, "I breathe in a long breath"; or breathing out a long breath, he understands, "I breathe out a long breath." Breathing in a short breath, he understands, "I breathe in a short breath"; or breathing out a short breath, he understands, "I breathe out a short breath." He trains thus: "I shall breathe in experiencing the whole body (of the in-breath)." He trains thus: "I shall breathe out experiencing the whole body (of the out-breath)."[9] He trains thus: "I shall breathe in, even though the bodily process (of the in-breath) is calming down." He trains thus: "I shall breathe out, even though the bodily process (of the out-breath) is calming down."[10]

Just as a skilled bellows-operator or his apprentice, when pressing a long [blast of air], understands, "I press long"; or, when pressing a short [blast of air], understands, "I press short"; so too, breathing in a long breath, a monk understands, "I breathe in a long breath"; ... or breathing out a short breath, he understands, "I breath out a short breath ...." He trains thus: "I shall breathe out, even though the bodily process (of the out-breath) is calming down."

---

[8] For the meaning of the phrase 'in front of his face' (*parimukha*), see p. 54.
[9] For the meaning of the phrase 'the whole body (of in-, out-breath)' (*sabba-kāya*), see p. 60.
[10] For the meaning of the phrase 'bodily process (of in-, out-breath)' (*kāya-saṅkhāra*), see p. 66.

(*INSIGHT*)

'In this way, in regard to the body, he abides observing the body internally, or he abides observing the body externally, or he abides observing the body both internally and externally.

Or else he abides observing the nature of rise in the body, or he abides observing the nature of fall in the body, or he abides observing the nature of rise and fall in the body.

Or else mindfulness that "there is a body" is established in him just to the extent necessary for bare knowledge and continuous mindfulness. And he abides independent, not clinging to anything in the world. That is how, in regard to the body, he abides observing the body.'

(*2. The four postures*)

'Again, when walking, he understands, "I am walking"; when standing, he understands, "I am standing"; when sitting, he understands, "I am sitting"; when lying down, he understands, "I am lying down"; or he understands accordingly however his body is disposed.'

(*INSIGHT*)

'In this way, in regard to the body, he abides observing the body internally, or he abides observing the body externally, or he abides observing the body both internally and externally.

Or else he abides observing the nature of rise in the body, or he abides observing the nature of fall in the body, or he abides observing the nature of rise and fall in the body.

Or else mindfulness that "there is a body" is established in him just to the extent necessary for bare knowledge and continuous mindfulness. And he abides independent, not clinging to anything in the world. That, too, is how, in regard to the body, he abides observing the body.'

(*3. Full Awareness of body movements*)

'Again, when going forward and returning, he acts with full awareness; when looking ahead and looking away, he acts with full awareness; when flexing and extending his limbs, he acts with full awareness; when wearing his robes and carrying his outer robe and bowl, he acts with full awareness; when eating, drinking, consuming food, and tasting, he acts with full awareness; when defecating and urinating, he acts with full awareness; when walking, standing, sitting, falling asleep, waking up, talking, and keeping silent, he acts with full awareness.'

(*INSIGHT*)

'In this way, in regard to the body, he abides observing the body internally, or he abides observing the body externally, or he abides observing the body both internally and externally.

Or else he abides observing the nature of rise in the body, or he abides observing the nature of fall in the body, or he abides observing the nature of rise and fall in the body.

Or else mindfulness that "there is a body" is established in him just to the extent necessary for bare knowledge and continuous mindfulness. And he abides independent, not clinging to anything in the world. That too is how, in regard to the body, he abides observing the body.'

(*4. Reflection on the foulness of the body*)

'Again, he reviews this same body up from the soles of the feet and down from the top of the hair, enclosed by skin, as full of many kinds of impurity thus:

> "There are, in this body, head-hairs, body-hairs, nails, teeth, skin, flesh, sinews, bones, bone-marrow, kidneys, heart, liver, diaphragm, spleen, lungs, intestines, mesentery, stomach, faeces, bile, phlegm, pus, blood, sweat, fat, tears, grease, spittle, snot, oil of the joints, and urine."

Just as if there were a bag with an opening at both ends full of many types of grain such as hill-rice, red rice, beans, peas, sesame, and white rice, and a man with good eyes were to open it and review it thus: "this is hill rice, this is red rice, these are beans, these are peas, this is sesame, this is white rice"—so too, he reviews this same body ... as full of many kinds of impurity thus: "There are in this body, head-hairs, ... and urine."'

(*INSIGHT*)

'In this way, in regard to the body, he abides observing the body internally, or he abides observing the body externally, or he abides observing the body both internally and externally.

Or else he abides observing the nature of rise in the body, or he abides observing the nature of fall in the body, or he abides observing the nature of rise and fall in the body.

Or else mindfulness that "there is a body" is established in him just to the extent necessary for bare knowledge and continuous mindfulness. And he abides independent, not clinging to anything in the world. That, too, is how, in regard to the body, he abides observing the body.'

(*5. Reflection on the elements of the body*)

'Again, he reviews this same body, however it is placed, however disposed, by way of the elements thus: "There are, in this body, the solid element, the liquid element, the heat element, and the air element."

Just as if a skilled butcher or his apprentice, having slaughtered a cow, were to sit at a crossroads with it cut up into portions, so too he reviews this same body .... by way of the elements thus: "There are, in this body, the solid element, the liquid element, the heat element, and the air element."'

(*INSIGHT*)

'In this way, in regard to the body, he abides observing the body internally, or he abides observing the body externally, or he abides observing the body both internally and externally.

Or else he abides observing the nature of rise in the body, or he abides observing the nature of fall in the body, or he abides observing the nature of rise and fall in the body.

Or else mindfulness that "there is a body" is established in him just to the extent necessary for bare knowledge and continuous mindfulness. And he abides independent, not clinging to anything in the world. That too, is how, in regard to the body, he abides observing the body.'

(*6-14. The nine charnel ground observations*)

(6) 'Again, as if he were to see a corpse thrown aside in a charnel ground—one, two-, or three-days dead, bloated, livid, and oozing matter—and he compares his own body with it thus: "This body too has the same nature; it will become like that; it is not exempt from that fate."

'In this way, in regard to the body, he abides observing the body internally... externally... internally and externally.

Or else he abides observing the nature of rise in the body, ... the nature of fall ..., or the nature of rise and fall in the body. And he abides independent, not clinging to anything in the world. That too, is how, in regard to the body, he abides observing the body.'

(7) 'Again, as if he were to see a corpse thrown aside in a charnel ground—being devoured by crows, hawks, vultures, dogs, jackals, or various kinds of worms—and he compares his own body with it thus: "This body, too, has the same nature; it will become like that; it is not exempt from that fate."'

'In this way, in regard to the body, he abides observing the body internally ... externally ... internally and externally. Or else he abides observing the nature of rise in the body, ... the nature of fall .... That, too, is how, in regard to the body, he abides observing the body.'

(8) 'Again, as if he were to see a corpse thrown aside in a charnel ground—a skeleton with flesh and blood, held together with sinews …

(9) ... a fleshless skeleton smeared with blood, held together with sinews…

(10) ... a skeleton without flesh and blood, held together with sinews…

(11) ... disconnected bones scattered in all directions; here a hand-bone, there a foot-bone, here a shin-bone, there a thigh-bone, here a hip-bone, there a back-bone, here a rib-bone, there a breast-bone, here an arm-bone, there a shoulder-bone, here a neck-bone, there a jaw-bone, here a tooth, there the skull—and he compares his own body with it thus: "This body, too, has the same nature; it will become like that; it is not exempt from that fate."

'In this way, in regard to the body, he abides observing the body internally ... externally … internally and externally. Or else he abides observing the nature of rise in the body, ... the nature of fall .... That, too, is how, in regard to the body, he abides observing the body.'

(12) 'Again, as if he were to see a corpse thrown aside in a charnel ground—bones bleached white, the colour of shells…

(13) ... bones heaped up…

(14) ... bones more than a year old, rotted and crumbled to dust—and he compares his own body with it thus: "This body, too, has the same nature; it will become like that; it is not exempt from that fate."'

(*INSIGHT*)

'In this way, in regard to the body, he abides observing the body internally … externally … internally and externally.

Or else he abides observing the nature of rise in the body, ... the nature of fall ..., or the nature of rise and fall in the body. Or else mindfulness that "there is a body" is established in him just to the extent necessary for bare knowledge and continuous mindfulness. And he abides independent, not clinging to anything in the world. That, too, is how, in regard to the body, he abides observing the body.'

(Observation of Feelings)

'And how does he, in regard to feelings, abide observing feelings?

Here, when feeling a pleasant feeling, he understands, "I feel a pleasant feeling"; when feeling an unpleasant feeling, he understands, "I feel an unpleasant feeling"; when feeling a neither-unpleasant-nor-pleasant feeling, he understands, "I feel a neither-unpleasant-nor-pleasant feeling."

When feeling a pleasant sensual feeling, he understands, "I feel a pleasant sensual feeling"; when feeling a pleasant non-sensual (spiritual) feeling, he understands, "I feel a pleasant non-sensual feeling"; when feeling an unpleasant sensual feeling, he understands, "I feel an unpleasant sensual feeling"; when feeling an unpleasant non-sensual (spiritual) feeling, he understands, "I feel an unpleasant non-sensual feeling"; when feeling a sensual neither-unpleasant-nor-pleasant feeling, he understands, "I feel a sensual neither-unpleasant-nor-pleasant feeling"; when feeling non-sensual (spiritual) neither-unpleasant-nor-pleasant feeling, he understands, "I feel a non-sensual (spiritual) neither-unpleasant-nor-pleasant feeling."'

(Insight)

'In this way, in regard to the feelings, he abides observing feelings internally ... externally ... internally and externally.

Or else he abides observing the nature of rise in feelings, or he abides observing the nature of fall in feelings, or he abides observing the nature of rise and fall in feelings.

Or else mindfulness that "there is feeling" is established in him just to the extent necessary for bare knowledge and continuous mindfulness. And he abides independent, not clinging to anything in the world. That is how, in regard to feelings, he abides observing feelings.'

(OBSERVATION OF THOUGHTS)

'And how does he, in regard to thought, abide observing the thought?

Here, he understands a thought with lust as a thought with lust. He understands a thought without lust as a thought without lust. He understands a thought with hate as a thought with hate. He understands a thought without hate as a thought without hate. He understands a thought with delusion as a thought with delusion. He understands a thought without delusion as a thought without delusion.

He understands a contracted thought (due to drowsiness) as a contracted thought. He understands a distracted thought (due to anxiety) as a distracted thought.

He understands an exalted thought as an exalted thought. He understands an unexalted thought as an unexalted thought. He understands a surpassed thought as a surpassed thought. He understands an unsurpassed thought as an unsurpassed thought.

He understands a concentrated thought as a concentrated thought. He understands an unconcentrated thought as an unconcentrated thought. He understands a liberated thought as a liberated thought. He understands an unliberated thought as an unliberated thought.'

(INSIGHT)

'In this way, in regard to thought, he abides observing the thought internally … externally … internally and externally.

Or else he abides observing the nature of rise in thought, or he abides observing the nature of fall in thought, or he abides observing the nature of rise and fall in thought.

Or else mindfulness that "there is thought" is established in him just to the extent necessary for bare knowledge and continuous mindfulness. And he abides independent, not clinging to anything in the world. That is how, in regard to thought, he abides observing thought.'

(Observation of Mind-Objects)

(1. *The five mental hindrances*)

'And how does he, in regard to mind-objects, abide observing mind-objects?

Here, in regard to mind-objects, he abides observing mind-objects in terms of the five mental hindrances. And how does he, in regard to mind-objects, abide observing mind-objects in terms of the five mental hindrances?

Here, if sensual desire is present in him, he understands, "There is sensual desire in me"; or if sensual desire is not present in him, he understands, "There is no sensual desire in me"; and he also understands how there comes to be the arising of unarisen sensual desire, and how there comes to be the abandoning of arisen sensual desire, and how there comes to be the future non-arising of abandoned sensual desire.

If ill-will is present in him... If sloth and torpor is present in him... If restlessness and remorse is present in him... If doubt is present in him, he understands, "There is doubt in me"; or if doubt is not present in him, he understands, "There is no doubt in me"; and he understands how there comes to be the arising of unarisen doubt, and how there comes to be the abandoning of arisen doubt, and how there comes to be the future non-arising of abandoned doubt.'

(*INSIGHT*)

'In this way, in regard to mind-objects, he abides observing mind-objects internally … externally … internally and externally.

Or else he abides observing the nature of rise in mind-objects, or he abides observing the nature of fall in mind-objects, or he abides observing the nature of rise and fall in mind-objects.

Or else mindfulness that "there are mind-objects" is established in him just to the extent necessary for bare knowledge and continuous mindfulness. And he abides independent, not clinging to anything in the world. That is how, in regard to mind-objects, he abides observing mind-objects in terms of the five mental hindrances.'

(*2. The five aggregates of mind and matter*)

'Again, in regard to mind-objects, he abides observing mind-objects in terms of the five aggregates of clinging.

And how does he, in regard to mind-objects, abide observing mind-objects in terms of the five aggregates of clinging?

Here, he understands, "Such is the material body, such its arising, such its passing away; such is feeling, such its arising, such its passing away; such is perception, such its arising, such its passing away; such are the mental formations, such their arising, such their passing away; such is consciousness, such its arising, such its passing away."'

(*INSIGHT*)

'In this way, in regard to mind-objects, he abides observing mind-objects internally … externally … internally and externally.

Or else he abides observing the nature of rise in mind-objects, ... the nature of fall ..., or the nature of rise and fall ....

Or else mindfulness that "there are mind-objects" is established in him just to the extent necessary for bare knowledge and continuous mindfulness. And he abides independent, not clinging to anything in the world. That is how, in regard to mind-objects, he abides observing mind-objects in terms of the five aggregates of clinging.'

(*3. The six sense organs and sense objects*)

'Again, in regard to mind-objects, he abides observing mind-objects in terms of the six internal sense organs as well as the external sense objects.

And how does he, in regard to mind-objects, abide observing mind-objects in terms of the six internal sense organs and external sense objects?

Here he understands the eye, he understands visible forms, and he understands the *mental fetter* that arises dependent on both; and he also understands how there comes to be the arising of the unarisen mental fetter, and how there comes to be the abandoning of the arisen mental fetter, and how there comes to be the future non-arising of the abandoned mental fetter.

He understands the ear, he understands sounds... He understands the nose, he understands odours... He understands the tongue, he understands flavours... He understands the body, he understands tangible objects... He understands the mind, he understands mind-objects, and he understands the mental fetter that arises dependent on both; and he also understands how there comes to be the arising of the unarisen mental fetter, and how there comes to be the abandoning of the arisen mental fetter, and how there comes to be the future non-arising of the abandoned mental fetter.'

(*INSIGHT*)

'In this way, in regard to mind-objects, he abides observing mind-objects internally ... externally ... internally and externally.

Or else he abides observing the nature of rise in mind-objects, ... the nature of fall ..., or the nature of rise and fall ....

Or else mindfulness that "there are mind-objects" is established in him just to the extent necessary for bare knowledge and continuous mindfulness.

And he abides independent, not clinging to anything in the world. That is how, in regard to mind-objects, he abides observing mind-objects in terms of the six internal sense organs and external sense objects.'

(4. *The seven factors of enlightenment*)

'Again, in regard to mind-objects, he abides observing mind-objects in terms of the seven factors of enlightenment.

And how does he, in regard to mind-objects, abide observing mind-objects in terms of the seven factors of enlightenment?

Here, if the enlightenment-factor of mindfulness is present in him, he understands, "There is the enlightenment-factor of mindfulness in me; or if the enlightenment-factor of mindfulness is not present in him, he understands, "There is no enlightenment-factor of mindfulness in me; and he also understands how there comes to be the arising of the unarisen enlightenment-factor of mindfulness and how the arisen enlightenment-factor of mindfulness comes to fulfilment by development.

If the enlightenment-factor of investigation of phenomena is present in him... If the enlightenment-factor of energy is present in him... If the enlightenment-factor of rapture is present in him... If the enlightenment-factor of tranquillity is present in him... If the enlightenment-factor of concentration is present in him...

If the enlightenment-factor of equanimity is present in him, he understands, "There is the enlightenment-factor of equanimity in me"; If the enlightenment-factor of equanimity is not present in him, he understands, "There is no enlightenment-factor of equanimity in me"; and he also understands how there comes to be the arising of the unarisen enlightenment-factor of equanimity and how the arisen enlightenment-factor of equanimity comes to fulfilment by development.'

(*INSIGHT*)

'In this way, in regard to mind-objects, he abides observing mind-objects internally … externally … internally and externally.

Or else he abides observing the nature of rise in mind-objects, ... the nature of fall ..., or the nature of rise and fall ....

Or else mindfulness that "there are mind-objects" is established in him just to the extent necessary for bare knowledge and continuous mindfulness. And he abides independent, not clinging to anything in the world. That is how, in regard to mind-objects, he abides observing mind-objects in terms of the seven factors of enlightenment.'

(*5. The Four Noble Truths*)

'Again, in regard to mind-objects, he abides observing mind-objects in terms of the Four Noble Truths.

And how does he, in regard to mind-objects, abide observing mind-objects in terms of the Four Noble Truths?

Here, he understands as it really is: "This is suffering"; he understands as it really is: "This is the origin of suffering"; he understands as it really is: "This is the cessation of suffering"; he understands as it really is: "This is the practice leading to the cessation of suffering."'

(A. The noble truth of suffering)

'And what is the noble truth of suffering? Birth is suffering, ageing is suffering, death is suffering, sorrow, lamentation, pain, grief and distress are suffering; union with what is displeasing is suffering; separation from what is pleasing is suffering; not to obtain what one wants is suffering; in brief, the five aggregates of clinging are suffering.

'And what is birth? The birth of beings into the various orders of beings, their coming to birth, their precipitation [in a womb], generation, the manifestation of the aggregates, obtaining the sense organs—this is called birth.

'And what is ageing? The ageing of beings in the various orders of beings; their old age, brokenness of teeth, greyness of hair, wrinkling of skin, decline of life, weakness of faculties—this is called ageing.

'And what is death? The passing of beings out of the various orders of beings; their passing away, dissolution, disappearance, dying; completion of time, dissolution of aggregates, laying down of the body—this is called death.

'And what is sorrow? The sorrow, sorrowing, sorrowfulness, inner sorrow, inner sorriness, of one who has encountered some misfortune or is affected by some painful state—this is called sorrow.

'And what is lamentation? The wail and lament, wailing and lamenting, bewailing and lamentation of one who has encountered some misfortune or is affected by some painful state—this is called lamentation.

'And what is pain? Bodily pain, bodily discomfort; painful, uncomfortable feeling born of bodily contact—this is called pain.

'And what is grief? Mental pain, mental discomfort; painful, uncomfortable feeling born of mental contact—this is called grief.

'And what is distress? The trouble and distress, the tribulation and desperation, of one who has encountered some misfortune or is affected by some painful state—this is called distress.

'And what is union with what is displeasing? Here, whoever has unwanted, disliked, unpleasant visible forms, sounds, odours, flavours, tangible objects, and mind-objects, or whoever encounters ill-wishers, wishers of harm, of discomfort, of insecurity, with whom they have concourse, intercourse, connection, union—this is called union with what is displeasing.

'And what is separation from what is pleasing? Here, whoever has wanted, liked, pleasant visible forms, sounds, odours, flavours, tangible objects, and mind-objects, or whoever encounters well-wishers, wishers of good, of comfort, of security, mother or father or brother or sister or younger kinsmen or friends or colleagues or blood-relations, and then is deprived of such concourse, intercourse, connection, or union—this is called separation from what is pleasing.

'And what is not to obtain what one wants? To beings subject to birth there comes the wish, "Oh, that we were not subject to birth, and birth would not come to us!" But this is not to be obtained by wishing, and not to obtain what one wants is suffering.

To beings subject to ageing... subject to sickness... subject to death... subject to sorrow, lamentation, pain, grief, and distress, there comes the wish, "Oh, that we were not subject to sorrow, lamentation, pain, grief, and distress! That sorrow, lamentation, pain, grief, and distress would not come to us!" But this is not to be obtained by wishing, and not to obtain what one wants is suffering.

'And what are, in brief, the five aggregates of clinging that are suffering? They are the material body aggregate of clinging, the feeling aggregate of clinging, the perception aggregate of clinging, the mental formations aggregate of clinging, and the consciousness aggregate of clinging. This is called the noble truth of suffering.

(B. The noble truth of the origin of suffering)

'And what is the noble truth of the origin of suffering? It is craving, which gives rise to rebirth, is accompanied by delight and lust, and delights in this and that; that is, craving for sensual pleasures, craving for existence, and craving for nonexistence.

'And where does this craving arise and establish itself? Wherever in the world there is anything agreeable and pleasurable, there this craving arises and establishes itself.

'And what is there in the world that is agreeable and pleasurable? The eye in the world is agreeable and pleasurable, the ear..., the nose..., the tongue..., the body..., the mind in the world is agreeable and pleasurable, and there this craving arises and establishes itself.

'Visible forms ... sounds ... odours ... flavours ... tangible objects, mind-objects in the world are agreeable and pleasurable, and there this craving arises and establishes itself.

'Eye-consciousness, ear-consciousness, nose-consciousness, tongue-consciousness, body-consciousness, mind-consciousness in the world is agreeable and pleasurable, and there this craving arises and establishes itself.

'Eye-contact ... ear-contact ... nose-contact ... tongue-contact ... body-contact ... mind-contact in the world is agreeable and pleasurable, and there this craving arises and establishes itself.

'Feeling born of eye-contact ... ear-contact ... nose-contact, tongue-contact ... body-contact ... mind-contact in the world is agreeable and pleasurable, and there this craving arises and establishes itself.

'The perception of visible forms ... sounds ... odours ... flavours ... tangible objects ... mind-objects in the world is agreeable and pleasurable, and there this craving arises and establishes itself.

'Volition in regard to visible forms ... sounds ... odours ... flavours ... tangible objects ... mind-objects in the world is agreeable and pleasurable, and there this craving arises and establishes itself.

'The craving for visible forms ... sounds ... odours ... flavours ... tangible objects ... mind-objects in the world is agreeable and pleasurable, and there this craving arises and establishes itself.

'Thinking of visible forms ... sounds ... odours ... flavours ... tangible objects ... mind-objects in the world is agreeable and pleasurable, and there this craving arises and establishes itself.

'Pondering on visible forms ... sounds ... odours ... flavours ... tangible objects ... mind-objects in the world is agreeable and pleasurable, and there this craving arises and establishes itself.

This is called the noble truth of the origin of suffering.

(C. The noble truth of the cessation of suffering)

'And what is the noble truth of the cessation of suffering? It is the remainderless fading away and ceasing, the giving up, the relinquishing, the letting go, and the rejection of that same craving.

'And how does this craving come to be abandoned, how does its cessation come about? Wherever in the world there is anything agreeable and pleasurable, there its cessation comes about.

'And what is there in the world that is agreeable and pleasurable? The eye in the world is agreeable and pleasurable, the ear ... the nose... the tongue... the body... the mind in the world is agreeable and pleasurable, and there this craving comes to be abandoned, there its cessation comes about.

'Visible forms ... sounds ... odours ... flavours ... tangible objects ... mind-objects in the world are agreeable and pleasurable, and there this craving comes to be abandoned, there its cessation comes about.

'Eye-consciousness, ear-consciousness, nose-consciousness, tongue-consciousness, body-consciousness, mind-consciousness in the world is agreeable and pleasurable, and there this craving comes to be abandoned, there its cessation comes about.

'Eye-contact ... ear-contact ... nose-contact ... tongue- contact ... body-contact ... mind-contact in the world is agreeable and pleasurable, and there this craving comes to be abandoned, there its cessation comes about.

'Feeling born of eye-contact ...ear-contact ... nose-contact, tongue-contact ... body-contact ... mind-contact in the world is agreeable and pleasurable, and there this craving comes to be abandoned, there its cessation comes about.

'The perception of visible forms ... odours ... flavours ... tangible objects ... mind-objects ...; volition in regard to visible forms ... sounds ... odours ... flavours ... tangible objects ... mind-objects ...; craving for visible forms ... sounds ... odours ... flavours ... tangible objects ... mind-objects ...; thinking of visible forms ... sounds ... odours ... flavours ... tangible objects ... mind-objects ...; pondering on visible forms ... sounds ... odours ... flavours ... tangible objects ... mind-objects in the world is agreeable and pleasurable, and there this craving comes to be abandoned, there its cessation comes about.

This is called the noble truth of the cessation of suffering.

(D. The noble truth of the practice for the cessation)

'And what is the noble truth of the practice leading to the cessation of suffering? It is just this Noble Eightfold Path, namely, right view, right thought, right speech, right action, right livelihood, right effort, right mindfulness, and right concentration.

'And what is right view? It is the knowledge of suffering, the knowledge of the origin of suffering, the knowledge of the cessation of suffering, and the knowledge of the practice leading to the cessation of suffering—this is called right view.

'And what is right thought? The thought of renunciation, the thought of non-ill-will, and the thought of non-cruelty—this is called right thought.

'And what is right speech? Abstaining from lying, abstaining from divisive speech, abstaining from harsh speech, and abstaining from idle chatter—this is called right speech.

'And what is right action? Abstaining from killing living beings, abstaining from taking what is not given (i.e. stealing), and abstaining from sexual misconduct—this is called right action.

'And what is right livelihood? Here a noble disciple gives up wrong livelihood and earns his living by right livelihood — this is called right livelihood.

'And what is a right effort? Here, one rouses his will, makes an effort, stirs up energy, exerts his mind, and strives to prevent the arising of unarisen evil, unwholesome mental states. He rouses his will... and strives to overcome evil, unwholesome mental states that have arisen. He rouses his will... and strives to produce unarisen wholesome mental states. He rouses his will, makes an effort, stirs up energy, exerts his mind, and strives to maintain wholesome mental states that have arisen, not to let them fade away, to bring them to greater growth, to the full perfection of development. This is called right effort.

'And what is right mindfulness? Here, in regard to the body, he abides observing the body, ardent, fully aware, and mindful, having put aside covetousness and grief for the world. In regard to feelings, he abides observing feelings, ardent, fully aware, and mindful, having put aside covetousness and grief for the world. In regard to thoughts, he abides observing thoughts, ardent, fully aware, and mindful, having put aside covetousness and grief for the world. In regard to mind-objects, he abides observing mind-objects, ardent, fully aware, and mindful, having put aside covetousness and grief for the world. This is called right mindfulness.

'And what is right concentration? Here, quite secluded from sensual pleasures, secluded from unwholesome states, one enters upon and abides in the first *jhāna*, which is accompanied by applied and sustained thought, with rapture and bliss born of seclusion.

With the stilling of applied and sustained thought, he enters upon and abides in the second *jhāna*, which has self-confidence and singleness of mind without applied and sustained thought, with rapture and bliss born of concentration.

With the fading away as well of rapture, he abides in equanimity, and mindful and fully aware, still feeling bliss with the body, he enters upon and abides in the third *jhāna*, on account of which noble ones announce, "He has a blissful abiding who has equanimity and is mindful."

With the abandoning of bliss and pain, and with the previous disappearance of joy and grief, he enters upon and abides in the fourth *jhāna*, which is beyond pain and bliss, and is purified by equanimity and mindfulness. This is called right concentration.

This is called the noble truth of the practice leading to the cessation of suffering.'

(*INSIGHT*)

'In this way, in regard to mind-objects, he abides observing mind-objects internally … externally … internally and externally.

Or else he abides observing the nature of rise in mind-objects, ... the nature of fall …, or the nature of rise and fall ....

Or else mindfulness that "there are mind-objects" is established in him just to the extent necessary for bare knowledge and continuous mindfulness. And he abides independent, not clinging to anything in the world. That is how, in regard to mind-objects, he abides observing mind-objects in terms of the Four Noble Truths.'

(CONCLUSION)

'If anyone should develop these four establishments of mindfulness in such a way for seven years, one of two fruits could be expected for him: either final knowledge here and now, or if there is a trace of clinging left, non-returning.

Let alone seven years ... six years ... five years ... four years ... three years ... two years ... one year ... seven months ... six months ... five months ... four months ... three months ... two months ... one month ... half a month ... if anyone should develop these four establishments of mindfulness in such a way for seven days, one of two fruits could be expected for him: either final knowledge[11] here and now, or, if there is a trace of clinging left, non-returning.

'So, it was with reference to this that it was said (in the beginning), "This is the direct path for the purification of beings, for the overcoming of sorrow and lamentation, for the disappearance of pain and grief, for the attainment of the true method, and for the realisation of Nibbāna—namely, the four establishments of mindfulness".'

This is what the Blessed One said. The monks were satisfied and delighted in the Blessed One's words.

[11] Final knowledge, *aññā*, is the knowledge of the final liberation of a Worthy One (*Arahaṃ*). Non-return (*anāgāmitā*) is the state of the non-returner (*anāgāmi*), who is reborn in a higher world where they attain the final Nibbāna (*parinibbāna*) without ever returning to the human world.

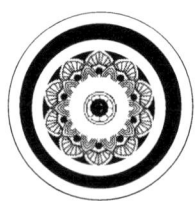

BIBLIOGRAPHY

BISCHOF, MARCO (2005), "Biophotons - The Light in Our Cells", Institute for Future Science & Medicine, Journal of Optometric Photography. https://www.researchgate.net/publication/280714672_Biophotons-_The_Light_in_Our_Cells.

BODHI, BHIKKHU (1993, 1999), *A Comprehensive Manual of Abhidhamma - The Philosophical Psychology of Buddhism*, Buddhist Publication Society, Kandy, Sri Lanka.

BODHI, BHIKKHU (1981), *Nibbāna. A condensed transcript of The Buddha's Teaching As It Is,* Lecture six, https://buddhistuniversity.net/content/essays/nibbana_bodhi.

BODHI, BHIKKHU (2009), "*Nibbāna*" in the Introduction to Majjhima Nikāya. *The Middle Length Discourses of the Buddha*, 4th ed., Wisdom Publications, Boston, USA.

BODHI, BHIKKHU (2007), *The All-Embracing Net of Views*, Buddhist Publication Society, Kandy, Sri Lanka.

BRONKHORST, JOHANNES (1993), *The Two Traditions Of Meditation In Ancient India*, Motilal Banarsidass Publication.

DE NICHOLAS, ANTONIO (2003), *Meditations Through the* Rig*Veda*: *Four-Dimensional Man*, ISBN 978-0595269259.

EVERLY, GEORGE S. LATING, JEFFREY M. (2002), A *Clinical Guide to the Treatment of Human Stress Response,* ISBN 0-306-46620-1.

FOWLER, JEANEANE D. (2012), *The Bhagavad Gita: A Text and Commentary for Students*, Sussex Academic Press, ISBN 9781845193461.

JAMES, WILLIAM (1890), *The Principles of Psychology,* Forgotten Books, ISBN 9781330274156.

MAHONY, WILLIAM (1997), *The Artful Universe: An Introduction to the Vedic Religious Imagination*, State University of New York Press, ISBN 978-079143 5809.

MORRIS, BRIAN (2006), *Religion and Anthropology*: *A Critical Introduction*, Cambridge University Press, ISBN 978-0-521-85241-8.

NICHOLSON, ANDREW J. (2013), *Unifying Hinduism: Philosophy and Identity in Indian Intellectual History*, Chapter 9, Columbia University Press, ISBN 978-0231149877.

NYANATILOKA, MAHATHERA (1980), *Buddhist Dictionary - A Manual of Buddhist Terms & Doctrines,* Buddhist Publication Society, Kandy, Sri Lanka.

OLIVELLE, PATRICK (1992), *The Samnyasa Upanisads: Hindu Scriptures on Asceticism and Renunciation*, Oxford University Press, ISBN 978019-5361 377.

OLIVELLE, PATRICK (2011), *Ascetics and Brahmins: Studies in Ideologies and Institutions*, Anthem, ISBN 978-0-85728-432-7.

SRINIVASAN, DORIS (1975), "The So-Called Proto-Śiva Seal from Mohenjo-Daro: An Iconological Assessment", George Mason University.

TAYLOR, EUGENE (ed.) (1999), "Introduction" in Murphy, M. Donovan, S. *The Physical and Psychological Effects of Meditation: A Review of Contemporary Research with a Comprehensive Bibliography 1931-1996*, p. 1–32.

VAJIRAÑĀṆA, PARAVAHERA (1962), *Buddhist Meditation in Theory and Practice*, Introduction by Francis Story, Charleston Buddhist Fellowship edition 2010.

WERNER, KAREL (1994), *The Yogi and the Mystic*. Routledge, ISBN 978-0700-702725.

WHITE, DAVID GORDON (2014), *The Yoga Sutra of Patanjali: A Biography*, Princeton University Press, ISBN 978-0691143774.

WALLACE, B. ALAN (1998), *The Bridge of Quiescence: Experiencing Tibetan Buddhist Meditation*, Carus Publishing Company.

INDEX

About the author

The Greek-born Buddhist monk Nyānadassana or Ñāṇadassana (Ioannis Tselios) has been a monk in the ancient Buddhist Theravāda tradition for over 40 years and lives mostly in Sri Lanka.

Born in 1959 in Serres, Greece, he finished high school in Thessaloniki and studied sociology at Goethe University in Frankfurt, Germany. In 1981, at the age of 22, a trip to India became a turning point in his life when, looking at a tourist brochure, he read these memorable words of the Buddha:

> This is my last birth. I have crossed the ocean of existence.

Reflecting deeply on these words and determined to learn more about the Buddha and his Teaching, he visited Kusināra, the place where the Buddha attained his final rest in *Nibbāna* (*Parinibbāna*). Here, under the guidance of an elder Indian Buddhist monk, the director of the Kusināra Museum, Ioannis Tselios not only practised meditation but also read about Buddhism. With increased interest, he decided to seek the original and authentic teachings of Buddha, eventually arriving in Sri Lanka.

In 1982, at the age of 23, he was ordained as a novice by his preceptor (*upajjhāya*), Venerable Kaḍavedduve Shrī Jinavaṃsa Mahāthera, a state-recognised scholar (*rājakīya paṇḍita*), and entered the monastic life for full-time study and practice. For four years, he trained under the guidance of Venerable Mātara Ñāṇārāma Mahāthera, a state-recognised scholar (*rājakīya paṇḍita*) and renowned meditation teacher at the Nissaraṇa Vanaya Monastery in Mītirigala.

In 1986, he received higher ordination (*upasampadā*) from his preceptor, Venerable Kaḍavedduve Shrī Jinavaṃsa Mahāthera. He then studied the ancient Indian language of Pāḷi and the Buddhist Triple Canon (*Tipiṭaka*), as well as its Commentaries and Subcommentaries, under three learned Elders (*Mahāthera*) at the Gnānārāma Dharmāyatanaya Monastery in Mītirigala, where he stayed for 16 years.

In 1997, after written and oral examinations, he received the title of *Vinayācariya* (Teacher of Monastic Discipline). Inspired by his teacher, he began teaching the Pāḷi language and the Tripiṭaka for several years. From 2003 to 2007, he practised meditation in Myanmar (Burma), and then returned to Sri Lanka. He has been repeatedly invited by Buddhist centres in Singapore, Indonesia, Malaysia, and Taiwan to deliver Dhamma talks and classes on meditation.

He is the author and translator of more than ten Buddhist books in German, English, Sinhalese (the official language of Sri Lanka), Pāli, and Greek. An experienced speaker, he has given numerous lectures in English, Sinhalese, and Greek.

His monastic name *Ñāṇa-dassana* means 'Knowing and Seeing' and he is considered Most Senior monk (*Mahāthera*) in his tradition.

Made in the USA
Las Vegas, NV
29 March 2025

20210040R00180